Commodity Speculation for Beginners

Commodity Speculation for Beginners

A Guide to the Futures Market

**Charles Huff and
Barbara Marinacci**

Macmillan Publishing Co., Inc.
NEW YORK

Collier Macmillan Publishers
LONDON

Macmillan Publishing Co., Inc.
866 Third Avenue, New York, N.Y. 10022
Collier Macmillan Canada, Ltd.

Library of Congress Cataloging in Publication Data
Huff, Charles.
  Commodity speculation for beginners.
  Bibliography: p.
  Includes index.
  1. Commodity exchanges. I. Marinacci, Barbara, joint author. II. Title.
HG6046.H83   332.63'28   80-18343
ISBN 0-02-555450-6

10   9   8   7   6   5   4   3   2   1

Printed in the United States of America

*To the speculator in life—
that is, to all of us,
including our Mr. E.*

"In a modern market contracts are not confined to sales for immediate delivery. People will endeavor to forecast the future and to make agreements according to their prophecy. Speculation of this kind by competent men is the self-adjustment of society to the probable. Its value is well known as a means of avoiding or mitigating catastrophes, equalizing prices and providing for periods of want."

Justice Oliver Wendell Holmes, Jr.

Contents

Foreword: Be Realistic!   xi
Acknowledgments   xv

PART I: An Introduction to Trading
   1. Meet Mr. E., Who Wants to Get More Money Somehow   3
   2. Making More Money with Money by Banking, Gambling,
      and Insurance   10
   3. Real Estate and Stocks: For Investment or Speculating? 20
   4. Considering Commodities   28
   5. Hedgers and Speculators: What Each Is Doing   37

PART II: Welcome to the Marketplace
   6. Looking at a Commodity Exchange   51
   7. Out on the Trading Floor   68
   8. A Visit to the Clearinghouse   82

PART III: A Short Course in Speculating
   9. Starting with Fundamentals   101
  10. About the Commodities   115
  11. Contracts and Prices   140
  12. Price Charting   152
  13. More Technical Tools   168

14. The Business of Speculating   187
15. Trading the Actuarial Way   203
16. A Commodity Speculator's Guide to Myths and Truths   222
17. Mr. E. Goes Off into the Sunset   237

Appendix
    For Further Reading   239
    About Brokerage Firms   240
    Commodity Pool Operators   242
    Advisory Services   242
    Charting Services   243
    Commodity Information Packages   244
    Wire Services   244
    The Commodity Futures Trading Commission   245
    The Commodity Futures Exchanges in the United States   245

Index   249

Foreword:
Be Realistic!

This book may not resemble most other "how-to-make-money" books that you've seen.

Why? Because it does not promise to help you acquire riches overnight. You know the kind: *How to Make a Fortune in . . . Real Estate, Roulette, Mail Orders, Coins, Blackjack, Stocks.* You name it.

Don't keep chasing the illusion of easy money. In the following chapters we'll show you mathematically why, in all probability, making large amounts of money in such get-rich-quick endeavors is virtually impossible for the ordinary person with limited assets. If you consider the arguments briefly presented here, you may spare yourself from wasting energy and suffering financial misery. Earning money takes time and work.

But don't give up on the possibility of earning money through wise money management. Although an investor with modest resources cannot build up a huge fortune through the available legal routes, you can quite possibly add appreciably to your annual income, with little physical effort on your part.

How? By speculating in commodities.

Many people think that the commodity market and its exchanges operate just for the well-entrenched rich and for the big-scale entrepreneurs trying to corner the market on a particular commodity and then squeeze profits from the public through higher prices. Although prevailing, this belief isn't true.

COMMODITY SPECULATION FOR BEGINNERS

As a matter of fact, the commodity exchanges were designed expressly for trading by the individual with limited capital: *you*. And on them you may earn anywhere from 50% to 200% of your investment or even more per year—*if* you exert the proper efforts to obtain background information and undergo a preparatory period in which you school yourself in certain skills that are essential for successful trading.

Our book will introduce you simply, clearly, and gradually to commodities and their exchanges and clearinghouses and to futures contracts and the brokerage houses that handle them. It will consider in detail the aspects and stages of trading in the commodity marketplace. It will consistently advise you to design a trading program for yourself that is prudent and conservative while speculative.

Trading in commodities has attracted many novice speculators who were wiped out within their first year of trading. Lured by the possibility of earning high profit percentages, most of them perhaps did not bear in mind that the market is fast playing, risky, and tough. Although a large payoff can be won through a shrewd or lucky investment, it can just as readily be lost overnight. Speculators should know what they are doing, and why, at all times. They must be ever alert to the requirements of decision-making situations. They should also possess a resilient nervous system, for often the wisest traders cannot accurately predict what's going to happen. The commodities are hardly a safe arena for beginners who have a poor understanding of the market mechanisms. Speculators who have taken the time to learn first have stayed in—and have been successful.

Even if you yourself have no intention of speculating, you'll probably find the basic information about commodity trading instructive and intriguing if you know little or nothing about this form of financial activity, which is connected with many of the basic goods produced and used around the world. In the past few years the futures market has been overtaking the stock market in volume and value of trading, partly because it is more directly geared to the current economy.

Or if you are on the commercial side of commodities—involved with their production, storage, processing, or marketing—you may learn more about the "hedging" process that decreases financial risk from unfavorable price changes.

We hope with this book to dispel the bad or shady reputation—based on the unpleasant experiences of novice or irresponsible speculators poorly prepared for action—that hovers over commodity speculation as a financial endeavor so far as the American public is concerned. We also intend to provide a readable introduction to the commodity market, since poor knowledge of or misinformation about futures trading is partly caused by the lack of suitable literature. The commodity exchanges themselves and a few brokerages dealing in futures contracts have prepared attractive and informative booklets that do try to caution potential speculators, but these booklets can't, of course, provide more than superficial coverage. And although there are numerous books on the subject, most of them are highly technical—written for experienced speculators by specialists and usually confined to particular aspects or techniques of trading that would be incomprehensible to beginners.

The few fairly current general books fall into two main groups. There are well-done, serious tomes that are dry and difficult to read. Textbookish in appearance, they have no "counter appeal" and doubtless turn off all but the most determined novices wishing to pursue the subject. Then there are those phony "get-rich-quick" publications that claim to reveal the magic formula for making millions in commodities in ten easy steps. Lacking real substance, they achieve a limited sale and soon depart. Unfortunately, the information and advice that their authors dispense can cause large financial losses when readers act on them. Furthermore, since the commodity market has changed considerably in the past few years—especially since the addition of the so-called "soft commodities"—international currencies and financial instruments like Treasury bonds, GNMAs, and commercial paper—the majority of books published before then will be badly out of date.

Commodity Speculation for Beginners is written expressly for uninformed general readers, not for those already knowledgeable about commodity trading. We have assumed at the start that readers may not know much either about various forms of income-producing activities. We believe that before you can speculate wisely in commodities, you must first consider why this particular approach to financial improvement may be better—more sensible and appealing—for you than other ways of making money, such as changing jobs, getting a second job, investing in real estate or stocks, or (seriously) straight gambling. We will introduce—or review, for readers already acquainted with such subjects—some basic points about the nature of money itself: what it is, where it comes from, how it can be used. We will consider some easy and practical mathematics connected with probabilities, speculation, risks, and insurance—because these all enter into commodity trading. We will briefly explore the history and function of commerce in commodities in society to learn how the exchanges came about.

We have included these preliminary matters so that you will have a firm groundwork for understanding the commodity market itself and will be better able to follow and understand the discussions of a number of market mechanisms and trading specifics that come later.

To make the journey through the book's unfolding information more readable and, we hope, more enjoyable, we have contrived an approach that is informal and fictional. We have created an Everyman figure (or, we should say, Everyperson, for women certainly trade in futures contracts too). Our Mr. E. undergoes a succession of learning experiences, step by step, with four other characters engaged in one useful way or another in speculation or the commodity market. By going along with our Mr. E., a complete beginner, you too can learn things that you'll need to know if you're considering commodity trading as a future financial activity.

If you, like Mr. E., decide to join the ranks of speculators, we urge you to study well in advance of your first moves by applying yourself diligently to no-risk "paper trading"—that is, by learning by trial and error on work sheets before commiting real money to futures contracts. We also recommend that you move on to the more complex books on the subject written by reliable authors. The education process will take self-discipline, time, and effort. But if it ultimately enables you to prosper in the commodity marketplace, you will recognize that the investment has been worth your while.

TO THE READER: If you lose your nest egg by buying or selling gold or pork bellies or any other commodity futures contracts, you can't say we did not warn you of the possibility!

Acknowledgments

The authors are grateful to these people who assisted in the progress of our book: Jane Jordan Browne, our literary agent, who introduced us; Toni Lopopolo, senior editor at Macmillan Publishing Co.; Austin Hyde, the publisher's consultant; George Rach, a branch manager of E. F. Hutton & Co. in California; Irwin B. Johnson of the Commodity Futures Trading Commission; M. S. Hackett of Lloyd's of London; Connie Plaehn, interim manager, and John Geldmacher, staff writer, in the Public Relations Department at the Chicago Board of Trade; James T. Russell, director of compliance, and Robert Wettlaufer, account executive, who showed us around the Chicago office of ContiCommodity Services; and Edward F. Keiser, account executive at Garvey Commodities Corporation in Chicago and member of the Chicago Board of Trade, who took us onto the hectic yet fascinating trading floor.

For permission to reproduce various charts in the book, we would like to thank the Commodity Research Bureau, Spread Scope, and the Chicago Board of Trade. Also, North-Holland Publishing Company for granting permission to cite statistics from a study by H. S. Houthakker on commodity price forecasting in *Review of Economics and Statistics* (September 2, 1957).

PART ONE

An Introduction to Trading

CHAPTER ONE

Meet Mr. E., Who Wants to Get More Money Somehow

Mr. E. is an average American: a person who has worked hard for money for some years now. He has made sacrifices in order to save a portion of his salary, to use not just now for occasional pleasurable expenditures that reward his efforts but also in a future time when he no longer will wish to work so hard.

But what's happening? While he's building up funds, the ever-accelerating pace of inflation is sharply reducing the value of his assets kept in a savings account. So he has begun to look around for some way to protect his money from constant devaluation. And with family responsibilities to shoulder and taxes to pay, his fairly fixed salary keeps on shrinking in its capacity to cover expenses and leave anything at all for savings. He often feels utterly defeated and wishes he had some way to get the money he has set aside to work for him instead of just sit there. But in order to do so, he really needs to make more money.

No matter what potential plan Mr. E. considers for reaping profits from extra labor expended, he can't seem to find a practical solution. He is a rational person who normally regards things realistically and is able to separate facts from fantasies when determining the best moves to improve situations that bother him.

Mr. E.'s predicament is scarcely unusual. Many sensible and hard-working people confront a serious financial dilemma at some point in their lives. Frequently it comes midway along, when after years of apprenticeship in acquiring skills and of working experience in a particular profession, it appears that further financial advancement to any significant degree has become impossible. Now, with an occupation goal fulfilled, Mr. E. asks himself, how does one manage to earn more money in order to pay expenses that are starting to overtake income and to build up assets for the retirement years ahead—plus have a bit extra for comforts and even a few luxuries that enhance the quality of life?

Mr. E. realizes it won't be easy. People who work an eight-hour day may increase their incomes by working overtime or by "moonlighting" at other jobs. But unfortunately the income tax structure creates the problem of diminishing returns for labor expended. More earnings usually put one into a higher tax bracket, and therefore one earns a larger income but a smaller net hourly wage in take-home pay. Anyway, Mr. E. knows that most people are so tired after the normal workday that they need to spend their free time resting or in a leisure activity. And if they have families—as Mr. E. does—they generally prefer to be with them instead of out somewhere working for more money, however much it is needed. How can people enjoy extra income if they don't have the time to do so —and are too fatigued from working for it?

Of course, Mr. E. is thinking, one should be able to advance continually by obtaining better-paying positions elsewhere. But achieving that higher status may require more education and expertise, which cannot be easily acquired in one's spare time. Most people, in any case, reach the pinnacle of professional success appropriate for their backgrounds and intelligence, their skills and personality characteristics, by their middle years. It may be quite impossible for them to move upward, and to try is to court disappointment and failure.

Mr. E. recognizes that going into an entirely new field or occupation may offer better opportunities. But will such a move actually result in ultimate financial improvement? To start at the bottom in any profession generally requires financial outlay for tuition or training. Then there may be several years of on-the-job learning. Unless the special work itself is the attraction, such extensive retraining efforts may be ill advised. Mr. E. is convinced that with the limited human life-span, most people can only manage to pursue one serious career and become proficient at it. Wouldn't it be preferable for him to keep the job he has and knows and not be hasty in abandoning it for the sake of potentially better earnings in a field he isn't yet equipped to enter? Besides, Mr. E. actually *likes* his present job.

So why couldn't Mr. E. keep his employment with its steady salary and side benefits but initiate a sideline activity that might eventually add appreciably to his annual earnings? Ideally, this second enterprise would require little physical exertion and minimal spare-time hours. It might

4

even eventually involve his wife too as a partner, since she is currently busy with raising their children and does not work now in the outside world. And how convenient if it could be done at home, without going anywhere!

What Mr. E. is searching for, then, is some do-it-yourself endeavor, a profitable venture that could be launched from his desk, the garage workshop, or even the kitchen table. He ruminates about a number and variety of possible money-making schemes, trying to determine, by the process of elimination, the ones or one that seems most likely to produce substantial rewards with minimal output of time and energy—once the basic skills and knowledge are learned.

For instance, Mr. E. knows people who make handicrafts to sell for cash. Does he have an inherent talent or acquired ability, perhaps a pleasant hobby, he could convert into a paying, part-time profession? Well, he can do fairly presentable woodworking that may have some commercial merits if he concentrates on it. But then he's already seen the competition he'd have in all those boutiques and craft fairs and realizes that this would not be the way to keep the wolf from his door.

And what about that big story he has always intended to write? For years he has dreamed of writing the Great American Novel, thinking that he'd just sit down someday and start off, maybe typing for an hour or two each day until he finished, letting the story roll along. There would be a fat contract with a first-class publishing house, reprint rights sold for a half-million dollars, and the blockbuster film coming up, giving him a percentage. . . . But here Mr. E. brings himself up short and acknowledges that this is sheer fantasy. If he was really going to write that novel, he'd have written it by now. He suspects that he may not have what it takes to compete with the pros. And anyway, he's not a driven creator who forsakes everything and everybody to do his own thing.

Then Mr. E. examines another great American dream he has long nourished: becoming an inventor. He has always been a garage and backyard tinkerer, figuring that sometime he'd hit upon some clever and indispensable device nobody yet thought of that could bring in a fortune. Trouble is, Mr. E. hasn't yet found that unique and wonderful invention that would assure his future as an inventor. Also, he would be competing with large corporations that have professional-caliber research staffs. Such firms already know what the public needs—and will buy. They also have the marketing resources denied to the free-lance gadget maker and the capital to develop new products to perfection and then produce and promote them out in the public marketplace. If Mr. E. ever did come up with something, he might be able to patent it after long months of application, then sell it to some company for a considerable sum. . . . But isn't this daydreaming just another distraction from the real business of trying to think of a way to make more money, now? No, Mr. E. is simply too practical to be able to convince himself of the wisdom of pursuing any of these courses.

Then one Friday night Mr. E. takes part in a neighborhood poker game, one of those casual, semiregular get-togethers that he always enjoys because he likes card playing, poker and blackjack in particular. And he knows that he plays quite well compared to most other people. He's not sure why. It isn't that he's always lucky and gets better hands. It's more that he knows what to do with what he's got. He concentrates on the action and instinctively manages to combine intelligence and skill with expert bluffing. He also thrives in the fast decision-making process.

So this night, anyway, Mr. E. takes in almost the entire winnings of the evening. Not wishing to run off early with the spoils, he stays to give others the chance to win some of their own money back. But right up to the end, Mr. E. still keeps winning. The money is no big deal compared to Las Vegas takings, but it's impressive for that bunch of poker players. The game's host, a casual acquaintance, invites Mr. E. to stay on for coffee after the game breaks up. Mr. E. accepts. He knows Dr. M. is a mathematician, and he has always wanted to hear more about the work Dr. M. does as an actuarial expert with an insurance company. Mr. E. is often interested in fields other than his, especially those he knows little about.

As they sit down at the kitchen table to drink their coffee, Dr. M. comments that tonight Mr. E. even broke his own previous records for winning. He admits that he always likes to watch Mr. E. play, for he is intrigued with things like luck, probability, and patterns of winning or losing. Mr. E., he has concluded, is awfully good at risk taking; he seems to have a natural bent for appraising situations and their potentials for profit or loss.

Has Mr. E. ever tried gambling with the real professionals? asks Dr. M. out of curiosity. Well yes, Mr. E. supposes he has, if Dr. M. is talking about a place like Vegas that attracts the hard-core gamblers. But he's always been too cautious to get caught up in the play for high stakes. Much as he'd like to win, he's inclined to be aware of what he might lose.

Dr. M.'s question triggers that money-seeking urge in Mr. E. Tonight, he confesses, he has begun to realize that he could get hooked on gambling—not just at cards, which usually require skill as well as luck, but also at roulette and dice, which operate more on chance or probabilities. Mathematics, he admits, has never been his forte, yet he somehow seems to know the chances of something's happening or not and how much it's worth. Perhaps, he now suggests to his companion, he could make a good side living off gambling, the way some people seem to do.

He's read a few books by gaming-table experts who have broken the bank at Monte Carlo or wherever and are now telling others how they did it. Perhaps if he threw caution to the wind, took his little nest egg to Vegas for a weekend, and played to the hilt, he'd find a way to increase his income that suited his own inherent abilities.

Dr. M. almost starts to laugh, but the expression on Mr. E.'s face informs him that he is very serious indeed. Oh yes, Dr. M. says, one can always *try* to make a decent living by gambling. But he doubts that it can be easily done. And he himself is extremely wary of any supposedly guaranteed technique of making big money at it. One must always be alert to aspects of human nature that may be flaws—and thus resist their impulses, Dr. M. observes. It's perfectly normal to be attracted to somebody's well-advertised formula to assist you, at a price, in becoming wealthy: just put your money into a new but "proven" fast money-making scheme. But look at it this way. The once-secret formula is laid out in a book that is hawked to people who naturally respond to this chance of improving their financial conditions as swiftly as possible. The author of such a book and the publisher who markets it are leading people on because they hope to make big money on book sales. They aren't operating out of altruistic reasons, revealing surefire methods of money making so that everybody in the world can become wealthy by simply purchasing their book and then applying its advice out in the real world.

If such methods really worked consistently, Dr. M. goes on, we might all become millionaires and poverty would vanish overnight. Perhaps some clever schemes have at first worked well for individuals. But by the time they are disclosed to the public at large, their unique value is considerably diminished. Gaming rules might even be changed. And anyone who has invested in the book and followed its recommendations religiously might end up angry—and broke. That goes for gambling and a lot of other activities in which money is involved.

Sure, says Dr. M., we'd all like to be rich. And the richer the better! We'd like to do it quickly, with little physical effort, and at no risk to our lives or the few assets we've managed to acquire. So if someone or something comes along that stirs up these all-too-human hopes for some financial easy street, we're apt to buy the instruction plan. We may follow it blindly and forget to think. It's okay if we keep our fortune-capturing daydreams, but acting them out on other people's advice can get us in real trouble. Investing money, time, and labor in a new commitment may lead to disaster if we don't thoroughly investigate and think through the venture in order to become aware of drawbacks and pitfalls as well as possible profits. Unrealistic people are the best prey for con men. The essence of a confidence game, Dr. M. explains, is to lure an unwary victim into parting with money now for the promise of much greater money yields in the future. All too often, real money is spent in return for false hopes. This is what continually hooks the compulsive gambler.

But what is the average person to do? asks Mr. E. in utter frustration. Inflation and mounting expenses keep chopping away at basic salaries. He himself can't seem to think of a sensible way to increase his own income. Perhaps he should become a nighttime bandit, put on a mask, and start raiding liquor stores!

Dr. M., of course, realizes that his guest is kidding, but the underlying tone sounds worried to extreme exasperation. Concern over money isn't a laughing matter, he admits. Almost everyone has it to some degree or another. And that's why, out of sheer desperation, some people actually resort to criminal activities. Oh, not robbery and theft, the outright crimes. But otherwise upright and ethical people may suddenly or gradually become associated with dubious or illicit enterprises—often becoming enmeshed before they comprehend what they are doing or what the consequences and penalties may be. Even if their involvement is only indirect, perhaps financial in nature, they will be subject to investigation, arrest, and imprisonment—and also to possible blackmail and public exposure. And certainly they'll always have their own worries and guilt. There is big money in crime because it supplies certain goods and services to the public, as legitimate businesses do, except that these are illegal— and therefore cost much more. Law-breaking competitors are ruthless, vindictive, and devious. And since one's own associates are criminals, they are untrustworthy by definition. However lucrative a connection may appear, it's exceedingly doubtful that one will ultimately benefit from dealing with any branch of crime. There are some gambles and investments that aren't worth taking or making, Dr. M. pronounces somberly. Quite apart from morality and the commonweal, there's the element of risk—whether of personal safety or total financial loss.

And to make things even more difficult, Dr. M. concludes, time and effort aren't usually enough just by themselves. To get onto most paths leading to wealth, you've got to bring some cash along with you—and risk losing part or all of it along the way.

Mr. E.'s becoming very aware of this by now, which is why he has really begun to consider risking the small assets he has on a weekend at Las Vegas or some other gambling resort. With any success, he'll add to his pile and then go back again in a month or two and do it all over again. Eventually, he may be able to accumulate enough money to invest in something that will bring in a good, steady, extra income, though he's not sure yet what that would be.

Whoa! cautions Dr. M. He knows that Mr. E. now means what he says. Mr. E. is a nice guy. And though he's a good card player, he may very well get skunked when playing against the pros, at blackjack or whatever. Come back tomorrow and talk further, Dr. M. tells him. Then they can discuss gambling, probabilities, risk taking, and expectation. They'll even do a few mathematical exercises. In the process, Mr. E. may begin to think differently about trying to earn his way to fortune by putting his money down on the green felt of a gaming table.

CHAPTER TWO

Making More Money with Money by Banking, Gambling, and Insurance

History shows certain economic breakthroughs that have contributed to the progress of human society, proclaims Dr. M. as he offers his visitor, Mr. E., a cup of tea and a doughnut. Settling upon a definite medium of exchange has been basic to most cultures. Doing so was actually simpler, he observes, than bartering one object for another or paying for labor in goods. Buying and selling could be done by exchanging some accepted token of value: a shell or bead, a substance like salt or spice or gold, a manufactured metal disk or coin. Money could also be transported and stored. A person who managed to accumulate a lot of such tokens became wealthy and powerful.

The concept of banking was another breakthrough, Dr. M. goes on. A bank was a safe place for storing money. But there was an even greater benefit to the money's owner: he could lend the money out at interest to other people who wished to use it, giving the depositor a percentage on the transaction. Of course, explains Dr. M., this fluid use of available funds proved better for both the depositor and society than burying them in the ground, which would remove money from circulation. Banks could also combine small sums held in many individuals' accounts to make reasonably safe investments for everyone's benefit.

So Mr. E. can see, then, that money and banking institutions came about naturally, says Dr. M. That is, a need had arisen for their functions. As civilization developed and assets mounted, financial mechanisms evolved into more complex forms. Commodities or goods sold in the marketplace, that central place in towns and cities, were acquired by money. There the common people could purchase essential and special goods whose prices generally changed according to the fundamental economic law of supply and demand. If there was plenty of something, the price was low. But if there was a shortage and interest in a particular commodity remained strong, the cost was high.

People became increasingly interested in buying a variety of goods, Dr. M. continues. Some were willing to pay a lot of money for certain exotic products, and so the merchant-trader assumed an important role, especially toward the end of the Middle Ages. Some adventurers traveled to faraway foreign lands by caravan or sailing ship to bring back new and desirable goods. Others just invested money to back these ventures. People who declined to take part in this speculative commerce could always keep their money in banks, where risks—and returns on their investments—were comparatively low.

But why should this make such a difference in earnings? Mr. E. asks. High-risk endeavors are invariably attached to greatly increased profits, Dr. M. replies, since their outcomes are uncertain and unpredictable. It sounds, then, rather like gambling, Mr. E. comments. Dr. M. agrees. Large risks can be undertaken on the chance that a successful expedition or a clever or lucky play will result in great profits when compared with modest payoffs in situations in which there is more certainty of winning. But speculating is very different from gambling in that speculating comes from and affects society in some large or small way, whereas gambling exists only for the sake of gamblers.

The attraction of risking money to make much more money, especially when the outcome can be known within a short span of time, is age-old and universal, Dr. M. says. For many humans gambling is irresistible. You'll find some form of it in almost every culture in any corner of the world, no matter how primitive. It's the simplest, most direct manifestation of the get-rich-quick impulse. But the play of probabilities —some people call it "luck"—that is often mixed with skills of various kinds also fascinates many people and helps them pass time in otherwise dull circumstances.

Wouldn't some people do better to gamble directly rather than to invest their money in trading ventures or in banks, though? Mr. E. wants to know. Not for very long, Dr. M. answers, unless they're running the gambling house or a crooked game. To make money consistently at gambling is virtually impossible because each game, in its ultimate form anyway, has been devised so that no one can keep on winning. Betting and payoffs are closely connected with the odds. For example, take the basic game of flipping a coin, in which the coin will come up either heads or tails. . . .

At this, Dr. M. removes a penny from his pocket to demonstrate his points. If one ruled that a $1 bet on tails would result in a $1 gain if tails came up and that a $1 bet on heads would result in a $2 gain if heads came up, would Mr. E. bet on tails? Of course not! says Mr. E. Sure, says Dr. M., everybody would bet on heads and nobody would bet on tails. And that would end the game. To get people to play on both sides of a gambling game, the payoff must equal the risk if the odds themselves are 50/50. As the odds against the player's winning increase, so must the payoff —to make the gamble worth the risk.

Dr. M., while he talks, continues to flip his coin and record the results—*H* or *T*—on a pad of paper. Contrary to common belief, he says, gambling isn't necessarily a "sucker's game." In a coin-flipping game played with an honest coin, like this one, the chance of winning equals the chance of losing. If a person keeps betting on heads, half of the time he wins, half of the time he loses. At least that's how it will average out in time. No matter what clever system of progression he has—doubling his bets if he loses, doubling if he wins, or whatever—the player will eventually break even if he keeps on playing. Every time the coin flips through the air there's a 50/50 chance that it will land on the player's choice. The coin doesn't know what will happen to it any more than the player can predict the outcome. Look! Dr. M. announces conclusively. He has flipped the coin twenty times altogether and has gotten eleven tails and nine heads. If he keeps on like this, the totals should remain similarly close to even. But he sets the penny down, commenting that this form of gambling can become dull very fast.

That's why games like roulette and craps have appeal: they are far more variable and complicated in their probabilities. Therefore betting and risk-taking opportunities result in an increased size of payoffs. These gambles are just complex enough to make players think they can cleverly design a "system" that will enable them to win on the whole. Usually gamblers believe that they are playing against the "house," or casino. But actually they're really playing against the other customers: red against black, pass against don't pass. The "other side" may not be there at the same time, Dr. M. observes, but all in all any player is, in reality, betting against other players' positions and not against the house. What the house does is to exact its commission—a reasonable one, say about 5%—during the plays, as with the two green slots on a roulette wheel among the thirty-six red and black numbered slots. That's how the house takes care of its running expenses and earns good profits. Basically, then, the players themselves gamble against one another. And their money, not the house's, is being risked. The casino is only running a profitable business by providing the place, equipment, and supervision for gamblers.

But what about games like blackjack or poker? Mr. E. wants to know. After all, playing them involves more than sheer chance or probabilities. Oh yes, Dr. M. agrees. Certain gambling pursuits that take skill or knowledge, like those and horse racing, allow for an increased odds of winning by a gambler with experience. For example, in racing a bettor must have good information about horses, jockeys, racetracks, and weather conditions. But such study can take almost full-time work and concentration if one goes at the gambling pursuit seriously as a money producer. It then becomes a job—though an undependable source of income. Also, Dr. M. points out, in order to gamble one usually has to go somewhere, and doing so requires spending time and more money in traveling.

But still, asks Mr. E., isn't it possible to take a fairly small amount of money, say $1,000, and turn it rapidly into a large fortune—maybe $1 million? After all, on all sides we're told of people who've done it through gambling, investing in real estate, or speculating in stocks or commodities.

Well, offers Dr. M. looking rather dubious, *theoretically,* of course, such things are possible. But in actuality things are bound to work out otherwise. To consider the odds or probabilities of doing so, they must first examine some mathematical mechanisms involved in gambling games. Most books and articles that show the ''right way'' to make a financial killing, Dr. M. asserts, are essentially proposing *parlaying.* This means winning once, using the gains to bet and win a second time, then using the larger amount to bet again and win again, and so on. Thus by buying and selling always at a profit, investing the profit in another trade, and winning on that trade, one can continue on up to accumulate that $1 million.

To demonstrate the principle of parlaying to Mr. E., Dr. M. begins to write down some figures. He chooses a very simple game in which the bettor doubles his money each time he wins and has a 50/50 chance of winning. This is an *even bet,* says Dr. M., because the player will receive $1 in winnings for each $1 bet. Coin flipping makes the easiest example. If our player bets $1 on heads and wins, he gets his $1 back plus $1 more. On the second bet he risks $2. If he wins again, he now has $4 to play with.

Dr. M. now shows his visitor how the figures work out:

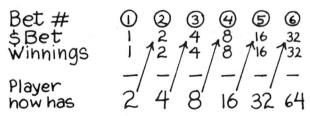

Mathematically, a parlay of this kind naturally looks appealing, Dr. M. admits. It appears that by taking $1,000 and repeatedly winning in an even-bet gambling or speculating situation, within ten successful successive plays this $1,000 can be parlayed into more than $1 million. A lure like this is difficult to resist, particularly when someone claims that he himself has done it and therefore knows that it is possible.

But in reality it won't work out that way, Dr. M. asserts. Can Mr. E. guess why not? Well, replies Mr. E. after a moment of thought, probably because nobody can be right all the time when betting or speculating— whether picking a horse or a stock. Everyone's bound to lose at some point. So if in Dr. M.'s parlay chart the player had lost anywhere along the line, he'd be back where he started. Worse! Dr. M. points out. For he'd have also lost his initial investment. Dr. M. is pleased that Mr. E. spotted the basic flaw in the parlay technique. Many people, in their desperate desire to acquire a fortune, put on blinders when they look at the neat mathematics and fail to consider that they may just possibly lose.

In all probability, then, Dr. M. goes on, an individual can't parlay a small amount and convert it by gambling or speculative trading into a fortune, since he can't always be correct. Even if the odds are stacked in his favor, he's going to lose sooner or later. What happens if a bettor is right 80% of the time? Dr. M. now proposes. These odds are very good indeed, compared to those in most gambling or speculative ventures.

At the first turn, says Dr. M., the player has an 80% chance of being correct, yes. But how about the second time? The probability of being *right* twice in a row becomes 80% multiplied by 80%—which is 64%, which is then the chance of being correct. And how about being right three times in a row, and four and five? Look—Dr. M. takes out his handy, trusty pocket calculator to do the multiples of 0.80, or 80%:

Bet #	①	②	③	④	⑤
Probability of winning	.8	$.8^2$ = .64	$.8^3$ = .512	$.8^4$ = .4096	$.8^5$ = .32768
in %	80%	64%	51%	41%	33%

Dr. M., having written out his calculations, shows Mr. E. how by the fourth turn the bettor has less than a 50/50 chance of winning once again. And by the fifth, only 33%. This, even though he is right 80% of the time! On a parlaying play entailing thousands of dollars, Dr. M. comments, the odds become unfavorable indeed, involving high risks that the player— if his life's assets hang upon winning—would be foolhardy indeed to undertake.

And yet the long parlay actually happens sometimes, Dr. M. remarks. That is, if you can believe what you read or hear. The people who get three exactas in a row or throw seventy straight passes or "break the bank" at Las Vegas are the ones who get the publicity. But nobody is told about the twenty thousand others who lost their shirts to make such wins possible.

Practically speaking, then, says Dr. M., it is exceedingly unwise for the ordinary person, a person like Mr. E., to continue to hope that he can take a few thousand dollars in hard-earned savings and, by risking them in gambling or chancy investments, parlay them into a fortune—or even a half-fortune. If someone is already well endowed and enjoys taking such risks, win or lose, it's just a game to them. But the gambling urge in a person who has few cash assets can become highly self-destructive in the frantic quest for riches.

Speculation, after all, Dr. M. observes, takes place over events and situations that are quite uncertain in their outcome. Inevitably, and invariably, the larger the payoff or reward for guessing correctly or winning, the more unfavorable the odds and the lower the probability of winning—and therefore the higher the risk. What happens, he concludes, is that each player in economic life ends up deciding personally whether certain risks are worth taking in order to gain profits.

But does one actually have to speculate in order to increase one's assets appreciably? asks Mr. E. Dr. M. gives a good-natured chuckle. Mr. E. sounds as if he thinks there may be something . . . well, a bit wicked or devious about speculation. But does he realize that he's actually speculating right now just by being here? Mr. E. looks startled. Think of it! Dr. M. commands. Clearly Mr. E. believes that the odds are favorable that he'll live for quite some time yet. For if he really felt or knew that he was going to die tomorrow or even next week, he would hardly be laying plans for his own financial future. It's an outrageous example of speculation, perhaps, but true nonetheless.

Yet why is that speculation? Mr. E. wants to know. Dr. M. guesses that they should now examine the meaning and applications of the word *speculation,* which has acquired an undeserved bad reputation. People somehow seem to think that it's an activity that a nice person doesn't do, that it isn't legitimate work. *But speculation is simply analyzing the probability of winning, offset by the consequences of losing, and then determining if the gains to be received are worth the risk.*

In essence, Dr. Mr. goes on, speculation involves betting that events will go a certain way. Proceeding through life, we are all speculating most of the time. But the ongoing process is usually subconscious, except when risks seem considerable to us. At any moment, if one wants to look at it that way, we are liable to lose something, get injured, harm somebody, become ill, even die. Engaged in normal goal-seeking activities, we take risks that we dismiss automatically from our minds, having implicitly decided that the gain or reward for our efforts considerably offsets and outweighs that risk taking.

Mr. E. has noticeably perked up at this interesting revelation. A woman who drives to work each morning, for example, is subconsciously betting that she won't be involved in a serious auto accident, Dr. M. continues. If she knew that she would be maimed or killed, or if she suspected that there might be a 50% chance of this happening, she obviously wouldn't go to work. Whatever the salary to be received for that day's labor would hardly compensate for serious injury. Even though the worker can't know for sure that she will *not* be in an accident, she normally feels that the odds are so greatly against it that the payoff, or wage, is worth the small risk in traveling. By inadvertently analyzing the risk versus the reward, she is, in a sense, speculating on the favorable outcome.

Ah, remarks Mr. E., Dr. M. obviously is now entering his special realm of expertise: the insurance business! His host genially admits that this is so and asks his visitor to follow a few simple mathematical equations before they move on to the connection between insurance, probabilities, and money.

Note that there are two parts of speculating, he tells Mr. E.: first, the probability of winning, or the odds, and second, recognizing what you win when you win and what you lose when you lose. A mathematician wraps this up in one word: *expectation*. Expectation is the probability of winning multiplied by what is won, minus the probability of losing multiplied by what is lost. Or, as he writes it down now:

$$E \times P = P_W \cdot \$W - P_L \cdot \$L$$

So what is the expectation in flipping a coin and betting $1 each time? asks Dr. M. rhetorically. It is zero, like this:

$$\tfrac{1}{2} \cdot \$1 - \tfrac{1}{2} \cdot \$1 = 0$$

In other words, a player should break even after playing for a while.

And what's the expectation in betting $1 on a single number on a roulette wheel—say with no green slots, thirty-six numbers, and a payoff of thirty-five to one? Mr. E. thinks he's not up to calculating that as yet. It's easier than you think, says Dr. M. as he writes it:

$$\tfrac{1}{36} \cdot \$35 - \tfrac{35}{36} \cdot \$1 = 0$$

Zero again, he remarks, which means that the payoff fits the odds. Now there are situations in which there's a positive expectation, as with the coin-flipping game in which heads paid $2 on a $1 bet:

$$\tfrac{1}{2} \cdot \$2 - \tfrac{1}{2} \cdot \$1 = \tfrac{1}{2}$$

Negative expectation would be simply demonstrated by the situation in which tails paid only $1 on a $2 bet:

$$\tfrac{1}{2} \cdot \$1 - \tfrac{1}{2} \cdot \$2 = -\tfrac{1}{2}$$

A negative expectation, such as a driver's likelihood of being injured on her way to work, Dr. M. says, may be a high-risk situation without compensatory rewards. A zero expectation, with the reward for winning properly geared to the odds, is fair enough. A positive expectation, which most of us normally have in just going about our business in the world, may contain favorable odds, minimal risks—and a very small payoff. A positive expectation is slanted toward the individual's benefit. That's why the driver goes to work. Yet she may recognize the risk involved, however improbable. So to protect herself, she can *transfer the risk*.

Of course, Dr. M. exclaims, a person cannot take a physical injury and spread it out over many people—take three of her broken bones, for example, and transfer them to three other people, one apiece! A financial risk, however, can be spread out. A driver can significantly reduce her financial liability in case of a serious accident by buying *insurance*.

Ha! says Mr. E. He has been waiting for this. Financial risk is transferred from the person who buys an insurance policy to the company that supplies it, Dr. M. continues. Since most people don't want to speculate on being wiped out financially by a disabling accident—to themselves or to others or to property—they buy insurance from a firm willing to accept this risk. The cost is the payment premiums.

Some individuals do not buy insurance unless it is compulsory, Dr. M. says, though often, of course, corporations have insurance policies for employees. People who choose not to have insurance either accept all the financial risks themselves or else irresponsibly deny any probability of accidents. But isn't this unwise? asks Mr. E. Certainly! Dr. M. agrees —though of course he's biased because he's in the business. But he recognizes that almost everyone is apt to lose money when buying insurance. Mr. E. frowns. He hasn't thought about that, he admits. Dr. M. explains that people are likely to lose money because the premiums set by the insurance company are figured actuarially, so that the sum of all premiums received is greater than what the company must pay out collectively to the injured or deceased insured. From this difference the company extracts its working expenses; what remains is profit. And it's the profit that makes this risk-accepting business worthwhile.

But don't the expert actuaries like Dr. M. arrange for the whole system to work out that way? asks Mr. E. Yes, Dr. M. admits. They and now their computers, into which are fed the most astounding accumulation of statistics collected over the years, having to do with all sorts of facts, people, and circumstances. And imagine! he adds. The very first insurance policies in Europe were created for trading ventures, for those high-risk maritime commercial voyages that could bring such wealth to the trader-speculators involved if the ships came back into port. And if they didn't, at least there was an insurance payoff as a consolation. Such insurance worked out so well in practice for everyone concerned that eventually it also began to cover losses from fires and risks to people's lives.

But if the insurance companies always figure on making net profits on their policies, why do people keep on buying insurance even though they are paying out money they'll never see again? asks Mr. E.•Because, explains Dr. M., they are willing to pay out a small amount that they *can* afford to lose in order to protect themselves from the possibility of paying out a large amount that they *cannot* afford to lose—or that their families will somehow have to earn if something happens to them. So one might say that insurance companies are rather like casino banks, Dr. M. remarks. They take money in on premiums from many thousands of individuals and pay out chunks of it when a client "wins"—if you can call it that —by becoming a casualty in an unlikely or low-odds accident or illness. People who purchase insurance contracts in effect accept what is mathematically a built-in loss so that they can live and work normally, retaining their peace of mind without constantly fearing financial disaster. As far as the probabilities work out, for them it's a form of negative expectation —but one worth investing in. And for the profit-seeking insurance company, the net transaction involves positive expectations, since if the actuarial calculations are correct, the company will win more than it will lose, even though it has assumed other people's risks.

The insurance business, then, is essentially based on speculation, Dr. M. observes. It is institutionalized speculation, however, compared to the speculation done by individuals who invest in real estate or stocks. Their money has actually worked for them. People traditionally conceive of labor as the main source of income. But they find it hard to acknowledge that business has always required risking assets or capital, sometimes at unfavorable odds, in order to achieve significant profits. And money can sometimes accomplish what labor alone cannot. But it must be handled prudently, not gambled away.

So, says Mr. E., realizing that their discussion is drawing to a close, what Dr. M. seems to be telling him is that he would be wiser and safer to put any accrued capital into some established form of business speculation, certainly not into blackjack or roulette, which as gambling games are unconnected with the interests and needs of society.

Yes, Dr. M. agrees. What it can be will depend upon Mr. E.'s resources and inclinations. He himself invests in property, believing that as the population increases and the amount of available land decreases, the basic law of supply and demand will inevitably assure that real estate will do much better than simply keep pace with inflation. Working with numbers all day long, he is happy to switch to the realities of land ownership in his spare time. Altogether, he has a quite positive expectation of the rewards of this endeavor and experiences little risk.

Well, Mr. E. remarks, speculating does sound a lot more sensible than gambling! He now thanks Dr. M. for giving him a morning's minicourse in money, risk taking, and probabilities—with a side trip into the insurance business, which Dr. M. knows so well. As he departs, he says he hopes to see Dr. M. at the next poker-playing session when, with any luck, he'll once more show his skills at gambling. But, following his host's advice, he is going to stay in the minor league. He will have to find some other way than high-stakes gambling to put the money he has to work at making more money for him.

CHAPTER THREE

Real Estate and Stocks: For Investment or Speculating?

Some people get lucky breaks in life, Mr. E. often has reminded himself. Maybe they come into them wholly by chance, without exerting any special effort or even determining to be successful. This happens when people are born into well-to-do families that have already blazed the trail ahead, and even paved it, leading to good fortune. Such people, Mr. E. observes, may be apt to take their fortuitous situations for granted—quite as if they deserved them.

And yet Mr. E. has also seen that usually the most energetic, innovative, and ambitious people are "self-made," using their own initiative and the educational and employment opportunities in the United States to achieve their goals, whatever their family backgrounds have been. Mr. E. himself has had only modest aims: he never set out to become a great entrepreneur. But from time to time, he inevitably wishes that his own road through life could be both more secure economically and more mentally challenging. He is aware that much of the time he is simply plodding along, trying to get the household budget to conform with his earnings.

Mr. E., then, wasn't born with the proverbial silver spoon in his mouth. Like most of us, he gets along—by the skin of his teeth. He isn't looking for a lucky break; he's searching for opportunities.

And suddenly, out of the blue, he gets both. His favorite aunt dies, unexpectedly, and leaves him the bulk of her estate. Not that she was wealthy. But she had some solid assets, and the trustees convert them into a handsome amount that is paid by check to Mr. E., the beneficiary. He deposits it in a special savings account and begins to consider how he may best invest it in the future.

Mr. E. will treat this money in the same way he would had he earned it himself. He hardly intends to fritter it away foolishly. He'll put some of it into long-term bonds and education trust funds for his children. He figures that after he takes care of the essential financial responsibilities right now and for the future, he'll have $10,000 to do with as he pleases. No, it isn't a lot of money, the way things are nowadays, but it should be enough to get started in some sideline enterprise that offers an opportunity to increase his income.

He knows what he doesn't want to do. He doesn't want to purchase a franchise to open some fast-food service in another part of town. He doesn't want to put it into any of the "collectibles" that increasingly intrigue people who like to have something attractive yet solid in which to invest their money. Old West paintings, antique furniture, postage stamps, rare coins, Persian rugs, gemstones, Depression-period milk glass—he doesn't need them. Mr. E. also doesn't want to keep his money in a bank account, even one that pays 10% interest. He figures he can do better than that.

Mr. E.'s friends and associates invariably advise him to purchase real estate. That's what most of them do. After all, it's *real,* not just something on paper. And losing on it is difficult because of the rapid rise of property values across the nation. Mr. E. doesn't want to buy land that's still cheap, somewhere out in the sticks, and then wait for years to see it escalate in worth. So he begins looking for a building—a house, an apartment complex, or an office structure—to rent out for a while before being able to sell out at a profit. This way he can bring in a dependable income while he's waiting for his investment to appreciate.

Well, now. The usual down payment required to buy real estate is 20%. Therefore, Mr. E.'s $10,000 will enable him to purchase something costing $50,000. He starts looking around town and discovers that he really can't get much at all for that price—at best, a small, older house in the less desirable section. But such a purchase could work out as a starter on the route to future riches, especially since certain signs of activity—new buildings and refurbished old ones—indicate that the property's value will soon rise. He decides to buy.

Mr. E., of course, doesn't know what he's getting into until he gets into it. There are innumerable forms to fill out (which he always hates doing), insurance to buy, charges to pay for title searches and escrow. The project takes much more time and trouble than he expected. Cleaning and basic repairs indoors and out have to be arranged for, inspected, paid for. There will be additional maintenance problems and costs later on, he realizes. A for-rent ad has to be run in the classified section of the local newspaper, resulting in annoying phone calls and time-consuming interviews, until Mr. E. finally finds what seems to be the right tenants. Then the property tax is raised just after he takes over ownership. Mr. E. is deciding early on that he doesn't like being a landlord at all. Real estate is full of hassles and responsibilities and costs that he hadn't anticipated. A middle-of-the-night phone call over an emergency plumbing problem is the last straw. Come profit, come loss, Mr. E. wants out.

Mr. E. sells the house less than a year after he bought it. He is lucky. The value of the property has increased by 10% in that interval. Making a $5,000 profit on his $10,000 investment gives him a return of 50%. Not bad. Until he begins thinking—and subtracting. He pays the current real-estate broker's commission of 6%, amounting to $3,300, leaving him only $1,700. (Why hadn't he tried to sell it himself? he now wonders, much as he would have disliked the chore.) Then he realizes that all along he has been paying 10% interest on the $40,000 mortgage held by the bank: that's $4,000 (though there's also a penalty charge levied by the bank because he sold early). Now he's into the red on this deal, with a loss of at least $2,300.

But wait! Of course there was the monthly rent that Mr. E. took in: that good, steady payment, which puts him back in the black again in his calculations. But then he adds up what he has spent to repair, maintain, and pay taxes on the house. These "operating expenses" threaten to overtake the rent receipts. When he calculates his own time spent, Mr. E. becomes really upset. Well, he failed to profit from the whole business of becoming a real-estate operator. So much for real estate! he concludes.

Mr. E. figures, though, that he can still assemble a $10,000 chunk of money for another investment venture. This time he follows his brother-in-law's advice and goes to talk to a reputable stockbroker in town. He is taken around the brokerage quarters, given some pamphlets with lots of impressive charts and statistics, and shown the perpetual electronic contact maintained with the New York Stock Exchange.

Mr. B., the knowledgeable and amiable broker, has a knack for assessing the personality characteristics of prospective customers so that he can steer them toward the type of investing appropriate for them. What course can he recommend to this new client? Obviously, discovering the right route for Mr. E.'s money will take time. But yes, Mr. E. is invited to open an account here with his $10,000. It will allow him to buy almost any kind of securities of interest to him, as a modest start in a new side career as a stock investor.

Mr. B., after listening to Mr. E.'s account of his recent real-estate deal, tells him frankly that although Mr. E. is intelligent, he is noticeably lacking knowledge of various fundamentals in money-making. Mr. B. would do him a disservice if he did not acquaint him with the general terrain, for although Mr. E. has come in to see about buying stocks, some other form of investment or financial speculation may well be more suitable for him.

Mr. B. starts off by introducing Mr. E. in a preliminary way to the procedure of buying and selling *corporate stocks*—those shares available to the public that make them partner-participants in American business. A stock market, Mr. B. explains, is nothing mysterious. Like all markets —the local grocery store, for instance—it is simply a locality where people meet to buy and sell items. These items may be cans of tuna, pairs of shoes, tubes of toothpaste—or shares of stock.

The stock market is really a matter of convenience, says Mr. B. Any person wishing to buy one hundred shares of General Motors, say, does not have to do so on a stock market. He can advertise his desire in the newspapers if he wishes. But buying stock at a market expressly conducted for exchanging stock for money is much easier.

Mr. E. wonders whether a specific marketplace—like the New York Stock Exchange—is being referred to when people talk about what the "stock market" is doing. In that sense, Mr. B. answers, the term refers to a specific sort of economic activity going on in society, not to an actual marketplace. And in that usage it means the whole nationwide transactions connected with the ever-fluctuating values of corporate stocks as shares are bought and sold by millions of Americans. An important index like the Dow Jones Average can indicate the relative health of the nation's business community as it reacts to current news and future forecasts. Or one should say as the American public reacts, Mr. B. corrects himself, for it is they who buy and sell stocks and determine their values.

For many investors, Mr. B. tells Mr. E., investing in the stock market is preferable to putting money into bank accounts. Banks determine for themselves where and how they will lend out the money deposited by account holders. Stock buyers can select the enterprise in which they would like to invest. Their money is pooled with that of many other stockholders and used by a company to establish or maintain what is hoped will be a successful enterprise. Shareholders receive dividends when there are profits to be shared. These dividends are usually not much more than what one's money might earn on bank interest and may be less than the yield on a bond. But stocks seem more attractive to many investors because they are geared to the economy and can rise in value, sometimes rather quickly. Bank accounts and bonds do not normally react in this way.

Stocks, however, Mr. B. points out, can be riskier than the more steady investments. Poor management, a lack of widespread interest in products, unpredictable happenings that affect operations, even rumors —all can cause a drop in the value of some company's stock, so that a shareholder loses instead of gains on an investment. But there are limits to such losses, Mr. B. says. One cannot lose any more money than what the stock was originally purchased for. This includes not only the customer's margin but also whatever was borrowed from the brokerage handling the account.

Margin? Mr. E. asks Mr. B. to define the word as it's used in the stock market. Patiently, Mr. B. explains that the government, through the SEC (Securities and Exchange Commission) periodically sets particular "down payments" on the purchase of stock. Usually this figure is around 50%, but sometimes it could be much more. This percentage determines the amount that a buyer must put up when acquiring the shares. The remainder can be borrowed from the brokerage at interest, using the stock itself as collateral.

But does one have to buy at margin? Mr. E. wants to know. No, Mr. B. tells him. But then he shows how, by buying at margin, an investor can make an investment go much further because of *leverage.* What's that? Mr. E. asks, not sure he knows. Leverage is a way of controlling a comparatively large amount of value with a small amount of cash, Mr. B. answers. By putting up only 50% of the purchase price of some stock, the customer can earn a 20% profit from only a 10% rise in value. Say Mr. E. acquires 100 shares of stock at $20 per share at a 50% margin, investing his own $1,000 and borrowing another $1,000 from the brokerage. If the stock's value rises 10%, or $2 per share, his total investment is then worth $2,200—giving him a $200 profit. Without the brokerage loan, he could only have bought half as much. With the loan, he will also receive twice as much in dividends—which help to pay the loan interest. The brokerage itself makes money from commissions and interest. All profits belong to Mr. E.

Yet what if the stock goes *down* 10% in value? Mr. E. inquires. Ah, then he sustains a $200 loss, Mr. B. admits. He'll draw a diagram to show this to him better:

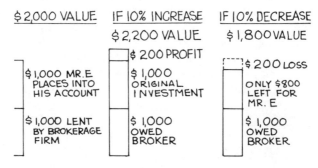

Mr. E. says that he sees now what Mr. B. meant by leverage. A $200 gain, or loss, would be $200 compared to his $1,000: 200 ÷ 1,000, or 20%.

If the price does go up, can he take his $200 profit out right away? Mr. E. asks. No, replies Mr. B., because he won't receive the money representing the rise in the stock's value until he actually sells it. And, he adds, if the price goes *down* substantially, Mr. E. will have to come up with the extra money to cover the loss to avoid violating SEC regulations.

Anything else he should know about? Mr. E. wants to know. Well, Mr. B. says, of course there will be certain debits along the way—like the loan interest and the fees or commissions to the brokerage for buying and selling his shares. How much will these fees amount to? Mr. E. wonders. Figuring on a year between purchase and sale, Mr. B. calculates about $100 for the loan interest, which might be canceled out by dividends. The buy-and-sell commission will probably exceed $100.

Mr. E. is surprised: Why such high commissions for such a small amount of money? Because, Mr. B. tells him, a share represents a part ownership in a corporation. Buying stock involves a lot of paperwork done mainly by the brokerage firm. The investor may be wholly unaware of the complicated transactions regarding changes in ownership and in the transfer of titles and arrangements for dividends and the votes or proxies at stockholders' meetings. This paperwork requires the broker to do signings and sendings already familiar to Mr. E. from his real-estate experience. The more shares an investor purchases, the less proportionately he pays in such commissions over market transactions.

What about the stories Mr. E. has heard through the years about big "killings" made on the stock market? Usually, says Mr. B., such large and quick profits are made by speculators in *volatile stocks:* stocks of new or perhaps risky business ventures that rarely pay dividends to stockholders but can rapidly escalate in value if the companies' operations seem promising or are successful. Then new buyers want to get in too, paying prices much higher than the price of the original shares. If someone buys one hundred shares of such stock at $20 and sells them afterward for $80, that person will make about $6,000 in profits. On the other hand, if the company goes bankrupt, its stock becomes worthless. And unless it has assets in salable properties that can benefit its shareholders in some small way, the unlucky investor will lose $2,000. This kind of chance many investors never wish to take, however appealing the prospect of big profits.

But isn't this speculating on price changes what the stock market is really for? Mr. E. inquires. After all, he has come in to see Mr. B. because he wants to get in on this kind of action. He wouldn't mind risking a portion of his $10,000 on some stock that might double in value in a year or so. Stable, long-term investments don't really grab him so far as this nest egg of his goes. He really enjoys taking chances whenever he stands to make significant profits—especially if he can know the outcome fairly quickly, whether it's win or lose. Perhaps he's a gambler by nature, adds Mr. E., remembering his conversations with Dr. M.

But the stock market was not set up as a gambling mechanism, Mr. B. points out at once. Gambling games are contrived for gamblers alone and are not connected with any possible economic or social benefits to society at large—unless they are tied into state-run lotteries, in which a government, in order to raise money for worthwhile functions, operates virtually as a casino in a legitimate "numbers racket." The idea behind stock shares, says Mr. B., is to allow many small investors to pool their resources so as to start a large business. Later they can sell their shares and new investors can buy them—through the convenience of a stock exchange, if they wish. And these investors, Mr. B. continues, plan to make money on the dividends that the corporations pay their shareholders.

But it's true, isn't it, Mr. E. interrupts, that a lot of these people are really hoping to make the big profit by selling at a higher price than they bought? Yes, Mr. B. sighs, but people who hope to profit by a price change should really be called speculators. The ones content to receive a steady return on their capital are investors.

Mr. E. now admits that he must really want to speculate, not gamble or invest, though somehow the term *speculator* bothers him and will take getting used to. But can't he speculate on the market, if that's what he wants? Of course he can, says Mr. B. Millions do, so why not he? He might be better advised, however, to go to a market mechanism already set up for speculating. Speculating on the stock market is, in a sense, abusing its original purpose—and not really to Mr. E.'s advantage anyway.

Mr. B. is beginning to comprehend Mr. E.'s disposition, he announces. Clearly, Mr. E. knows himself and has already taken care of his financial needs and responsibilities. Now he wants some fast action at higher stakes than those available in regular investments. Since Mr. E. is apparently the speculating type, Mr. B. wonders whether he has ever considered trading in commodities. The commodity market, he points out, is properly set up for speculation. And that seems to be what Mr. E. really intends to do. There would be definite advantages to him, which they can discuss later.

Mr. E. seems shocked. What he has heard about commodities isn't good at all. He knows that Mr. B. is an honest, expert broker, and so he is surprised that Mr. B. might suggest, even recommend, this course of financial betterment. Does Mr. B. actually handle commodities at this brokerage? Indeed he does, says Mr. B. But he is careful in accepting clients who wish to open accounts, for many people are financially and psychologically unsuited for commodity speculation. Also, he always asks that would-be speculators undergo a learning process about commodity trading before they actually enter and take positions in the marketplace. He never wants them to rely upon his own knowledge or advice, for although he has many good sources of information, which his clients are welcome to draw upon, he can be wrong just as often as he can be right. This is true even of expert professional traders. His clients must make their own decisions; he acts upon their instructions. They do much better if they really know what they are doing. As a broker he may suggest techniques: how to get out if a trade seems to be going wrong or how to follow up a seemingly correct guess and work at it to one's advantage without overextending and risking all profits earned thus far. But his main role, as Mr. B. sees it, is to introduce a client to the pros and cons in commodity speculation, to explain how the market originated and how it works now, and to help a new customer prepare a program of serious study before jumping in.

Mr. E. seems reassured, even impressed. But he tells Mr. B. that the commodity market, despite its name, has always seemed very phony, unsubstantial—and, yes, disreputable. Is it really legal? At this, Mr. B. has to laugh. What could be more substantial, more real, than commodities? They are visible, actual, tangible, weighable, countable things. They involve 50,000 pounds of potatoes, 5,000 bushels of oats, 38,000 pounds of pork bellies, or 25,000 pounds of copper. Not just figures in a ledger, they can't be shifted around and lost in the bookkeeping shenanigans of embezzlers, as often happens in corporations' finances. And certainly commodities are just as real as the property bought, maintained, and sold in real-estate speculations. The contracts regarding them are just as valid, negotiable, and legal as property deeds and stock certificates! As for their being "disreputable," this reputation has been unjustly earned because the commodity market is a quick-buck, hard-playing arena. Its potential profits attract all sorts of new speculators. Most of them burn out within their first year at trading—mainly because they do not understand the mechanisms in the market and fail to use conservative money management techniques. Both of these matters can be learned.

But people are sometimes peculiar, Mr. B. observes. They can put years of study and preparation into a profession, yet so many of them seem to think that making money with money should be swift and effortless, requiring no education at all! Then when they fail at something, they blame *it*, not themselves. And that's why the commodity market is frequently considered shady or even evil.

Mr. E.'s head is reeling with the many things that the broker has been telling him. And it's starting to churn up more questions. Saying that he wants to know more about commodities, he makes an appointment with Mr. B. for the following day.

CHAPTER FOUR
Considering Commodities

The stockbroker, Mr. B., offers Mr. E., the novice speculator, the chair by his desk. Today they will talk about commodities, trading commodities on the market, and the role of the speculator, he announces. Since Mr. E. seems to know little about the field, Mr. B. will present it as simply and generally as he can. He welcomes any questions that his visitor may wish to ask during the course of this informal lecture. Then, if Mr. E. continues to be interested in commodity speculation, they can discuss the specifics of trading and design an education program for him at a later meeting.

First of all, asks Mr. B., does Mr. E. know what commodities are? Well, commodities are goods, of course, says Mr. E. Mr. B. explains that the goods traditionally presented on the commodity market itself are mostly "raw": things grown on the land, like produce and livestock, or removed from the ground, like certain minerals. They are animal, mineral, or vegetable products—most of them in heavy demand by industries or consumers, though many must be transformed before they are moved out to the consumers. They are usually produced, shipped, and stored in large quantities. They are fairly uniform in size and substance. They can be precisely measured, weighed, or counted. Properly stored, they are not quickly perishable. They are apt to be seasonal in supply, and their prices fluctuate according to the basic law of supply and demand. Widely marketable, many have worldwide producing and consuming networks.

How are these commodities usually classified? Mr. E. wants to know. The best way to consider them initially is to break them down into general kinds of goods, says Mr. B., taking out a pen and writing down a rough list for his visitor to look at:

GRAINS-- wheat, corn, oats, barley, soybeans, etc.

LIVESTOCK-- cattle, hogs, poultry, pork bellies

FIBERS-- cotton and wool

FOREST PRODUCTS-- lumber and plywood

FOODS-- potatoes, sugar, frozen orange juice, coffee, cocoa

METALS-- silver, gold, copper, platinum, paladium

FINANCIAL-- treasury bills and bonds, commercial paper, foreign currencies

OTHER-- fuel oil, propane, U.S. silver coins

That's quite a lot of things, comments Mr. E. But why these particular ones and not others? He notices that Mr. B. hasn't mentioned rice. But surely that is a major cereal grain? Mr. B. explains that although many traders through the years have tried to get rice put on the American commodity market, a move that would doubtlessly benefit consumers, so far they have failed. Mr. B. suspects that the rice merchants around the world prefer to control the supply themselves—hence the prices too. However, there is a rising demand for rice to be traded openly, and so we may soon see a government-regulated rice market.

And how about onions? asks Mr. E. Aren't they a large-bulk, storable form of produce that is much in demand, like potatoes? Mr. B. tells him that actually they were entered on the market for a few years but then disallowed—possibly resulting in higher prices to consumers.

But don't the commodity speculators themselves actually drive the prices continually upward? Mr. E. opines. That's what the public tends to think, Mr. B. admits. People generally fail to understand the function and the benefit of commodity trading to them. Speculators themselves, as Mr. E. is aware, are surrounded by myths portraying them as malicious meddlers in the American and international economies. In fact, speculators usually keep the prices *down* through their constant buying and selling. And because speculators can take opposite positions, price changes rarely go to extremes. Speculators introduce into the market a considerable and necessary *liquidity*—the ready flow of cash money into production and marketing. At any one time there are so many buyers and sellers that they make a smooth transition from one price to another, leaving no large gaps between price changes in large-volume trading. Most importantly, though, speculators provide what amounts to insurance for *commercials*—those individuals and companies whose businesses are directly connected with growing or using basic commodities. Commercials depend upon speculators to furnish the financial umbrellas that shield them from adverse price changes.

Insurance? The term used here utterly baffles our Mr. E. Oh yes, says Mr. B., a special kind of insurance. Without it, many businesses would fail. And think how such a constant financial crisis would swiftly affect almost everybody—above all, the consumers who need commodities for food, clothing, shelter, and a stable and prosperous economy.

Mr. E., however, can't imagine how such insurance is provided by speculators. Insurance itself, he knows—especially since talking with Dr. M.—involves speculation on the part of both insurance companies and the insured, who must concern themselves with probabilities, risks, expectations, profits, and losses. But how does all this connect with commodities? he wants to know.

Mr. B. points out that all the commodities on the market have one thing especially in common. Does Mr. E. care to guess what it is? Well, Mr. E. volunteers, he expects it has to do with the price changes that Mr. B. already mentioned. That's right! Mr. B. commends him. They are all subject to unpredictable fluctuations in prices or values. After all, that's why they are put on the market to begin with. The near-constant rise and fall in value affects those commercials who produce, store, or process commodities differently. Those at one end—the farmers, ranchers, loggers, and miners, who produce the raw commodities and initially sell them—will not be affected in the same way as those at the other end—the grain elevator owners, food processors, meat packers, lumber dealers, and manufacturers, who generally buy goods to resell them, use them, or convert them into other forms. If supply is short and cannot keep up with demand, a producer can charge a higher price for a raw commodity and get it, sometimes reaping unexpectedly big profits. And at the same time, a buyer who needs this commodity and has to pay more for it may suffer large financial losses, particularly when the processed product's price has already been set so that the difference cannot be passed on to retailers and consumers.

Mr. E. expects that the opposite effect takes place when there is an oversupply. Yes, Mr. B. agrees, if a commodity has been overproduced and demand slackens, commercial buyers can obtain it at a much lower price than was previously figured into business costs. They can consequently reap higher profits, while the producers sustain a considerable loss in revenue, wiping out their small but essential profits in the process, perhaps causing them to go bankrupt. Either way, one commercial side or the other is in peril when a price moves up or down, especially widely.

But now where do speculators come in? Mr. E. inquires. They interpose themselves within selling and buying transactions among commercials, who well in advance of delivery of a commodity are making contractual agreements that set their costs, Mr. B. explains. Commercials in the business of some commodity thereby transfer the risk of a price change to speculators. Speculators accept this risk in the hope of profiting from a price change that goes up or down according to their predictions and the positions they have taken in obtaining future contracts. The whole process virtually insures commercials against financial losses.

Mr. E. confesses that he is still confused. He doesn't understand how this insurance happens. Is Mr. E. acquainted with *syndicated insurance?* asks Mr. B. Is this very different from the regular insurance supplied by the large, familiar insurance companies? asks Mr. E. in reply. Mr. B. wants to know if his visitor knows about Lloyd's of London. Mr. E. has heard of it, of course, but that's about all. Do they insure commodities? Mr. B. laughs gently. Not against the risk of adverse price changes, he says. No company in the world has resources vast enough to do that, and probably no combination of companies either. Why? Mr. E.'s expression is asking. Because there's too much money involved, Mr. B. declares. Sure, goods normally can be insured against theft, loss, and damage from fire or flood. For a price, insurance companies provide such coverage for individual or corporate owners of things subject to risk; crop insurance, for example, is available to farmers.

But when it comes to commodities, Mr. B. goes on, the huge quantities of goods grown and traded widely, there is one risk that simply cannot be transferred to insurance companies: those unpredictable price changes that go against people or parties directly involved in producing and selling or in processing and marketing the commodities.

A price change itself may seem small enough, Mr. B. suggests, like 10¢ per bushel of wheat, more or less. But when considering 50,000 or 150,000 bushels of wheat grown on a farm, the figure becomes significant, for the total value can go up or down by $5,000 or $15,000. That means either more money for the farmer and more expense to the company buying his wheat or less money for the farmer and less cost to the wheat buyer. Although both commercial sides in trading want to make profits on their separate labors, neither wishes to be put out of business because of a disastrous price change coming unpredictably from the workings of supply and demand, which themselves are affected by hundreds, even thousands, of random events.

COMMODITY SPECULATION FOR BEGINNERS

Commercials, Mr. B. continues, are not in the business of trying to earn high profits from taking big risks. That is speculation—the speculators' business. Ordinary insurance companies, who *do* make a business out of speculation, cannot involve themselves in this form of risk taking: protecting commercials from adverse price changes. The quantities of goods dealt with around the world are too large and the sums of money attached to their valuations are too gigantic. Companies have reserve funds to insure many thousands of automobiles, houses, and people's lives. But the dollar volume in commodities is much too great. In the United States, Mr. B. gives as an example, about 3 billion bushels of wheat are supplied annually. If the wheat sells wholesale at, say, $4 per bushel, that adds up to $12 billion. Not even governments have that kind of money at their fingertips! And that figure is just for wheat. What would you have if you added in other essential, highly tradable commodities, like corn, oats, cotton, sugar, soybeans, cattle, pigs, chickens, lumber, orange juice, coffee, potatoes, copper, and silver? The supply of commodities can be suddenly reduced by bad weather, a widespread and uncontrollable plant or animal disease or infestation, or some new government decision. A surplus can create almost equivalent financial stress in the world economy, despite the seeming availability at the time of foodstuffs for hungry populations.

So what commodities do require, Mr. B. asserts, is a special form of insurance available to commercials at a nominal sum (they have enough costs to contend with as it is) that will protect them from calamitous price fluctuations—the fear of which can distract them from the proper work of producing or processing goods. Such an insurance would not be easy to achieve through the ordinary channels, for not only are the risks involved in commodity price insurance too huge financially, but they are also unpredictable. There are too many unknowns—such as world weather conditions in six months' time—that prohibit price forecasts to be made in the way that insurance actuaries can fairly precisely calculate the incidence of accidents or deaths in a given population group.

Another factor of great importance, Mr. B. adds, is that a price change in any commodity is worldwide in effect. If the Russian wheat crop fails, all bushels of wheat everywhere actually change price at the same time once the news is confirmed, since the Russians must arrange to buy their wheat from another source, naturally increasing the value, and price, of wheat throughout the world. The reverse is also true with surpluses. When, for example, a great excess of wheat that has been grown in Australia is offered on the world markets, the overall supply increases, thereby lowering the price to all buyers. The owners of a large bakery in, say, Saint Louis may want the cheapest wheat available, no matter where it comes from. They would rather pay $4.00 per bushel for the Australian wheat plus 40¢ per bushel shipping costs, than put out $4.50 per bushel for wheat coming from nearby Kansas. Thus the supply, demand, and consumption of commodities cut across national boundaries, linking improbable sellers and buyers because each seeks the best deal.

But isn't the same commodity actually quite different if grown in another land? asks Mr. E. Not in effect, Mr. B. answers. There are different varieties and different grades, of course; but basically wheat is wheat. Wheat grown in the United States has the same general characteristics and nutrients as wheat grown in Russia or Australia. As a shortage in one place is made up by supply from another, prices shift accordingly, so long as there are no stringent restrictions on free trade among nations. It's like water seeking its own level.

Then there's yet another thing to consider about grain prices, Mr. B. goes on. Grains can often be substituted for one another, especially in livestock feed, for which millions of bushels each year are used. A scarcity in one kind, say wheat, will run up the price and induce its regular buyers to purchase another, maybe corn, resulting in more demand for corn—and therefore a price increase in that too. Wheat usually costs more than corn, but though their prices need not be the same, they tend to move in the same direction, whether up or down. Thus if corn goes up, wheat will soon follow its lead, or vice versa.

Now, says Mr. B., to get back to the insurance issue. Companies can insure many cars because not every one insured will be involved in an accident within the year, and many houses because not all of them will burn down at the same time. The probabilities of a single car's being in an accident or a particular house's burning are worked out actuarially. The insurance premiums are based on remote likelihoods of some disaster. A life insurance firm can prosper because few customers are likely to die each year. The many other customers continue to pay their premiums, costing nothing and virtually supporting the payments to beneficiaries.

But one can recognize how different it is with the price of commodities, says Mr. B. Since the prices on all bushels of wheat change the same way at the same time, what normal insurance company would insure 1,000 bushels against a price decrease, expecting only two or three of these bushels to be so affected? None. Multiply this risk by the 3 billion bushels of wheat grown in the nation, and you can see that such insurance would be utterly unthinkable, at any premium price, for any insurance company.

Mr. E. now reminds the broker that he mentioned Lloyd's of London. If it doesn't insure commodities against adverse price changes, why is the "syndicated insurance" it offers of significance? Because, says Mr. B., it's a different form of insurance. Lloyd's can take greater financial risks than normal because it is composed of many individual insurers, each of whom accepts and bears only a small part of the entire risk. Suppose a $20 million tanker must be insured against collision and running aground. To obtain a policy, the shipowners' quest begins in a cubicle at Lloyd's Coffeehouse. There, one insurer may agree to take on that portion of the whole policy he feels he can comfortably carry, at an agreed-upon price. Or he may simply decline any part in it. From there the policy makes the rounds to other cubicles until it is at last completed. The heavy risk will be shared by literally dozens of individuals, who have reduced a venture with attendant perils and profits to manageable financial risk taking.

And this, Mr. E. surmises, is what speculators must be doing in the commodity market. Mr. B.'s face brightens: his new client is alert. Yes, syndicated insurance covering a vast financial risk is actually achieved by speculation in commodities. In commodity exchanges, risks are accepted because of the possibility of future profits. These exchanges are markets in the true sense: places where many people can meet to trade goods for money. In local markets, customers enter, select merchandise, pay for it, and usually take it away with them. In commodity exchanges, people also get together to buy and sell. But what they trade are not the actual goods or commodities the market deals in. No, they buy and sell *contracts*, which commit them to deliver or accept delivery on a specific quantity of a particular commodity at a certain date in the future, at a price set at the time by public bidding.

Mr. E. gives Mr. B. a look of surprise. They trade in contracts, not goods? Mr. B. nods. These contracts, which are standard and have very explicit specifications, are called *futures contracts*. And that is why the whole busy exchange of money and commodity contracts is called the *futures market*, which is another name for commodity speculation.

Mr. E. asks for an example of such a contract. Well, offers Mr. B., suppose a flour mill will need to purchase some wheat in December, and it's now April. Since its managers need to figure in the price they will be paying at that time, they arrange to purchase one contract of December wheat on the commodity exchange, paying the current price for it. This commits them to accepting delivery of and paying for 5,000 bushels of wheat when December comes. At the same time, a farmer or a grain elevator operator may have *sold* a December wheat contract, obligating him to deliver 5,000 bushels.

Mr. E. still seems confused. Mr. B. now adds to his confusion by saying that such contracts are seldom acted upon. The seller of a commodity does not usually intend to deliver as specified. Nor does the buyer actually plan to accept delivery and pay for the goods in the forward order. Sometimes it does work out that way, but such happenings are very rare—taking place about only 3% of the time. The great majority of contracts are canceled out by the time the delivery month arrives.

Then what *is* going on? asks Mr. E. inevitably. Well, his informant explains, the commercials are "hedging" while the speculators speculate on future prices. *Hedging?* Mr. E. isn't sure what this means. Is it like putting a hedge around oneself for protection? Very apt! says Mr. B. The commercials are protecting themselves from price changes unfavorable to them by entering into these contracts. They secure a guarantee of a particular price that is realistic and acceptable to them and is somewhat in line with the current cash price.

The commercials' separate functions and needs initiate the whole business in the commodity marketplace, in which sellers and buyers are always evenly matched in contracts, Mr. B. goes on. Commercials who secure contracts to cover themselves are abdicating the chance for big profits. But they are also removing the risk of heavy financial losses. So this insurance type of protection is known as a *hedge* and the commercials who use it are *hedgers.*

Mr. B. takes a booklet from his desk. He's going to read to Mr. E. the official definition of *hedging,* according to the Commodity Futures Trading Commission, or CFTC. Hedging, is, Mr. B. quotes, "taking a position in a futures market opposite to a position held in the cash market to minimize the risk of financial loss from an adverse price change; a purchase or sale of futures as a temporary substitute for a cash transaction that will occur later."

Mr. B. sees Mr. E. eyeing him rather glassily. Okay, he says, that means that the flour mill managers, who would like to buy wheat at a low price in December, protect themselves against a rise in price by *buying* a contract that will increase in value if the price of wheat goes up. And the farmer and grain elevator operator, who hope for a high wheat price, protect themselves against a drop in price by *selling* a wheat contract that can be bought back at a cheaper price, earning them a profit, if the price of wheat does fall below expectations or requirements. If the price to pay or to be paid in cash is unsatisfactory, the profits made in the futures contract transaction will make up for it.

But where do speculators fit into this scheme? Mr. E. wants to know. Well, they are the ones who take on the risks that commercials decline, Mr. B. explains. But what kind of profits can they make by doing this? asks Mr. E. Sometimes very large ones, says Mr. B. These are what lure speculators, of course. Some fantastic profits have been made—on the order of 5,000% a year! But heedlessly going after such remote returns on capital is what ruins most novice traders at the outset. Speculators hope to make a big profit from a price change in their favor. Depending on the position they have taken on a particular commodity—for speculators, like hedgers, can be contract sellers as well as buyers—they stand to make money if the price goes up, or down, according to their predictions. If they guess wrong they lose—the risk they run for profit's sake by taking over the commercials' equivalent risk. By offsetting their cash positions, the producers or processors have actually transferred that risk—thereby satisfying the basic purpose of the commodity futures exchange.

Speculators who use prudent and conservative trading methods combined with a full understanding of the market can withdraw a reasonable, steady profit percentage from commodities, Mr. B. maintains. Commodity trading is a form of financial speculation that can be far more appealing, interesting, and indeed successful for certain types of people than real estate or stocks can be.

Mr. B. may be right, says Mr. E., partly convinced now. But he admits that he still doesn't know how the insurance works in the speculation process over commodities. To tell him, to show him, Mr. B. declares, will take another day. In the meantime, he suggests, the student speculator might read a few booklets on the subject. He picks up a few from his desk top and hands them to Mr. E. as Mr. E. rises to go. The subject may look very complicated to him in the beginning, Mr. B. warns. But in many ways it's really simpler than the stock market. And just think! In stocks there are maybe forty thousand different enterprises offering shares. It's hard to know much about even a few of them at once. But in commodities there are only about fifty different kinds actively traded. So keeping track of what's happening in the whole arena is much easier.

And with that said, they shake hands—and part until the next day.

CHAPTER FIVE

Hedgers and Speculators: What Each Is Doing

Eager to know more about the commodity futures market, Mr. E. comes in right on time for his appointment with Mr. B. at the brokerage firm. He has looked at the booklets that Mr. B. gave him the day before but still feels uncertain over his grasp of the essentials. Learning the mechanics and details of trading takes time, study, and practice, says Mr. B. The most important thing at the start, really, is to get a good overall look at the field, from both the individual's and the economy's perspectives.

People—both the commercials concerned with producing or processing commodities and the speculators watching the movements of prices—go about their business of trying to make money for themselves, Mr. B. explains. Meanwhile, there is always a far bigger and more important activity going on that is the summation of their activities and the explanation for them: the well-being of society. Understanding the separate roles or functions of hedgers and speculators—why they do what they do at a particular time—can be baffling at first, Mr. B. agrees. He has found that it always helps to work out on paper some simple transactions that demonstrate the main positions taken in commodity trading. They'll do this today, after which Mr. E. can decide whether or not to pursue the whole endeavor further on his own.

Mr. E. first asks to learn a bit about the history of futures contracts. Has this form of speculation gone on for very long? Mr. B. assures him that the basic mechanism has existed for many centuries, in both Western and Oriental civilizations, stemming from the time when merchant-traders frequently contracted in advance to purchase certain crops or goods. Often, however, one side of the transaction would renege on a verbal promise or even a written order if the price on a commodity changed in a way that was significantly advantageous, or disadvantageous, to that side's position as seller or buyer. It was realized in some places that both parties in an exchange should deposit a sizable sum of money with a third party to guarantee their word or good intention to deliver or take delivery of goods at an agreed-upon price at a definite time in the future. Then if one side failed to come through as promised, the injured party received the forfeited deposit.

Until the Chicago Board of Trade was established in mid-nineteenth-century America, however, says Mr. B., there was no systematized way of handling many commodity transactions so vital to the public needs. The town of Chicago, in a central location with access to waterways and rail and road transport, became overrun at harvest time by hordes of people involved with the growing, storing, and shipping of grains from the vast new tracts of fertile land in the Midwest. Grain merchants arrived. Inevitably, speculators came too; they hoped to earn profits by buying or selling in the right way at the right time through anticipating price changes over current surpluses or future shortages. Many deals took place in the smoke-filled back rooms of saloons and hotels, a practice not always fair to farmers or honest merchants. Even then, some people gave the whole speculating enterprise a bad name.

So in 1848, Mr. B. continues, a group of Chicago businessmen recognized the need for a large market, or exchange, in which the grain transactions could go on in full view of everybody, be subject to public auction at which offers and bids could be done by both hand signals and outcry, and be regulated by disinterested officials employed by the exchange itself who would oversee the activities and guarantee their fairness to both commercial sides. The methods, rules, and financial mechanisms used since then, with variations, in commodity markets around the world were largely originated by the Chicago Board of Trade.

Commodity exchanges are actually one of the greatest democratizing institutions anywhere, Mr. B. now asserts with strong feeling. Mr. E., of course, must ask why. Because, says Mr. B., these exchanges allow many thousands of ordinary citizens to participate in the buying and the selling that help to set realistic prices on goods. Buying and selling commodities would take place anyway without the exchanges, but they permit all transactions to be open to everyone and to be scrutinized carefully for any unethical or illegal tactics that end up affecting the people themselves in unfavorable ways. Exchange officials and government representatives are constantly watching what goes on. All prices—current, offers, bids, acceptances, changes—are called out. All new prices are recorded on an electronic board visible to traders on the floor and sent on ticker tape, followed by final figures on the day's trading, throughout the nation to brokerages, wire services, and newspapers; thus information is spread to anyone who wants it, almost instantaneously.

So who should really love the markets? Mr. B. asks rhetorically. The "little guys"! And who doesn't care for them much? Those "big guys," who would prefer to get together and maybe form cartels that could control different commodities in order to set prices. The way it works out now, in our economic democracy based on free but supervised trade, everyone is equal in the commodity marketplace. In the trading pits, when your order goes in, you can be white, black, or brown; old or young; male or female; rich or poor; a Ph.D. or a high-school dropout; a lawyer or a truck driver. It doesn't matter who you are when it comes to buying or selling futures contracts for commodities. Those 5,000 bushels of September wheat or those 42,000 pounds of feeder cattle are not concerned about your identity. Hedging or speculating on them, you'll have an equal chance, no more and no less, with anybody, to win, lose, or break even. Meanwhile, without realizing it, you are performing the role you are really there for: keeping the American economy out of the hands of manipulators and monopolies, assuring the production and dissemination of commodities among the people.

Mr. B. makes quite a hero out of the speculator, Mr. E. observes. It would surprise the general public to know that speculation in the commodities has the makings of a noble profession, rather than being some shady pursuit of the greedy. Mr. B. responds that he looks upon it for its utility, not nobility. To aspire, to compete, and to seek always to improve one's condition are basically human. He attributes the trading impulse to these instincts and maintains that they unquestionably led humankind toward civilization—and now help to keep us there.

Mr. E. admits that he's quite attracted to the role of the trader, particularly if he doesn't have to get involved with the legal and book-keeping paperwork, the responsibilities, and the extra costs that had bothered him when he tried to speculate in real estate. But he still isn't sure that the commodity market has more advantages for him than the stock market.

Does Mr. E. remember their conversation yesterday, when they were discussing leverage? Well, says Mr. B., this leverage factor is highly important in considering the pluses of commodity trading. Leverage allows a small amount of money to control a larger unit of value. The smaller the percentage of initial investment or deposit, the greater the leverage. If some stock shares require a margin of 50%, which is about as low as one can get, then the owner can control twice as much value. In real estate the down payment of 20% gives the property owner a much greater leverage, a factor of five to one. But a commodity contract is even more impressive: it's usually about ten to one. Generally, Mr. B. remarks, leverage of this sort involves taking greater risks in order to achieve large profits. Your money can increase your profits by a factor of ten, in contrast to the five of real estate or the two of stocks. But when you lose, you lose bigger too. Still, your $10,000 can theoretically control $100,000 worth of commodity contracts but only $50,000 in property or $20,000 in stocks!

How is this leverage in commodities figured? asks Mr. E. Mr. B. replies that it is based on the margin requirement, which is usually about 10% of the contract's value. The *margin* in a futures contract, however, is not like the margin in stocks, he explains. It's not a down payment or an option payment. It's a deposit, a performance bond; and since it belongs to you, it's returned to you when the contract is closed out or liquidated. But who keeps it until then? asks Mr. E. The brokerage hands it over to the clearinghouse connected with the commodity exchange on which a trader buys or sells a futures contract, Mr. B. answers. *Clearing-house?* asks Mr. E. Oh, that's the central business office and credit corporation connected with each commodity exchange, Mr. B. says.

But then where's the big risk? Mr. E. wants to know. Ah, Mr. B. replies, that comes when you have to put more money to *maintain* your margin according to the current value of your contract. Say in early spring you purchase a futures contract for 5,000 bushels of oats at $2 per bushel, to take delivery in the month of September. So it's referred to as September oats. The contract was worth $10,000 when you purchased it, requiring a margin maybe of $1,000. But then the oat price begins to fall. If it falls by 25¢, your position will obviously be less valuable—less tenable. Figure it this way—and Mr. B. writes:

$$\$.25 \times 5{,}000 = \$1{,}250$$
$$\$10{,}000 - \$1{,}250 = \$8{,}750$$

Your contract, Mr. B. says, will be worth only $8,750 on the market now, since it has lost $1,250. So to maintain your end of the contract transaction, you've got to put in that additional amount of money: $1,250. This is called a *margin maintenance*. And if the price goes down again, you'll have to keep paying in, unless you want to sell the contract and get out, figuring that the situation will only get worse. The loss you'll take comes from maintaining the margin. The margin money itself you'll get back after selling the contract, unless you haven't come up with the proper maintenance sum before the contract is sold.

Mr. E. shakes his head in bewilderment. Then who gets the profit if he takes the loss? That's easy, says Mr. B.: the trader on the other side of the contract, who was betting that the price would go down instead of up. So he sold a contract instead of buying one. But doesn't he have to own the oats in order to sell them? asks Mr. E. No, says Mr. B., because a futures contract is only a *promise* to deliver or accept delivery on a commodity, at a prearranged price and time. So for as long as he stays in this spot, he just "owes" oats. Nobody has to own anything, really, except money. The hedgers usually have enough oats to sell and buy among themselves, as things go.

And when can a trader take out his profit if he has any? asks Mr. E. Oh, replies the broker, whenever he wants it. His commission house or brokerage, which marks each trader's commodity account to the closing market price every day, gets the money indirectly from the losing speculator's brokerage account, through the exchange clearinghouse. Does this mean, then, that a trader doesn't have to liquidate the contract first in order to enjoy his profit? Mr. E. is amazed. How different this is from stocks and real estate, where you have to sell out in order to benefit from the profit! But remember, Mr. B. cautions, that the price can very well change again, going against a trader and wiping out any profit he's made and then demanding a margin maintenance.

And what about the 5,000 bushels of oats that the contract is based on? Mr. E. wonders. Don't those really exist somewhere? Sure they do, Mr. B. assures him. There are lots of oats to be hedged on the market. And none of them gets forgotten or goes to waste. Sooner or later the oats end up with the people who really wish to buy them, to accept delivery—sold by the farmers who grew them in order to sell them.

Mr. E. looks perplexed. But then what is all the speculation that has gone on over these oats and all the other commodities about? Most of the activity back and forth, Mr. B. explains, goes on during the months, weeks, and days preceding the delivery time, when price movements fluctuate as speculators try to guess the exact situation of supply versus demand in the coming period. And by the time that the delivery month arrives, when that month's futures price virtually becomes the *spot*, or *cash price*—the price at which the actual commodity is now selling in the current market—almost all contracts have been closed out by opposite, offsetting transactions. And how is that done? Mr. E. inquires. Well, says Mr. B., the sellers buy back and the buyers sell. That is how they cancel out or liquidate their contractual obligations to deliver or to take delivery. Mr. B. promises to explain this more fully later on.

But what if there are more buyers than sellers? Is somebody going to get stuck holding one side of a contract? Mr. E. wants to know. Mr. B. tells him that this cannot be. Each contract needs one buyer and one seller. The exchange clearinghouses make sure, daily and for each commodity, that the contracts sold are exactly balanced by the contracts bought. Whether these contracts are entered into by hedgers or speculators does not matter. What matters is that the commitments on either side are precisely even.

Mr. E. now wants to know whether hedgers themselves can be considered speculators. Not if they have completely covered their financial positions by selling or buying futures contracts, Mr. B. replies. Then they will just break even at delivery time, having lost—or won—nothing in the overall process. They hedge because they need small profits from their normal businesses involving commodities, not because they wish to risk them by speculating.

But don't commercials ever speculate? Mr. E. asks. Mr. B. admits that many of them actually do—the ones who don't hedge at all or the ones who don't hedge enough. Mr. B. now proposes to show his visitor in a simple and graphic way how the hedging function works in practice. Let's take two different candy makers, he says, named X and Y. It is now January and each of them is figuring on buying 10 metric tons of cocoa— that's a contract's worth—in September, in time to make goodies for Halloween. Now X, who's a cautious and careful fellow, decides to buy a September cocoa contract on the New York Cocoa Exchange. Even though the futures price is higher than the current cash price, he believes that speculators who follow the cocoa market are more knowledgeable than he in forecasting the probable value of the contract come September. But Y, on the other hand, wants to keep things simple by figuring that the price nine months from now may be close to what it is now; it may even be less, which will work to his benefit. So he doesn't purchase a contract and calculates and sets the price for his candy on the basis of the present price of cocoa.

Well, says Mr. B., let's see what might happen from January through September. And he draws a straight horizontal line X to represent the price paid for the futures contract, then a somewhat lower line Y for the cash price Y had figured on paying for cocoa later on. Then Mr. B. makes two random, up-and-down, wiggly graph lines: a dotted one to follow the futures price and a broken one to chart the changing cash price. Now look what happens in September to our candy makers! he declares. Unhappily for Y, the price has gone up quite a lot. The distance between his original figure and the cash price in September, Y', is in essence a loss because *he* had already set the candy price based on the lower cocoa price. But X, on the other hand, makes out okay. He has to pay more for the cocoa he'll buy, sure. But that amount is exactly made up by X', the profit he makes when selling his September cocoa contract, which has increased that much in value because of the price rise!

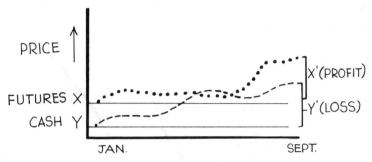

But why should commercials ever decide not to hedge, then? asks Mr. E., convinced now of the wisdom of doing so. It's understandable, says Mr. B. A farmer may be strongly tempted to take a big chance on his corn crop. Hoping that the price of corn will go very high this year, he can avoid hedging completely, unless he needs cash now and his bank refuses to lend him money until he proves he hedged his future crop. But he's assuming a large risk because if the price goes down by the time he gets around to selling his corn, he'll make less, maybe much less, than he needs to make for his profit. He should have sold corn futures contracts to cover his entire crop, he'll tell himself then. And probably next year he'll become a confirmed hedger.

Let's follow through a "selling hedge" with this same farmer, Mr. B. proposes. Say it is now April, his seeds are planted, and he anticipates growing 25,000 bushels of corn by the autumn. He plans to market them in December. He needs to get at least $3.00 per bushel to guarantee getting his costs back plus a profit for his efforts. For now, he will sell five December corn futures contracts at the present market price of $3.00 a bushel. Then, as the delivery month approaches, he will offset these futures contracts by buying them back at the price they are currently trading at. He will sell the real corn through his normal channels, perhaps to a nearby grain elevator. And this, says Mr. B., is what has happened with the selling hedge:

FARMER

ACTUALITY	CONTRACT	VALUE
IN APRIL: PLANS TO PRODUCE 25,000 bu. OF CORN FOR DEC. DELIVERY	SELLS 5 DEC CORN CONTRACTS ON THE CHICAGO BOARD OF TRADE AT $3.00 PER bu	25,000 × $3 OR $75,000
NEAR DEC.: SELLS 25,000 bu. OF CORN TO GRAIN ELEVATOR	BUYS BACK 5 DEC. CORN CONTRACTS ON THE EXCHANGE	?

The contract value, says Mr. B., will be determined by the current market price that he has to pay to buy back the five contracts. Say the corn price has gone up to $3.10: the farmer will have to pay 10¢ more per bushel on the five contracts—so that he sustains a loss of $2,500. But it's made up by the 10¢ more per bushel he makes when he sells the corn itself. And what if the price goes down 10¢? Mr. B. asks Mr. E. Well, then it should work in reverse, Mr. E. volunteers. He'll make less money on his corn than he wanted to, but when he buys back the five contracts he earns a profit of $2,500. Right! Mr. B. agrees. So in this example of a "perfect hedge," the farmer has broken even, no matter which way the price goes—assuming his crop came out as planned.

And how about an example of a "buying hedge" now? Mr. B. offers. While our farmer has been growing his corn, a chicken feed producer sets his costs for December feed sales. In May, let's say, he purchases four December corn contracts. These may even be the very ones that the farmer initially put on the market and that have been bought and sold by various speculators. When December comes near, the chicken feed producer will offset his futures contracts by selling them at the current price for December corn—and then will buy the real corn from his normal supplier. When he offsets his position, if the corn price has gone up, his contracts will be worth more when he sells them—thereby making up for the greater price he must pay for the actual corn. And if the price has gone down, his contracts won't bring in as much as he paid for them, but he'll pay less for the corn. Figuring on the same 10¢ above or below the $3.00 he might have paid for the contracts that the farmer sold:

$$10¢ \text{ PRICE} \rbrack \text{ IN 4 CONTRACTS (20,000 bu): } + \$2,000$$
$$\text{RISE} \rbrack \text{ IN BUYING REAL CORN : } - \$2,000$$

$$10¢ \text{ PRICE} \rbrack \text{ IN 4 CONTRACTS : } - \$2,000$$
$$\text{DROP} \rbrack \text{ IN BUYING REAL CORN : } + \$2,000$$

Mr. E. is intently studying all of Mr. B.'s figures. He notices a discrepancy. Where? asks Mr. B. There's a missing contract! Mr. E. declares. Ah, replies Mr. B., grinning, not at all perturbed. Out of the farmer's original five, he means. Well, where does Mr. E. suppose it went? So the omission was intentional, Mr. E. realizes. It was done, then, to remind him of the speculator's role in hedging. A speculator had bought it!

In fact, says Mr. B., many more speculators are involved in trading than the commercials who are hedging. They help to fill in the spaces between the hedgers who are buying and those who are selling—especially in large quantities that need an immediate contractual response on the market. Yes! Mr. B. goes on. We should never neglect to notice the speculators' important role in commodity trading or to consider it as less than welcome to the commercials. Why, even government agencies—such as the Department of Agriculture—encourage the public to speculate and furnish it with a flood of information. Yet many people continue to think that commodity speculation is somehow disreputable.

But don't speculators behave differently than hedgers? Mr. E. asks. Yes, generally they weave in and out of the market action, taking positions according to how they think prices will go in the future. Commercials can enter the action at any point but generally do so early, while they are figuring costs and production. And they tend to stay put, whether in selling or buying hedges, until the time comes for them to sell or buy the actual commodity—when their futures contracts are canceled out by offsetting transactions.

But how would the speculators make out in the corn-trading situations that the hedgers were in? asks Mr. E. Well, says Mr. B., it would all depend on when they got into the trade and at what price and for how many contracts—and whether their position was bullish or bearish. "Bulls" and "bears": Mr. E. at least knows that much from the stock market. The *bulls* are the traders who believe that the price will go up, so they buy and plan to sell later at a higher price to make a profit. The *bears* are the traders who bet that the price will go down, so they sell out, planning to wait and buy back later if and when the price drops. Are these the same roles in commodity trading? Mr. E. asks. Yes, in a way, says Mr. B., except that the bears actually hold on to "selling" positions by entering into contracts to sell. And the speculators move around a lot more, partly because there's more money at stake: remember the 10% leverage in contrast to the 50% one in stocks. There's plenty of room for them, and everybody encourages both kinds. But they have to move fairly fast at times when they're in the wrong spot—to get out quickly.

Often it's the stubborn bulls and bears, those who refuse to budge from a poor position that's costing them just to stay there, who take the worst financial beatings, Mr. B. goes on. Or else they put all profits into new contracts in the same position, risking everything in a pyramid that then starts to crumble. And when they finally have to buy or sell themselves out of a contract predicament, it's going to hurt. Sometimes they just convince themselves that they stand to make a huge profit when the current price trend reverses itself, so they hang in there, expecting to make millions. Probably Mr. E. has heard the expression "Bulls make money, bears make money, but hogs get slaughtered."

COMMODITY SPECULATION FOR BEGINNERS

Speaking of the bulls and the bears and their respective positions, says Mr. E., does Mr. B. know where the terms came from? No, he doesn't, Mr. B. admits, but he has often wondered. Nobody has been able to tell him. Everyone uses the expressions, he guesses, without having the faintest idea how such curious characterizations originated. Ha! says Mr. E. Now *he* can tell Mr. B. something interesting for a change. He read sometime ago that the terms began with the bull-and-bear fights that the Mexican Californians put on for entertainment and gambling purposes in the mining camps during the Gold Rush. They'd go out and lasso a wild bear and drag it into camp, putting it into a special pit or ring. They would then bring in a mean long-horned bull and chain its front leg to the bear's hind leg. They would clear out and let the two beasts tear at, stomp, and gouge each other, until one finished the other off. The men who had bets on them would yell for the bull or the bear to be victorious. They noticed that the bear's best fighting tactic was to get down as low as it could, maybe even digging a hole, and try to bring the bull down to its level so it could grab the bull with its teeth and claws. The bull, though, kept working at raising the bear up so it could pierce the bear with its sharp horns. When the gold miners went on to San Francisco or back East with their gold, or anyway with their experience, they vividly remembered the bear's low stance and the bull's high one—and they used these terms in stock market speculations.

Well, exclaims Mr. B., that's positively fascinating! He can hardly wait to give his associates this historical explanation for the words they use dozens of times each day without knowing why. He also wonders about the words *short* and *long* that characterize buyers and sellers in both stocks and commodities. Does Mr. E. have interpretations for them? No? Well, he guesses that a "short" trader is one who is in an owing position, whereas a "long" one has bought whatever it is, figuring it will go up in value.

But now, says Mr. B., they must get back on track. Traders may do well with commodities if they can guess right 40% of the time. That low a probability in good prognostication? asks Mr. E., amazed. Then how do speculators make any profits? Shrewd traders usually get out as quickly as they can from their wrong guesses, taking a small loss now instead of a big one later, Mr. B. explains. They can make up for the losses and bring in good profits as well by riding along with the right guesses. There are some traders, though—with a great deal of information, experience, and capital behind them—who can stay in the game for the long gamble, reasonably confident that the adverse price will ultimately reverse itself and go as they originally predicted while they maintain margins in losing positions. However, this sort of figuring is very unwise for small and novice speculators to indulge in.

How do the positions of speculators differ from those of hedgers? Mr. E. wants to know. Actually, says Mr. B., "short" hedgers—farmers, say, who fear the price may fall and want to protect themselves from losses—and "short" speculators, who *want* the price to fall so that they can buy back the contracts they sold and make profits, are doing the same thing, selling contracts, for totally opposite reasons. This is also true of "long" hedgers and speculators, who both buy contracts. Hedgers, if they have hedged their positions adequately, don't care whether the price goes up or down.

But the speculators' positions are precarious, Mr. B. points out. The speculators are either going to win or lose. By risking their money in the commodity market, however, they have enabled both sides of the hedging action to arrive at neutral or safe places, while setting the final value on a futures contract coming due, soon to coincide with the cash price. Their funds, too, contribute liquidity, assuring smooth transitions of prices, with no big gaps in the movement.

It sounds rather like a "zero-sum game," Mr. E. ventures, remembering his talks with Dr. M. about gambling. Is that when the total sum lost by the losers equals the total sum won by the winners? asks Mr. B. Mr. E. nods yes. Except, Mr. B. says, that we'd have to figure in the miscellaneous expenses sustained by all the players in the brokerages' commissions and other fees. These, though, can be looked upon as normal business-operating costs by both hedgers and speculators. And actually these commissions don't really add up to much compared with those for the same amount of money transactions in the stock market. Take those five corn contracts, for example, worth around $75,000: a speculator buying or selling them all and then closing out his position—a *round turn*, it's called—would have started out with a margin of around $7,500. Once his profits or losses in the deal are completely calculated, he'll get it back, for it was just an "earnest money" deposit. He might have to pay the brokerage about $250 for handling the entire transaction, including *marking to market* each day—which means keeping track of the contracts' current value. On a stock trade for the same amount, buying and selling could cost him more than $1,000 in commissions, plus interest on the loan made by the brokerage.

But what does all this speculating on prices actually end up costing the public itself? Mr. E. wonders. If the winner wins and the loser loses and the commercials break even on their hedging while a price goes up, the public ends up paying, right? It does on a trade when the price rises, Mr. B. agrees. But in the following years the price may even go down. And if so, the public will benefit.

How can prices really go down through speculation? Mr. E. asks. Because, says Mr. B., a price rise will decrease demand. In the meantime, the increased production stimulated by higher prices will eventually create greater supply—and thus lower prices. And with futures contracts, price trends really assist the producer in determining or adjusting production. A farmer can decide on the basis of futures prices whether to plant more of one crop and less of another, for example. How does this happen? Well, if the futures price on wheat is low, the farmer may plant less. If many farmers plant less, there will be less wheat in supply. Therefore, there will also be higher prices for wheat in new futures speculating, which will persuade the farmers to plant more wheat again. And if meat prices are very high, ranchers will sell their feeder cattle at the high prices on an exchange and then increase production, a move that will eventually lead to more supply and therefore lower prices.

This self-correcting, constantly fluctuating rise and fall of commodity prices really ends up benefiting the public, says Mr. B., especially during inflationary periods, as now. Mr. E. looks at him quizzically. Mr. B. takes out some charts that demonstrate how the prices of certain basic commodities on the exchanges, such as copper, cotton, wheat, and eggs, have risen very little in the past two decades compared with prices of automobiles, housing, clothing, and most other goods. This, he says, is amazing when one realizes how taxes, wages, and other monetary elements have escalated. And meanwhile, the purchasing power of the dollar itself is worth less than half of what it was twenty years ago!

And what, asks Mr. E., has happened to the stock market in the same time period? Mr. B. brings out more charts, which show the overall decline in the value of various "blue-chip" stocks. And as far as volume is concerned, says Mr. B., the commodity market has far outstripped the stock exchanges, in terms of both quantity of transactions and money involved.

Mr. E. is convinced at last. He is going to speculate in commodities, he declares to Mr. B. He believes that by doing so he stands to make the best profits with the least effort, despite the greater risks involved. And he recognizes now that the speculator's role is both valid and valuable in the American economy. But he knows he has to do a lot of learning before he starts.

He thanks Mr. B. for the time and effort he devoted to this introduction.

PART TWO

Welcome to the Marketplace

CHAPTER SIX

Looking at a Commodity Exchange

Our novice speculator, Mr. E., has only begun to learn about the commodity futures market from Mr. B. A cautious fellow wherever his own money is concerned, Mr. E. won't just plunge in, as others have done, so that instead of just getting their feet wet at first, they get up to their necks or even far over their heads.

Also, in spite of his broker acquaintance's assurances and all the graphs and booklets given to him, Mr. E. feels uneasy. His wife and his friends looked shocked when he expressed a determination to speculate in commodities. They all have heard of people who did so—and failed miserably, ever afterward warning others against it. Mr. E. is reminded too of those evening news reports on television showing frenetic scenes in some commodity exchange in New York or Chicago. In them traders —gesticulating, shouting, grimacing, and even shoving—are driving the prices of wheat, pork bellies, soybeans, or gold up or down: always, it would seem, to the detriment of the American economy and of the poor American consumer. Is *he* going to get like them? Mr. E. wonders.

Mr. E., anyway, likes to stay in touch with reality. There's something unsettling to him about trading futures contracts back and forth, the way Mr. B. described it, especially when you never see them or the commodities they're connected with. It also bothers him that as a speculator he would be entrusting money and instructions to a network of people he doesn't know and whose functions he doesn't really understand. He would also have to trust machinery—communications systems, electronic equipment, and the market mechanisms themselves—that seems distant, impersonal, subject to breakdowns and foul-ups. And he somehow can't believe that tales he has heard about swindles and new attempts to "corner the market" don't contain some truth. Perhaps many speculators, especially those on the floors of commodity exchanges, are really a bunch of crooks after all?

Mr. E. takes his nagging doubts to Mr. B., who doesn't seem perturbed by such second thoughts. In fact, he says, he would be surprised if Mr. E. didn't have them. He advises Mr. E. to visit a commodity exchange if he possibly can, to see the action for himself. Commodity exchanges welcome visitors, of course, since they were set up for public usage. At an exchange he could get in touch with the real situation and meet professionals who could answer his questions.

Some people, Mr. B. acknowledges, do learn things better directly, from experience itself, than indirectly, from books or from what people tell them, especially when they must be convinced of the reality and stability of something widely doubted. Also, Mr. E. may find investigating an exchange an exciting adventure in itself. Yes, Mr. B. goes on, commodity markets really do exist—and so do futures contracts! As for the commodities themselves that the contracts are based on—including those new "soft" ones people talk about, the financial instruments—they are real too, Mr. B. declares. Most of them enter into everybody's everyday lives, whether we're aware of them or not. Their prices often respond like barometers sensitive to the national economic and political scene and, increasingly, to international situations. Once one is atuned to the commodity marketplace, watching how the latest news affects price fluctuations is simply amazing. But successfully manipulating these prices on the exchanges is exceedingly difficult, however much a few greedy traders may try. The system itself is too large, and there are too many safeguards and official scrutinizers from without and within to enable such practices to go on for long. And cheating and unethical behavior, once detected, are reacted against by other traders. They are punishable by legal means—by fines and expulsion from the exchanges.

Mr. E. goes away buoyed up, attracted to the possibility of going to an actual commodity exchange. There are none nearby, but he remembers learning that an old college chum of his, Mr. T., had become a member of the Chicago Board of Trade. It also happens that Mr. E.'s firm has business to be done in Chicago. So he volunteers to go, figuring that he'll have an opportunity in his free time to visit the very place where the modern commodity exchanges originated. Then if his experience there can convince him to erase his hesitations, he'll return home ready to undertake the study and work that will prepare him to be a part-time speculator.

So Mr. E. telephones his friend in Chicago, who is delighted to hear from him. When will Mr. E. be arriving? Of course Mr. T. will be glad to give him a personally conducted tour of the Board of Trade. It's the best thing possible for anybody thinking of becoming a speculator! They arrange an early breakfast date for the morning after Mr. E.'s arrival—after which they'll head for the CBT.

Mr. T. meets Mr. E. punctually in the hotel lobby. For a few minutes, after seating themselves in the coffee shop, they catch up on each other's personal lives since they last got together more than a dozen years ago. But quickly the talk shifts to that topic of keen mutual interest: commodity speculation. Mr. T. explains that he is no longer a regular securities account executive associated with his stock brokerage, as he was for some years. No, he became intrigued with futures contracts as the best upcoming form of fast-acting, high-yield return on capital. After a while he was made a commodity specialist by his firm. Then he acquired a membership at the Chicago Board of Trade so he could represent it there as a floor broker. Recently, though, Mr. T. has moved from that position, turning his work over to several younger men who can better handle the constant pressure from incoming customers' orders to be executed at various places on the trading floor. Retaining his membership, however, he is still a floor trader. He trades now for his own account but also earns commissions as a broker for a few big clients of his brokerage for whom he buys and sells futures contracts. Meanwhile, he has assumed a new managerial position with his firm.

Mr. E. is surprised that his friend would want to meet him so early in the morning. Mr. T. smiles. He likes to get to the exchange well before the trading starts, particularly when he's bringing a guest. They will have a lot to talk about and see before 9:30, when the big trading begins. Furthermore, the brokerage itself opens up much earlier than that in order to handle new orders coming in. Remember too that the New York exchanges start an hour earlier!

Mr. T. wants Mr. E. to see the Board of Trade's trading floor right before and after the trading starts, from a spot where he can look down on the big action. But how can he do that? Mr. E. wonders. Easy, says Mr. T. They'll go to the Visitors Center. Its glassed-in gallery is just above the trading floor. From it you can actually watch what's going on altogether better than if you were in the pits themselves. So he loves any reason to go up there, Mr. T. admits. Actually, he can't take Mr. E. onto the floor itself anyway until 10:00 since the rules forbid allowing visitors during the half hours just after trading starts and before it ends for the day.

COMMODITY SPECULATION FOR BEGINNERS

Mr. T. clearly enjoys his work and his place of work, Mr. E. observes. But won't his presence there today take Mr. T. away from any business he has to do? Mr. T. laughs and assures him that he doesn't have much on his trading agenda this morning that he can't transact with Mr. E. nearby. Mr. E. should find his visit to the trading floor both fascinating and instructive. He'll learn more this way about the details of real trading than if he spent all his time up in the gallery, where visitors remain if they do not know a member or an employee of the CBT who can take them on the floor itself. A guide is there, though, who gives an explanatory talk and can answer questions.

How many member-traders are there on the Chicago Board of Trade? Mr. E. asks. There are 1,402 regular members right now, says Mr. T., and over 100 associate members, with that number growing. But don't expect to see all of them trading here at once. Usually only a portion of that number—around 400 or 500—is present on any one day. Some members trade only for their own accounts. Some trade exclusively for a single large firm that employs them, whether as brokers or as hedging experts. Some, like Mr. T., combine personal speculating with trading for others. Can all traders do both? Mr. E. wonders. No, says Mr. T. In order to represent other people's accounts, one must be specially licensed as an agent or broker.

How does one get to be a member of the exchange? Mr. E. asks. By applying, Mr. T. replies, though there's no guarantee of acceptance. The CBT is self-regulating, and its board of directors is extremely careful in selecting new memberships, which are limited in availability. The exchange intends to maintain its historic reputation for fairness, honesty, and openness in a form of financial activity that is sometimes troubled by unethical business behavior. An applicant's qualifications are thoroughly investigated.

Furthermore, Mr. T. continues, since the current members don't want trouble in their midst, the membership committee requires not only a record of integrity but also considerable financial backing. Altruism can always be questioned, Mr. T. remarks, but self-interest cannot. It is to everyone's advantage to have honest exchange members who can meet their obligations so that trading proceeds smoothly.

But what is the exchange's own part in all the speculating that goes on there? asks Mr. E. Perhaps Mr. E. does not realize, Mr. T. answers, that the commodity exchanges themselves are not essentially profit-motivated enterprises. They are services, created as public marketplaces where the producers of commodities can trade with all other parties interested in the commodities, to the protection of everyone—whether the commercials desiring to earn or pay reasonable prices or the traders willing to invest capital in buying and selling contracts for future delivery during times of potential surplus or shortage that could disastrously affect prices. The exchanges derive their operating expenses from a variety of service fees that are based on transactions conducted within their premises, through individual brokers and traders or by corporations. But only members of the commodity exchange itself can actually trade on the floor.

Mr. E. imagines that the CBT is deluged by applications for membership, since the position must be both prestigious and lucrative as well as convenient for big traders. Does he want to guess at how much it now costs to join this very exclusive club? asks Mr. T. Probably what it would cost to belong to a first-class country club? ventures Mr. E. But how many are there that charge an initiation fee of almost $250,000—with the variable price generally rising—Mr. T. wants to know, plus an equal amount of solid assets behind the applicant? Mr. E. is flabbergasted at the money one must get together in order to purchase a seat on the exchange: that's about half a million dollars! Mr. T. chuckles while acknowledging that it costs far less even a few years ago and less than that when he himself joined.

But the old economic law of supply and demand is operating here in the commodity exchanges, Mr. T. points out. American money seems to be flowing away from the more popular, conventional investment media like stocks and bonds, he explains. Surely Mr. E. is aware of this phenomenon. Money is increasingly being put into futures trading, which allows successful speculators to keep better pace with fast-rising inflation. To many people, a market based on goods and the changing value of money may now make more sense than one based on business enterprises and their earnings. Since more and more professional money people want to be commodity traders with direct access to the exchanges, seats are in short supply at a time of great demand, and so inevitably they sell dearly, both at the CBT and at most of the other exchanges. But that same law of supply and demand means that new exchanges are being created and the established ones are expanding membership. As room is made for more traders, seats may eventually not be so costly. But after all, Mr. T. remarks, the investment isn't all that much when one considers how much it costs to start any business. And in essence commodity speculation *is* a business to traders. It's a highly legitimate and useful one, adds Mr. E., who says that a broker explained the insurance function to him.

Their breakfast over, the reunited friends go outdoors to hail a taxicab. Mr. T. instructs the driver to take the scenic route along Outer Drive, which will give his companion an inspirational perspective on the great city of Chicago. The city looks very different indeed from the way it looked in 1848, when the Board of Trade of the City of Chicago originated! Imagine the town then, suggests Mr. T., in the late summer and early autumn, when the farmers were bringing in their wheat and corn and oats in wagonloads over the plank roads from the farms to the west and south, or hauling bags in canal boats or river barges. Merchants gathered around to bid on the crops or to mill grains close by or transport them elsewhere. The railroads and extensive waterways made Chicago the hub of grain commerce and, soon, of the livestock and meat-packing industry too.

And all this activity, Mr. T. goes on, led to the creation of the Chicago Board of Trade, and later to that of the Chicago Mercantile Exchange, which deals in a number of commodities—notably meats and eggs—that the CBT doesn't handle. And there they are, he says, pointing toward the thriving business section called The Loop, which came about primarily because the city was the nation's, possibly the world's, busiest center for grain and livestock trading. Mr. T. guides Mr. E.'s eyes toward the Board of Trade's tall building, prominent within the skyline that they are swiftly approaching. The visitor feels that special excitement of being in the midst of a thriving metropolis.

Now they have arrived at their destination at the corner of Jackson and La Salle streets. Mr. E. gets out and gratifies his friend by standing and staring up at the building. It's no longer among the largest buildings in the city, Mr. T. admits, because it was built in the thirties. Yet it is still awfully big—containing not only the CBT but also the offices of many other firms, such as Mr. T.'s; a good number of them are connected with commodities. And wait until the new addition is completed! booms Mr. T., pointing toward the south, where construction is already in progress. Then the CBT will have the largest trading floor anywhere, comfortably accommodating more and more of the trading yet to come.

But Mr. E. thought that the CBT was already the largest exchange. Oh yes, agrees Mr. T, in terms of *volume*—the numbers and values of contracts traded both daily and annually. The CBT handles about 50% of the commodity trading done in the entire country! But just now in physical size the trading floor of the exchanges at the World Trade Center in New York is bigger. Yet the comparison is unfair, since the floor in New York has actually been occupied by four quite different, separate commodity exchanges, making up what's called the CEC or Commodity Exchange Center. The CBT is the only occupant here on the trading floor, though of course the large building around and above it contains dozens of different business offices—including those of Mr. T.'s firm, which Mr. E. will soon be seeing as part of his tour.

Walking through the revolving door at the entrance, Mr. T. halts inside the lobby to attach a black and yellow badge bearing his initials to his coat. Mr. E. notices that some of the men just coming in or standing out in the lobby, talking, are wearing similar insignias. Is this part of the trader's uniform? asks Mr. E. Actually yes, says Mr. T. That, along with a jacket and tie are the dress requirements nowadays. Traders traditionally wore light-colored jackets so that they could be easily identified, and some exchanges still maintain that more formal dress code.

Mr. T. is studying his watch. Good! he says, they'll have plenty of time to get to the Visitors Center and look around a bit before stationing themselves in a good spot from which they can watch the trading floor activities. Taking an elevator, they get off at the fifth floor and proceed to the gallery, where already a small crowd has collected in order to witness the opening of grain trading at 9:30. Mr. E. is drawn at once, of course, to the huge windows that span the width of the room and look out upon the great rectangular arena that is the trading floor. He does not believe, he says, that he has ever seen such a busy-looking place. There must be at least a thousand human bodies engaged in the business of readying the exchange for a day of trading, yet somehow people manage to move past others if headed somewhere or to remain in one spot if a stationary position is required. All this bustle of activity and talk and exchanging papers takes place in a room the size of—what? Mr. E. asks his friend. Almost the area of an ice hockey rink, Mr. T. volunteers, but more square. It's nineteen thousand square feet, but there's the smaller South Trading Room, too. And in a couple of years the trading area will be considerably expanded when the addition is completed.

Come and see the displays, commands Mr. T., before it's time for them to take up good viewing positions at the window. Mr. E. realizes now that when entering the gallery he had been so attracted to the floor show that he had failed to notice the exhibitions along the walls. So now with Mr. T. at his side ready to answer questions, he browses among the pictures and documents that cover the long history of the Board of Trade of the City of Chicago. Then at the information desk, the receptionist encourages him to pick up whatever booklets he wants among those offered there.

Mr. T. nudges his friend toward a vacant spot at the right side of the huge ceiling-to-floor picture window. Mr. E. sees that there will soon be competition for front-row positions. Standing now with the whole spectacle going on below him, Mr. E. remarks that it's surely sensible to keep visitors off the floor at first. They would get in the way and might even get crushed in the traffic! But the most amazing sight to him now is the kaleidoscopic crazy-quilt of colored coats—bright reds, blues, yellow, and greens predominating—that flows all around the room, forever shifting in patterns of combination. Now surely some of these are uniforms! he remarks. The big brokerages, which may have a dozen or more floor and pit brokers, sometimes have their brokers and also others on the staff, such as phoneclerks and messengers, wear the same kind of jacket so that they can spot one another easily, says Mr. T. The yellow coats, though, usually belong to runners. *Runners?* Mr. E. wonders. Oh, they are the messengers who travel from the phonedesks there along the walls, says Mr. T., pointing out the banks of tables lining nearly three sides of the trading room. Since they carry new orders into the pits, they really *do* run to get there as fast as they can. Even now, Mr. E. can see the runners scurrying here and there, carrying order slips to the right brokers so that the brokers will be able to execute the orders when the trading starts. And the brokers and traders themselves are already taking up firm positions within the pits, even though the gong won't sound for about ten minutes yet. Occasionally glancing up at a clock or down at their watches, they study their order slips or chat with one another. Mr. E. is aware of the underlying tension to get going.

So these are the notorious trading pits! says Mr. E. Yes indeed, Mr. T. agrees. And looking at them from above is the most dramatic way to get a first view. Of course, Mr. E. knows that traders in a particular commodity gather together in one pit to transact business. See their distinctive octagonal shapes? Mr. E. remarks that they resemble squat, hollow pyramids, with their four low steps that ascend to the top and then are repeated on the inside, going down to the center.

But isn't there a lot of commotion in some places already? asks Mr. E. Actually, says Mr. T., trading is going on now in some of the nongrain pits. He points to the trading areas for silver and gold in the distance, where busy trading action can be seen. These pits and several others open earlier than 9:30, Mr. T. explains, to keep pace with the New York exchanges. At the CBT, though, the biggest trading volume is generally in the grains, and their pits start up at the 9:30 gong and close at 1:15.

Is it an optical illusion or is that one pit larger than the others? Mr. E. now asks, pointing. That's the soybean pit, says Mr. T. It *is* the largest. He then identifies the wheat and corn pits that are only slightly smaller. The others are smaller still. A few of them are shared by several commodities, Mr. T. explains. Why? It has to do with the amount of trading that goes on in them. The ones that must accommodate the most traders of course have to be the biggest. And then there are the double pits for soybean meal and soybean oil.

And isn't it amazing about soybeans? Mr. T. begins rhetorically, eager to discuss them. For years people did not understand the value of this originally Asian crop, and now the United States produces more of it than the rest of the world. After being introduced on the CBT, it became a highly successful trading commodity. Mr. E. wonders why, for he himself doesn't eat soybeans. Actually he must, Mr. T. says, because soy derivatives, such as oil, are used in many processed products. And the meats he eats were made partly from soybeans, which are an important livestock and poultry feed. The soybean is an all-purpose "grain," like wheat or corn, useful in many ways for human consumption but also as animal food. But of course it isn't really a grain at all, though it's marketed and often used as one. It is a legume—a member of the bean tribe —and is therefore a good soil improver because of its nitrogen-fixing property. It has a high level of protein, which is most unusual in the vegetable kingdom. And it has many industrial uses too. But don't let him get really started talking about soybeans or other favorite commodities of his, or they'll never go anywhere today! Mr. T. exclaims.

Why are the trading areas called "pits," anyway? Mr. E. asks. Probably because of the depressed centers, Mr. T. answers, which made them rather like the ancient betting arenas in which humans or animals were put in the center, sometimes to fight to the finish, with the spectators around them wildly gambling on the outcome. In just a few minutes Mr. E. will see a bit of the same old competitive spirit going on in these pits, though now the noise is about contracts and prices!

This pit design, Mr. T. continues, originally made each commodity market self-enclosed. It also helped to contain some of the inevitable clamor of the traders, which got especially noisy when the proceedings were brought indoors, out of the open air. But the eight sides? asks Mr. E. Of what use are they? Mr. T. guesses that they are strictly traditional, built at first as sturdy steps made from local timbers. Perhaps they had some original use in separating traders into facing groups according to buyers and sellers arranged in delivery months. But a neat plan hasn't worked out in practice, he says, because most traders in any pit are both buying and selling and dealing with various delivery months all at once. In some other exchanges there are circular trading structures called *rings*. In them and the pits, traders generally arrange themselves temporarily on the inside steps according to the month they intend to trade in. The closest delivery month is generally conducted at the center; the "back," or farthest out ones, toward the top.

But what about any traders that really want to buy or sell the actual commodities themselves, now? Mr. E. wonders. Or is the CBT just for futures contract trading? Oh, there's a place for them too on the trading floor, says Mr. T., pointing toward the cash grain tables along the north windows. But this market is off to the side of the main action because the business transacted in cash commodities—also known as *spot* or *actuals* —is considerably smaller. Since the current spot price is already known, the variations on it have to do with other types or grades of that commodity, and the important issues of transportation, storage, and exact delivery time and place need to be settled by those commercials who agree to buy and sell the actual goods. Most commercials, though, as Mr. E. must realize, prefer to make their own deals directly, based on the current cash price, through established associations with growers, grain elevator operators, or processors. But the Board of Trade does offer commercials contacts and space for trading as an added convenience to its customers.

Now, what are those small platforms on the top of one face of each trading pit? Mr. E. wonders. They are for various people who have to know what's going on down there in the pit but are not themselves participating in the action, Mr. T. replies. See how the people sitting there usually wear brown coats? But who are they? asks Mr. E. Some are staff members of the exchange, who make sure that trades are proceeding according to the rules and regulations, answers Mr. T. Others are transaction recorders and auditors, who note down the details of each completed trade: number of contracts, delivery month, price, the initials of the traders buying and selling, and firms involved, if any. Still others are quotation reporters, who relay electronically any change in a futures price over to the master control center, which operates these giant quotation display boards on the opposite sides of the trading room's walls and also sends the price changes out to the world by wire, ticker tape, and telecomputers, allowing brokerages to provide customers with a near-instantaneous coverage of the latest prices on commodities.

Mr. E. looks now at the electronic boards, which report the price action below them. Mr. T. points out that they show the names of the main commodities traded here; the commodities are divided into contract months, which are abbreviated by first syllables. The numbers that range across the boards horizontally show the last trading day's closing price, today's opening price, the day's highs and lows thus far, plus, of course, the price at which the commodity was most recently traded. From time to time, here and when he's down on the floor, Mr. E. should watch these boards to see how quickly some of the figures change. Traders depend on them, so if a power failure knocks them out for more than five minutes, trading must cease. Nowadays you can't do much just by using blackboards, which were the old way of posting prices and occasionally are still used.

Only a few seconds to go now! announces Mr. T., who is studying a large wall clock as if supervising a rocket-launching countdown. Down below them the traders in the grain pits look like racers restraining themselves from jumping the gun. Mr. T. suggests that his friend survey the overall scene once trading begins, then concentrate on a single pit—the nearby wheat's probably the best one—so that he can notice the tactics and movements of particular traders in the midst of the commotion.

The gong is now sounded, and the bedlam that ensues passes—a bit muffled—right through the thick glass partition that separates the gallery from the trading floor. Mr. E. tries to catch individual voices, but doing so is difficult. What he mainly hears is the fantastic shouting from within each pit, combining to sound like a frenetic crowd at some crucially played sports event. But these are bids and offers, he knows, rather than cheers and boos and called-out requests for plays or goals. Hey! he remarks to Mr. T., one guy was actually elbowing another out of his way when he was trying to make some deal. And some even are jumping.

Mr. T. chortles. The traders often get overeager at the openings and closings, he admits, and also at times when some important price reversal or sudden movement takes place or when it is close to delivery time. But they are more intense than angry. Many a time he went home a bit bruised after a day in the pit, as well as hoarse and tired! But it's all in a day's work, and although sometimes it looks as if the traders are like sharks involved in a feeding frenzy, it's important to realize that much of this activity is ritualistic behavior that is inevitable in a highly competitive situation—rather like football players knocking one another about the field. You'd think these traders were ready to murder each other over certain scrimmages, but coming to blows is, of course, forbidden here. And when the trading day is over, you'll often see fellows who are fierce competitors in the pit drinking and exchanging tales together in complete camaraderie at the Sign of the Trader next door. But trading *is* a hard job, whether one is doing it for oneself or for others. No wonder the trading day is so short!

The guide at the Visitors Center is explaining over the public address system many of the features of the trading action that is going on below. Mr. E. listens to her description of the hand signals that the traders give one another. When the hand is held upward with the palm outward, the trader is selling; the palm inward means that the trader is buying. Each finger held up means one contract, so that five fingers would mean the trader wants to buy or sell five contracts—*except,* the guide makes clear, with the grains. With them, each vertically held finger stands for 1,000 bushels, so that five fingers designates 5,000 bushels, or *one* contract.

Mr. E. has noticed a lot of sideways gesturing with hands, and so he is glad that the explanation is given for that too. These movements indicate fractions above or below the current price, depending on whether a trader is buying or selling. Until a few years ago, the minimum fluctuation allowable in the grains at CBT was ⅛¢—which was shown by holding out one finger to the side. Now the minimum has become ¼¢—shown with two fingers. Four separated fingers indicate ½¢, and four fingers held tightly together show ¾¢. A closed fist means a change of 1¢.

The hand signals must always accompany the trader's outcry, and both uniquely belong to the commodity exchanges, where traders have always been required to vocalize and display in public, for all to hear and see, exactly what they are offering and bidding in the sale or purchase of contracts.

COMMODITY SPECULATION FOR BEGINNERS

For a time Mr. E. follows the path of one runner, who carries order slips to and from the phonedesk and the various trading pits in both directions. Watching the runner reminds him to ask Mr. T. about the ways in which customers' orders get to the floor itself. Well, says Mr. T., the best way to explain this to him is not to tell him but to *show* him. They've spent time enough here, haven't they? In a while they can go onto the trading floor itself, but right now they should really visit his brokerage office, where Mr. E. will be able to watch the process and even talk to a few people involved in it.

Mr. T. leads his friend back to the elevator. Entering it, the proper floor button is pressed and they are on their way up. When the door opens, Mr. T. exits with Mr. E. a step behind. They pass by a receptionist who greets Mr. T. cheerily as he heads down the corridor to the left, a wide white-walled thoroughfare branching off into various offices and then turning to the right. They enter a large and busy office containing people and machines that are producing one-way voice communications and different clacking and clattering sounds.

This, says Mr. T., is the order-receiving center from the outside world. Brokers at the other branches and hedger clients transmit orders here by two ways: phone and Teletype. It's a hive of activity right now, of course, because not only are customers around the country responding to yesterday's news and price quotations, but some are already reacting to the day's opening prices and initiating buying and selling orders to get into the action right away. It is primarily the job of the people here to receive, record, and time stamp these orders and then transmit them right away to one of the trading floors in Chicago: the Board of Trade downstairs, of course, but also to the Merc (that's the Chicago Mercantile Exchange up the street) and MidAmerica.

Mr. T. suggests that Mr. E. keep his eye on a young woman who is busily watching the output of a telex or Teletype machine, retrieving the sheet and running it through a small time-stamp device at her desk and then using her phone to relay the order by voice. When she completes this action, she gives the conveyed order to a young man seated next to her. As soon as the broker executes the order, says Mr. T., the details of it are phoned back to them here so that the proper brokerage or client can be contacted at once to confirm the completed order and its price. Then the order form is filed away, to be picked up later for clearing. What's that, exactly? asks Mr. E. Oh, he'll go into that when there's time to discuss it in detail, says Mr. T., but basically it involves making sure that the trade is okay.

Just how quickly can a trade be accomplished? asks Mr. E. Well, Mr. T. replies, he has known situations in which the time interval between when an out-of-towner gave an order to his broker and when the report of its execution was sent back took less than two minutes! Mr. E. is astonished, disbelieving. How can such speed be possible? Because of the rapid and efficient communication connections nowadays, Mr. T. explains, and also because of the efficiency of the professionals involved all along the transaction's route. In addition, the introduction of new setups that eliminate or speed up steps along the route has helped; one such setup is the "hot line," which they are just beginning to use, which puts major brokerage offices in direct voice communication with the phonedesks on trading floors, cutting down on the very order-receiving mechanisms Mr. E. is watching here.

Also, adds Mr. T., an order can be completed quickly if it's something a trader can handle easily. How does that happen? Mr. E. wonders. It depends, naturally, on how active trading is right at the time the order comes in, says Mr. T. If extremely busy, a broker may find it hard to be seen and heard amidst the uproar and motioning of many assertive traders. On the other hand, if the market day in that commodity or delivery month is a very sluggish, no other trader may be interested in or able to make the right exchange. Or if there's a squeeze going on, when many contract holders are attempting to close out their positions because of adverse price changes or because the delivery time is approaching, filling the order then may be difficult, even impossible. And, of course, the more precise an order is, the more difficult it may be to execute. So the easiest orders will be those from people willing to sell under the market or to buy over the market: such orders give the broker some flexibility and may gain attention from traders looking for bargains.

What's this "at," "under," and "over" the market? Mr. E. wants to know. Aren't all the contracts bought and sold right here at the market? Though Mr. T. laughs, he admits these are confusing expressions. Brokers saying "at the market" really mean "at the market price." "The market," then, is whatever the last price is right now on the floor, the going price—posted up on the board—since the last trade was made.

Oh yes. Mr. E. now recalls reading that definition. But he confesses that he finds remembering these special words and expressions difficult. This state of mind is true for almost everybody when they start out, Mr. T. reassures him. And then the terms begin to come readily and automatically, especially to the professionals, who really have to learn the lingo. Mr. T. promises to expand on the subject later, maybe when they are downstairs near the phonemen.

Phone*men?* says a voice nearby, and Mr. E. sees the young woman at the Teletype machine looking scoldingly at his friend. Mr. T. laughs good-naturedly. Phonepersons, he says, correcting himself. Better yet, phoneclerks—which is what they are. But he occasionally forgets that times have changed and slips back into the description used when one saw only men around the trading floor.

Of all the people to make such a mistake! the young woman remarks in her mock scolding. Before her Teletype machine completes its chattering, she informs Mr. E. that his friend here has personally been responsible for hiring many women—including herself—in the brokerage's commodity division here and elsewhere. Mr. T. is something of a women's libber around the CBT, she adds as she returns to her work. Oh? asks Mr. E., expecting further explanation.

Mr. T. ushers Mr. E. farther along the passageway until they come to a large area that is subdivided into a number of small stalls separated by partitions. Here are the firm's local brokers, he explains, as he takes Mr. E. over to meet one. Mr. E. and Ms. A., the broker, are introduced to each other just as her phone rings. Apologizing, she takes the call but gestures to Mr. E. to sit down at the chair next to her desk and motions for Mr. T. to bring over another chair for himself. But Mr. T. declines, telling his friend just to stay there to listen to and watch Ms. A. at work, while he goes off for a few minutes to check on some office matters.

When the broker hangs up, she turns to Mr. E. He explains briefly that his friend Mr. T. is giving him a tour of the building—the exchange floor and his brokerage—so that he'll know much more what commodity speculation is about. Right now he is interested in how orders come from customers and get onto the exchange floor. Well, Ms. A. comments, Mr. E. has come to an important step along the pathway all right: the account executive at a brokerage. Unless speculators themselves are members of an exchange, they must have registered commodity representatives initiate their orders for them. These brokers handle their trading accounts, keeping track of customers' contract positions and alerting them when delivery months are approaching. For example, says Ms. A., here's a print-out from the computer that shows which of her clients must be advised today of the need to make closing-out orders to liquidate long positions before they have to take delivery. Oh, says Mr. E., that's how brokers are able to know such things!

Computers, the broker agrees, are boons in the commodity business in many ways. They store an incredible amount of useful information and send it out in seconds. Just then, as if to back up her statement, the phone rings. It's obviously a client who wants to know what is going on with live hogs right now. Ms. A. begins pushing keys on the computer terminal and screen located on her desk and obtains a succession of price and news reports that come on line by line. While busily translating these things to her customer, she suddenly hears sounds coming through a small box sitting on the partition by her desk. Listen! she exclaims, standing up and holding the phone receiver right next to the voice, which comes through in a scratchy but audible way, though with a baffling background of noise. When the voice stops, the box goes quiet. Hogs are already limit down! exclaims Ms. A. to the person on the other end of the phoneline. They are a disaster at the Merc because yesterday somebody delivered fifty contracts of them in Nebraska and some were found to have a communicable disease and all were exterminated. The news got traders going long like crazy, figuring hogs would be scarce for a while, sending the price limit up by the closing time. But by this morning traders realized that even bigger new shipments would be coming in soon, and so the rush to unload began right away. What to do? asks Ms. A. of her customer. Whatever he wants. But if the contracts were hers, she'd just sit tight and ride out the blitz. His long position is probably secure. . . . And with that she replaces the receiver.

That, she says, pointing at the little box above her, is the "squawk box," which periodically—whenever something important is happening that brokers should know about—transmits messages from the brokerage experts on the trading floors. And that, she says, patting her telecomputer terminal, is the Quotron. The office also has a terrific device called a VideCom, which can give prices, lists, and charts down to the last detail for the past few minutes or the last year—and then print them, if you want. She shows Mr. E. a group of figures, reports, and price charts that she told the machine to reproduce for a client coming in later that day.

Once more the phone rings, and as the broker takes the call she reaches for a pad in front of her and starts writing on the top sheet. Tearing it off, she writes on the second, and then on a third. Checking them over for accuracy, she runs them through her time stamper, then picks up the phone and immediately recites the orders. Mr. E., hearing the numbers and abbreviations, can hardly understand a thing she has said—and tells her so. She shows him the order slips. The top part identifies the brokerage; broker and order number are stamped in, and the client's name is added. The small sheet has a line down the middle. The left side is BUY, the right side is SELL. Ms. A. had written within the appropriate place the buy or sell orders from the customer on the phone:

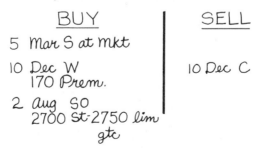

BUY

5 Mar S at mkt

10 Dec W
170 Prem.

2 Aug SO
2700 St-2750 lim
gtc

SELL

10 Dec C

But Mr. E. is still perplexed, admitting he doesn't yet know how to read, speak, or understand this peculiar language. Just then Mr. T. appears and hears him. Since the broker's phone has rung again, Mr. T. makes the translations: buy 5 March soybeans at the market. (Remember, he says, that's just 1 contract, not 5, since beans are traded as a grain in units of 1,000 bushels.) Buy 10 December wheat; sell 10 December corn; 170 premium on the wheat, good till canceled. (That one's a spread, Mr. T. comments.) Buy 2 August soybean oil, 2700 stop, 2750 limit, good till canceled.

Well . . . says Mr. E. dubiously. He supposes that helped a bit. It will take a while to learn what he needs to know, Mr. T. remarks reassuringly. But hang in there, because on the floor—where they're going now —he'll see and hear a lot more, spoken fast, that he won't comprehend either. Mr. T. will explain whenever he can whatever Mr. E. wants to find out.

Ms. A. is immersed in conversation with a client, pushing her computer keyboard, leafing through the current price chart book she keeps up daily. In a few seconds she finds what she wants and, running a finger along the latest ups and downs, remarks that the past few weeks now contain a "double reversal" that portends a price move that may mean "dynamite" for the client's present position. Seeing that she may be on the line for some while more, the two men catch her eye and wave good-bye, with Mr. E. briefly uttering his thank-you.

Now, says Mr. E. as they hurry away down the hallway toward the elevator, that was a most enlightening experience! In just a few minutes he began to understand what a broker's work must be like. And as the men negotiate the maze within the brokerage office, Mr. E. asks about women and commodities.

More and more women, of course, are entering the business world at all levels and in all arenas, including commodities, obviously, says Mr. T. Mr. E. will notice many female clerks, messengers, accountants, and phonepersons. There aren't too many account executives around yet. But they are no longer a rarity, as they were some years ago, and certainly not an impossibility, as they were a century ago, when the "gentler gender" was denied access to the palace of produce—a commercial hall where only men were permitted to trade. Women who liked marketplace activities could go out shopping for wheat flour and potatoes at the local grocer's. Women were not expected to be able to read contracts, let alone deal in them. If they ever signed them, their signatures weren't worth much, if anything, because the female brain, of course, was considered dim where money, business transactions, and even arithmetic were concerned.

Even today, says Mr. T., some brokers categorically refuse to take on any female customers' accounts, maintaining that women are too unstable emotionally and too ignorant about finance to make suitable commodity speculators. Mr. T.'s own experience has proved otherwise. Some of his shrewdest, most sensible, and most successful clients have been women! He doesn't want to sound like a sexist in reverse, but actually he believes that women as a group are more prudent and conservative and less ostentatious in handling money investments than men, when and if they are in a position to handle money with responsibility. He actively encourages women to enter the commodities field, whether as speculators or as brokers, economic researchers, or consultants. Often they achieve important professional positions by starting out in staff jobs at commission houses or commodity exchanges themselves and, like the men, working their way upward. But are there any women members of the exchange? Mr. E. inquires. Oh, several at least, says Mr. T. And Mr. E. may glimpse them today somewhere on the trading floor. A few years from now Ms. A. may well be among them!

The elevator has now deposited them right outside the large arena, from which the noise of human commerce and communication is issuing forth. Mr. T. leads his friend toward the entrance to his favorite place to be.

CHAPTER SEVEN

Out on the Trading Floor

Stopping at a large desk just outside the trading floor, Mr. T. fills out a visitor's form. A uniformed official hands Mr. E. a stick-on name tag to put on his coat. Now he too has a badge to wear that day on the trading floor. As at a convention, Mr. T. explains, it's useful to know who's who. Naturally the CBT does not permit unauthorized people to wander around the trading floor itself. There's too much congestion there as it is. And there are devices that might be tampered with, causing decidedly detrimental, wide-reaching effects on trade. Visitors unaccompanied by persons connected with the exchange's trading-floor operations can always see plenty and learn a lot at the Visitors Center upstairs.

The two men walk through the doorway. Even though he just saw the trading floor from above, Mr. E. is unprepared for the impact of entry into this vast, busy room. The trading floor of the Chicago Board of Trade is almost as wide as it is long and is several stories high. A row of large vertical windows on the north side of the room are letting in Chicago's morning sunlight. So here he actually is, in the great Temple of Trade! Mr. E. tells himself. Its occupants, though, are hardly worshipful. No, they are scurrying about on assigned tasks or their own business and are yelling at one another in the various large pits placed around the room.

There is no hushed reverence here before a throne erected to Mammon. The trading going on here, involving millions of dollars per day, requires exertion and noise. The tumult contains tension and vitality. A thousand voices must be joined in the incredible sounds arising from the pits, the phonedesks, the traffic upon the floor. The clamor of calls and loud conversations blends with the wild array of coat colors that Mr. E. had beheld from above. Trying to talk to his friend Mr. T., he realizes that he may have to shout to be heard. Sounds rise, bounce against the walls and the ceiling's acoustical boards, and multiply. He does not know how much his ears can take.

And now he can clearly read the gigantic, electronically operated boards that are beaming an assortment of recorded prices for today's contract trading. There are almost twenty commodities listed on the boards, subdivided into the delivery months for each, which of course carry a different range of prices, says Mr. T. He points out that for the commodities that have fractional price fluctuations, the fractions ¼, ½, and ¾ are designated by the terminal numerals 2, 4, and 6, respectively, following the price given in dollars and cents. Thus $6.99½ per bushel would appear on the board as 6.994.

Mr. E. tries to study this electrified collection of hundreds of red numbers in sequence, with many of them changing right before his eyes. The overall effect is dazzling—and well, overwhelming. He looks away, feeling disoriented. It *is* too much to take in all at once, admits Mr. T. To minimize his guest's stunned condition, Mr. T. leads Mr. E. over to several long rows of small, lined-up desks, each with a telephone. Nearly every slot is occupied by attentive men and women whose ears are next to phone receivers and whose hands are rapidly jotting down orders called in from elsewhere. Somewhat removed from the din in the pits, this area is a bit quieter, Mr. E. notes with relief.

This, says Mr. T., gesturing at the immediate vicinity, is the phone bank of his own brokerage house, where several phoneclerks—who acknowledge his arrival with a smile and a nod—are hard pressed to record, transmit, and then confirm back customers' orders received by the brokerage for execution today on the floor. Every few moments a yellow-jacketed runner scoops up a batchful of orders from the desks and charges off with them. The deluge, says Mr. T., sometimes never halts as long as trading goes on, and usually some commodities experience far more activity than others—predictably or unpredictably, but invariably in response to world and national news and to market experts' reports and recommendations.

Obviously, Mr. T. tells Mr. E., these phone jobs are crucial because they make the vital linkup between the outside world, with its many thousands of customers, and the inside one here, the commodities marketplace upon the trading floor, where broker-traders are expected to carry through these orders as best they can. As Mr. E. saw for himself upstairs in the brokerage office, the time factor can be critically important, and so the exact time of order receipt at each point along the route is recorded. In this way, should a customer or his own broker question a price given on an executed order, the transaction can be pinpointed to the time when the pit broker bought or sold the contract or contracts in the customer's behalf. If a price is considered unfair in contrast with those in similar transactions going on within that period, a customer may justifiably protest.

Does this happen often? asks Mr. E. Not really, Mr. T. replies, which is rather remarkable considering the terrific pressure that pit and floor brokers are under, especially if they are free-lancers, or "paper brokers," who virtually earn their livings on commissions coming from executing orders for other people. Each completed order yields a small fee of several dollars. So Mr. E. can well imagine how much hustling such brokers must do in a day of trading in order to take home a respectable wage! And if they fail sometimes to satisfy others' expectations by buying too high or selling too low in order to get orders filled speedily, they are apt to get dropped as an individual speculator's or firm's broker. Mr. E., watching from afar the brokers in action in the nearby pit, agrees that a floor broker's work must be strenuous to the point of exhaustion. But there are those who thrive on it anyway, Mr. T. maintains, and would not wish to do anything else for a living. For indeed here on the trading floor of the CBT one's fingers rest on the very pulse of the world's commerce.

Mr. E., listening to the repetitive calls of traders who are searching for opposite parties in contract transactions, wonders again about the special clipped phrases and abbreviations he hears and sees. About those order forms that Ms. A. wrote out and the ones written here too, he asks, What are all those letters used for the commodities themselves? He noticed a few—S, C, W, SO—which he was told stood for soybeans, corn, wheat, and soybean oil. How did these symbols get started?

The letter-symbol system began long ago with the exchanges themselves, Mr. T. explains. In those years orders were sent by telegram to the exchanges, and so brevity and precision were important. An order had to be given clearly and correctly so that a broker would not be likely to receive an erroneous order through the tapped-out transmission by wire. Now, however, there are special rates on open phonelines. The fastest way to send an order is by voice. But there are also ticker tapes, Teletypes, and telecomputers for sending and receiving orders and information—and all these methods can use a special shorthand in their keyboard systems. Ordinarily a speculator need not know them. If he's visiting his broker and wants to get the latest price quotation from an exchange floor, the broker just presses the proper sequence of letters on the computer terminal and lo and behold! there's the magic figure, plus maybe other things he would like to be alerted to.

While Mr. T. was talking, he was searching through his wallet for something, and now he pulls it out: a handy little card that translates most of the commodity symbols. He used to give it out to his clients, and Mr. E. can have this one. The list isn't complete, by any means. Also, the different exchanges sometimes use different symbols for the same commodity they both handle. But this card shows, anyway, the range of possibilities:

AU	troy gold	LB	lumber	PW	plywood
BO	soybean oil	LC	live cattle	RP	commercial paper 30-day
C	corn	LH	live hogs		
CP	commercial paper 90-day	M	GNMA mortgage interest	S	soybeans
				SI	silver
CR	copper	O	oats	SM	soybean meal
E	eggs			TN	Treasury notes
FC	feeder cattle	OJ	frozen orange juice	US	Treasury bonds
G	gold	P	potatoes	W	wheat
IB	iced broilers	PB	pork bellies		

Then there are all those letter symbols that stand for particular delivery months in commodities, Mr. T. goes on. Brokers and other people in the commodity business have to know them because they are frequently used in order sending and information retrievals. But there's no reason why Mr. E. himself should memorize them. To satisfy his curiosity, though, he can see what they are by reading that small chart taped on the desk next to him:

January	February	March	April	May	June
F^A	G^B	H^C	J^D	K^E	M^I
July	**August**	**September**	**October**	**November**	**December**
N^L	Q^O	U^P	V^R	X^S	Z^T

Reprinted with permission of the Chicago Board of Trade

COMMODITY SPECULATION FOR BEGINNERS

The small letters in each box, Mr. T. explains, refer to the more distant month of the same name in the following year—since some commodities have futures contracts that are bought and sold at least eighteen months in advance of delivery time. Sometimes *NXT*, though, will designate the same month, next year.

Now, says Mr. T., the really vital knowledge for small, at-home speculators is not the special lingo, the terms and abbreviations that brokers use among themselves regarding orders and commodities and so on. It is how to get the information they need to have in order to give the right order—and then how to state a precise order over the phone or in person to their brokers or commission house representatives. Brokers, once they understand what their customers want, will be able to translate the orders into the right abbreviations, symbols, and phrases so that the orders will be executed as the customers request and at the correct commodity exchanges. There are all sorts of trading expressions involved in order giving, such as *limits, stops, open orders, day orders, good till canceled, premium, market if touched, market on close, one cancels other,* and, of course, *at the market.* Many of them will be abbreviated during the transmission to the trading floor, but their meanings will be clear enough to the floor or pit broker.

Mr. E. looks a bit surprised, even stunned. So order giving isn't just a simple matter of either buying or selling? No indeed! Mr. T. comments. The wise speculator generally builds certain protections into a new order, for both now and later. When Mr. T. can, he'll go into more detail about how and why this is done. Just now, though, he sees that one of the phoneclerks is handing him an order just received, with the request that he handle it. Ah, this is the one Mr. T. was expecting to come in today! Well, it will give him an excuse to take Mr. E. as close to the corn pit as he's allowed to go, right to the foot of the steps. . . .

The two men have walked to the large pit located near the northeast corner of the room. Mr. T. shows Mr. E. where he can stand, close to the CBT personnel up on the platform overlooking the pit, while he himself mounts the steps, promising to return in only a minute or so since this is a simple order. Following Mr. T.'s progress, Mr. E. is aware that he is feeling more comfortable than before here on the trading floor. He's even becoming accustomed to the noise.

Mr. E. notices that as his friend starts down the inside steps, he begins making hand signals. He guesses that he wants to buy three corn contracts. Across the way another trader calls out "Sep corn" and holds his palms outward. But Mr. T. thrusts out four fingers—indicating, Mr. E. supposes, that he's willing to buy at ½¢ per bushel less than the current price up on the board. The other trader starts out again, this time sticking out two fingers for ¼¢ below. Now Mr. T. shouts his okay and the two men begin writing on their trading cards. Leaving the pit, Mr. T. summarizes with hand signals exactly what the deal was to the quotation reporter and auditors on the platform. He then hails a nearby runner, hands him the completed order form, and sends him off to the phone-desks.

What was that about? asks Mr. E. It looks to him as if Mr. T. has bought three contracts of September corn at ¼¢ below the last price, he says—judging from the signals. Precisely! declares Mr. T., pleased with the visitor's perception. And now, he says, watch the board up there and see how the latest price—his—will be on it, if not now, then in a few seconds. It's good that Mr. E. is learning how the auction trading is done with all contract orders.

Mr. T. goes on to say that a hedger client of his, a local baker, had wanted to assure himself that 15,000 bushels of corn would be available to him for making cornmeal when he needs it in the fall, at a price he can afford. This way, by buying the other trader's corn contracts today, all will be well. Who knows? They may even make and take delivery if it's convenient for both parties. For the opposite trader, Mr. T. declares, is actually a hedger. A nice fellow who really knows a lot about grains because he himself was once a farmer.

So trading isn't quite as detached and mechanical as one might think it would be, Mr. E. comments. His friend obviously knows and likes some of the other traders. Of course, says Mr. T. But while on the floor, business is business. If you're buying, you get the lowest price available. And if you're selling, you try for the highest—no matter who the traders may be. The first person who bids or offers an acceptable price gets your trade: that's how it must be at an auction.

Mr. E. has noticed that Mr. T. periodically checks one of the big quotation boards. Does he have more trading to do today? he asks. Maybe, Mr. T. replies. He is looking for the right prices, though, on some bean futures and they haven't appeared yet. In the meantime, though, they can just stand here at the side of the corn pit and watch the action inside.

Mr. E. wants to ask about prices themselves, the ones up on the boards and the numbers called out in the pits. All the quoted prices, says Mr. T., apply to the basic unit in each standard commodity contract. With soybeans and other grains it means cents per bushel, or dollars and cents with the decimal put in. For plywood it's dollars per thousand square feet. For iced broilers—chickens—it's cents per pound, and for soybean meal, dollars per ton. For silver it's cents per ounce, but for gold it's dollars per ounce. And of course each commodity contract has its own standard measurement system. All the grains on the major exchanges have 5,000 bushels per contract, by volume. Many commodities go by weight: 10 metric tons of cocoa, 112,000 pounds of sugar, 50,000 pounds of potatoes or cotton, or 40,000 pounds of live cattle. A few are counted, like shell eggs, which sell by the 22,500 dozen. The financial instruments go by face value per contract, and U.S. silver coins are considered in bags. The price of a contract is therefore calculated by multiplying the basic price by the contract size. Traders only concern themselves over the fluctuation in the unit price itself; they all know how it affects the total value.

Must traders start off each trading day using the previous day's closing price? Mr. E. wonders. No, Mr. T. tells him; it only serves as a reference base. Each day traders must stay within certain *price-move limits,* designated by the exchange for each separate commodity. For instance, if soybeans closed yesterday at 750, then with a 30¢ limit they could not be traded today above 780 or below 720. Occasionally the limit figure is changed: it's either tightened or loosened, as happens right before a delivery month is due, when greater flexibility in price moves can be essential. Though at times they restrict trading, these daily limits on prices are safeguards to traders when a price is moving up or down rapidly because many speculators are buying and selling—or trying to, anyway, whether eagerly or in desperation. Further, the limits allow the exchange clearinghouses time to collect money from the losers and deposit it in the accounts of the winners. And they protect speculators from sustaining huge losses before they can even try to get out; some foreign exchanges don't have this built-in safety feature. In soybeans, for example, a daily limit of 30¢ per bushel in the standard contract of 5,000 bushels would mean that a speculator can't lose more than $1,500 in one contract's devaluation during a day's trading. Knowing there is a set limitation on daily price moves enables speculators to calculate whether or not they can afford to take or keep a contract position in a particular commodity. However, exchanges sometimes do change these regular limits, as needed. Therefore limits are variable.

Mr. E., of course, is now fascinated by being closer to the traders with their odd hand signals and calls, what Mr. T. calls "shortspeak." Simultaneously gesturing and calling out was begun during the Board of Trade's earliest years, Mr. T. explains, when in order to establish a public auction for contracts, the various traders had to devise ways of being both seen and heard. The signals and outcry may seem odd to outsiders at first, Mr. T. knows, but they are an intrinsic part of the open, democratic bargaining and are actually required of the traders. No back-room deals go on here!

Mr. E. notices that when a transaction is completed, most traders simply nod acknowledgments at each other and start writing things down. So they don't even need to shake hands over the deal and converse about it, he remarks in amazement. They are busy fellows, says Mr. T., who have little time for sociability right now. See how most of them, once they've filled an order, move elsewhere in the pit or leave, probably headed for another one. When the trading day is over, though, the traders are as sociable a bunch as any business has, he can assure Mr. E.

But how does anybody know what has been done? asks Mr. E. Four records are usually being kept at the same time, answers his trader friend. The initiating order slip remains in the brokerage office, time stamped. The phoned-in order slip that goes to the trading floor, also time stamped, is filled out by the trader after it has been executed, and confirmation is telephoned to the brokerage, which notes it down on its own copy. The trader personally keeps a brief account of each transaction handled. And the personnel of the exchange up on the platform also note down what has happened: who and what and for how much and when. At the end of the trading day these transaction records are merged in the clearing firms, which handle the accounts of customers and traders, within the clearing corporation connected with the exchange. Any discrepancy in prices or other contract details or the omission of an opposite trader in a contract acquisition must be run down. Such unmatched trades are called *out trades,* and they have to be resolved by the clearing firms, traders, or brokerages involved before trading can begin in the morning. Then, in prices and quantities, those who bought evenly match those who sold in the final records kept by the clearinghouse itself.

Mr. E. can scarcely believe that such accuracy can be achieved from a system that appears so haphazard—and, well, wild. Why, he has noticed that some traders actually throw down the slips for the orders they have just executed! he exclaims. Mr. T. laughs. The runners will pick them up and take them to where they belong, he says. The trader, after all, needs his hands free for signaling! But if Mr. E. thinks that the place looks littered now, he should see it when a real trading spree is going on or at the close of a busy trading day. Then it can look as if a blizzard has hit the pit.

What things does a floor broker have to write on a customer's order? asks Mr. E. The price, the time of the trade, the initials of the opposite traders, and also a firm's name if he's connected with one, Mr. T. answers. That's why traders have big initials on their badges: so that they can be seen at some distance. But of course, says Mr. T., after a while one gets to know a lot of traders just by sight, so that after a few trades a trader's initials come automatically, without even consulting the badge.

How many traders here does Mr. T. know personally? Mr. E. wonders. His friend looks around. Probably two dozen of the regulars, he says, who tend to specialize in corn, whether they are speculator-traders or pit brokers. Then there are the floor brokers and floor traders who roam around more, moving in and out most of the pits. But the staying fellows are mostly scalpers.

Scalpers? Mr. E. acts repelled, and his companion chuckles. He agrees that it is a rather disagreeable term for a trader who really performs a highly useful service. How so? Well, he "scalps," or skims, off the current prices by buying for a fraction of a cent less or selling for a fraction of a cent more.

But how can one do much of anything with ¼¢? asks Mr. E. Spending time fiddling around with fractions hardly seems worthwhile. But figure it out, says Mr. T. His friend the Corn Pit Scalper—the man with the red beard and the plaid jacket who's standing on the second step across the way—is down there right now trying to buy twenty contracts. That's 100,000 bushels. Obviously he hopes the price will go up. And if it does, even by a ¼¢, he'll then try to sell them all at once or in several separate transactions. If all this happens within an hour's time he'll have made himself a small profit of $250. (In his head Mr. E. multiplies 100,000 by 0.0025.) Now, says Mr. T., if during the trading day the Corn Pit Scalper manages to buy and sell a number of such contracts for various delivery months, keeping track all the while of the current prices of each, he may make similar profits on at least a few deals. If he can earn $500 or more in a single day of work, that's not so bad, is it?

And besides, Mr. T. goes on, all the while the Corn Pit Scalper has been adding action and liquidity to the market. Because he's there, money is moving back and forth, and interest is kept steady. A hedger may come in or put through an order to buy or sell a number of corn contracts. These hedgers, remember, only trade on the commodity exchange as a small part of their overall operations. They cannot afford to spend a lot of time and energy in haggling over prices. What they need is somebody to buy or somebody to sell in opposite positions from theirs, at current prices they consider sensible enough. And, handily, the scalpers are usually quite obliging. After all, if a grain elevator has just bought 10,000 bushels of corn from a farmer, it may wish to hedge right away, at the market price, to protect itself from adverse price changes.

So the people most likely to accommodate hedgers' immediate needs are the scalpers. Because a scalper is willing to take his profits—or losses, if need be—on a purely fractional basis, he helps to keep price transitions up or down fairly smooth, without sharp jumps or gaps. He uses the smallest increments, or points, set by the exchange by which a price is allowed to fluctuate. He'll rarely keep any position overnight, closing out his various trades before the day ends. So look at his good friend the Corn Pit Scalper! orders Mr. T. Forgive him that ugly epithet "scalper." They'll just wave to him—he's looking in their direction now—and move on to the soybean pit. The prices are inching closer to the way Mr. T. wants them, and he wants to be nearby to make his move if he can.

He's glad, though, that Mr. E. got close to corn today. It is one of Mr. T.'s great favorites, he says in a burst of eloquence, with Mr. E. right at his side while they move toward the west. Corn is a good, old-fashioned commodity if ever there was one—that and wheat. But corn—maize, that is—came from the Americas, not the Old World, so Mr. T. feels a special partiality toward it. As they walk along, Mr. T. explains that he's the kind of trader who gets fascinated by whatever commodities he speculates in. He's not strictly a statistically oriented chart-and-graph man with his eye on the profit and loss columns. He gets involved—which, he admits, isn't always advisable when loyalties or instincts cause impulsive moves or stubborn stands that get in the way of cool and rational decision making. But he can't help it, that's how he is, and he takes his emotional peculiarities into account whenever he's trading for himself, knowing that a coldly reasoning part of him may have to take over when things start going wrong. Yet he has managed to do all right in spite of his . . . well, it's probably a passion for certain commodities, wanting to know everything there is to be known about them.

Take corn, say. (By now they have reached the octagonal frame of the bean pit.) Watching corn grow. Being conscious of the diseases it's subject to; the terrible pests that attack it; and the weather that burns or dries, or floods and rots, it. Aware of the techniques, expenses, and complications in sowing, harvesting, transporting, and storing it. And thinking about all the many wonderful things that have been done and can be done with corn—with many more yet to be found. And besides, Mr. T. adds, smiling at his friend as he glances up at the big quotation board to study it anew, he learned an awful lot about corn in the whole process of speculating upon its existence . . . and about soybeans too.

Perfect timing! Mr. T. announces as he sets a foot impatiently on the first step of the bean pit. Why right now? Mr. E. wants to know. Because, says Mr. T., the difference between the futures prices for July and November beans is spaced about as he'd want them to be for making his spread.

Spread? Now that's another word that Mr. E. has heard and read but whose meaning still escapes him. Mr. T. mentioned it upstairs when translating Ms. A.'s orders. A spread, his trader friend summarizes, is the taking of opposite positions, buying and selling simultaneously, in the same or related commodities for different delivery months or sometimes at different exchanges. A *straddle* is really the same thing.

Telling his friend to watch him, Mr. T. mounts the stairs and then commences his own signals and outcry. He is offering to sell five July bean contracts at the market. A few feet away another trader calls out his acceptance, and signals back. Mr. T. jots the information down on the red side of his trading card, explaining that this is the "sell" side. Then he gestures for Mr. E. to follow him around the pit. What will Mr. T. do now? He yells out, "Buy twenty-five Nov one-quarter under market." All the while he gesticulates in sign language. Another trader opposite shouts, "Sell twenty-five Nov a quarter above." Mr. T. shakes his head no, then repeats the bid to buy. Another trader then indicates willingness to sell five straight at the market. Mr. T. shrugs and acknowledges his acceptance with "Done!" Now he turns his card over to the blue side and fills in the basics about his purchase.

And that's all for him to trade today on the floor, says Mr. T., suggesting that they take a break. They walk upstairs to a room where Mr. T. gets two cups of coffee and some coffee cake. Now, he continues, about spreads. That is what he just accomplished. Did Mr. E. notice how he both bought and sold five bean contracts in separate delivery months? But why? Mr. E. inevitably wonders. Spreads are done for various reasons, says Mr. T. Many speculators use them to make their positions safer. For example, in this bean spread it's possible that by being "short" July beans—owing beans because he has sold them or, rather, sold contracts to deliver them—he may be able to make a nice profit several months from now if, as he anticipates, the basis widens well before July. *Basis?* Oh yes, Mr. T. explains, that's the distance between the futures and the cash prices: a very important figure for both hedgers and spread traders.

The bean price, Mr. T. goes on, may dip very low this year because the forecast is for a large crop, caused by overplanting and excellent growing weather so far. This plus an unprecedented carry-over supply from last year's stored crop will create a great surplus. And useful as soybeans are, good for exporting too, the past several years' prices shouldn't hold. Buyers of bean contracts, for the most part speculators, won't want to pay for and receive beans, and so they'll have to liquidate their contracts, offsetting their positions by selling out very low and sustaining big losses. Meanwhile, because of taking a bearish tactic now, Mr. T. stands to profit because he can purchase the contracts back for considerably less than he sold them for. And at the same time, for another round turn, he will probably sell the November futures he also bought today. He hopes, of course, that the price of July beans will fall further than the price of November beans and that he will therefore make a profit.

But what if some unforeseen disaster, like drought or disease, strikes out most of the soybean crop in the United States, so that the anticipated oversupply totally fails to occur? Mr. T. asks so that he can answer his own question. Well, then, notice how he has somewhat protected himself by taking two opposite positions in two different months. As soon as he realizes that July beans are in trouble, he knows his short position, owing beans, is highly vulnerable. He will have to buy the contracts back at a higher price, perhaps much higher, just to get out before there's worse trouble. But then he can also sell his November contracts, which will be much more valuable. Thus any loss sustained on the July contracts should be offset or at least partially offset by gains in the second trade. He may even do better than break even. Of course, he emphasizes, there are risks with spreads as well as with an outright net position of being either long or short. Spreads may diffuse some risk taking in commodities, but they aren't a magical way to make money by trading.

Mr. E. is impressed with the sequence of reasoning, as Mr. T. expected him to be. Spreads are fascinating to devise, Mr. T. declares. The novice speculator shouldn't try them, though, because they can be tricky. But they are a regular tool for the accomplished trader. There are other interesting *arbitrage* situations—like buying and selling contracts in similar kinds of commodities, as in grains or in metals, since a price change in one almost invariably affects the other in the same direction. Or one can trade futures in different months of commodities in which one is made from the other: soybeans and soybean oil, live hogs and pork bellies. Or one can buy September wheat on the Minneapolis Grain Exchange and sell September wheat in Kansas City. (They are both wheat, says Mr. T., but remember that the K.C. kind is No. 2 Hard Red winter wheat, which is grown in early spring and has a different gluten content than the Minneapolis No. 2 Hard Northern spring wheat. Such differences are important to various commercial buyers.)

What are other advantages to spreads? Mr. E. wants to know. Apart from protecting one's position by doing a double deal, says Mr. T., in the past spreads have given tax advantages to speculators looking for investment mechanisms, allowing them to move income or profits taken from one year and push them into the next tax year. But now the IRS is watching spreads closely for tax evasions. Spread orders, anyway, enable *rolling over* contracts. What's that? asks Mr. E. That means simply selling one contract and buying another one for a farther-out, or back, month, Mr. T. explains. Say when a March wheat contract comes due, you "roll over" by getting December wheat.

They have finished their coffee. What now? Well, before going away from the trading floor altogether, Mr. T. wants to take Mr. E. to see several other popular pits for trading. Such as the Ginnie Mae pit. Mr. E. doubts that he has heard him correctly, and Mr. T. grins. Ginnie Mae has one of the busiest pits in the house, he says. She hasn't been here very long, though, and she's kept in the South Trading Room off to the side, along with the other "soft commodities"—the *financial instruments,* as they're called. Though what's really soft about them all he can't figure, except that instead of being tied up with the land's firm products, these new commodities consist of paper and have interest rates that fluctuate and therefore cause wide variations in value.

But Ginnie Mae? asks Mr. E. Oh, that's just the nickname for GNMA, says Mr. T., laughing. It stands for Government National Mortgage Association, which put futures contracts on interest rates on the exchange in the mid-seventies. These and other financial instruments— such as Treasury bills, Treasury bonds, and commercial paper—have been enormously successful after being introduced in the past few years, so that more and more "paper" valuables subject to price changes are being considered for the commodity exchanges. State and municipal governments are actively entering into hedging too.

Mr. E. wonders whether he should start right now to learn about this new market in financial goods. Today there's no time even to get into the subject, says Mr. T. But certainly Mr. E. should learn about the "soft commodities" when he learns about the other commodities, and also about the trade in foreign currencies, which is fairly new. But they are all complex and usually require large margins, and so he shouldn't trade in them until he's fully experienced as a trader. Once he has studied them in detail, he may then find the financial instruments an interesting and straightforward form of speculation.

Having looked over the Ginnie Mae action, the two men migrate back to the main trading room, where there's considerable commotion among the gold and silver traders. People, traders especially, remarks Mr. T., gravitate toward these precious metals whenever there's the slightest economic threat, particularly an international one. He personally tends to steer clear of them. He realizes that many people have made fantastic profits by going long or selling short at the right times. But if they are unlucky and choose wrong, the losses can be devastating. So he advises fledgling speculators to be extremely wary of dealing in these contracts, however "solid" they seem as an investment. Just now, contracts are being bought up by those who intend to *take* delivery so "short" speculators are in trouble, because they do not actually *own* the metals! As Mr. E. will learn, the attractive leverage factor in commodity speculation can move just as readily *against* one as for one, and in precious metals probably more than anywhere else the innocents and the ignorant get clobbered, since they don't fully understand the market mechanisms.

Had enough of the floor now? asks Mr. T. Well, the best plan for them right now, he suggests, is to see some of the clearing activities before the close of the trading day. What exactly is a clearinghouse? asks

Mr. E. He keeps hearing about it but he doesn't know what it does or where it is.

Well, he'll be able to show him far better than just tell him, says Mr. T. Does he go there often? Mr. E. wonders. At this Mr. T. must laugh. Why, he goes there almost every day—every trading day, that is. Not many traders do, but he does. Hadn't he told Mr. E. that he is in charge of his brokerage house's clearing firm? That's his main responsibility nowadays. Come along and see!

CHAPTER EIGHT

A Visit to the Clearinghouse

As they wait for the elevator, Mr. E. asks Mr. T. to explain the connection between his own brokerage company and the exchange clearinghouse. His commission house, says Mr. T., is a member firm of the clearing corporation—which is the exchange's "clearinghouse." It acquires this responsible position through individual brokers like himself who have seats on the Chicago Board of Trade. Clearing firms prepare all the necessary financial and legal evidence to prove that contract trades executed during a trading day by their brokers and independent trader-clients are sound. They assume responsibility for errors and insufficient funds. And as Mr. E. may imagine, this whole process is complex, detailed, and sometimes burdensome.

By now the elevator has deposited them once more at the brokerage office. But this time, after nodding to the receptionist, Mr. T. goes off to the right, toward his own domain. Walking past an assortment of offices, he talks to Mr. E. about the importance of the clearing mechanism in commodity trading. If the American public itself could comprehend how the clearinghouse works, he maintains, it might feel more assured about speculators and the whole futures market. People see and hear plenty about what goes on on the trading floor, but they do not know about the clearing activities behind the dramatic scenes of price moves made by traders. Nor do they fully realize that there are real contracts—involving earnest money and legal obligations—that are being traded with each price rise or drop. Without the clearinghouse a commodity exchange could not function. It provides the fail-safe feature. The exchange itself is never the victim of defaults in payments or unmet contract stipulations. These must be assumed by the clearing firms themselves, through which trades have been made and traders' positions and financial assets have been verified.

Mr. T. urges Mr. E. to take a seat in the small but comfortable anteroom within the clearing-firm quarters. He'll see and learn more by sitting here, he explains, than if they went off right away to his private office, since through here, all day long, comes traffic in persons and papers—mainly connected with today's trades. Mr. T. points toward an open doorway into another, much larger room, from which emerges those constant sounds of various machines: the whirring of wheels within office calculators, the chugging of computer print-outs, the tapping of keys, the moaning of copying devices. And there are also human voices, indicating to Mr. E. that machines don't take care of everything.

Contracts, then, really do exist? asks Mr. E. Yet he hears that speculators never see them. Yes indeed there are contracts, Mr. T. asserts, and the clearing corporation and its member firms are repositories of the ones traded on that particular exchange. Few speculators, it's true, ever see them, but by entering into commodity trading speculators are in fact buying and selling contracts to buy and sell actual goods at a specific price and time in the future. So it's not just a matter of flashing price numbers, ticker tape, and shouting in the trading pits.

Mr. E., of course, wants to see one of these contracts, and Mr. T. will be happy to oblige him later. Just now he'd like to explain that whatever work goes on here now is vastly multiplied after 1:15, when the gong again rings, this time to stop trading on the floor. All the various order forms and trading cards are collected from brokers, phonedesks, and traders and brought here to be sorted, tabulated, checked over, and whatever else needs to be done when preparing programmed cards for the first computer run, which comes at about 4:00. If there are any *out-trades*—if some of the executed trades don't balance out—then more checking must be done until everything is finally cleared. This preliminary work takes a lot of close attention, communication, and calculations before the proper assurances can be conveyed to the clearinghouse headquarters. On extremely active trading days or if there are some baffling out-trades hard to run down, some of the firm's employees—including, often, Mr. T. himself—have to work overtime well into the night in order to get all transactions ''cleared'' before the succeeding trading day. Hundreds of contracts involving valuations in millions of dollars must be both legally and financially set—even though a number of them could be closed out in a day or two.

Furthermore, adds Mr. T., the clearing firm must make sure that all customers' and traders' margin accounts on previously taken contract positions have been added to when prices moved against them. The money must be deposited with the clearinghouse itself. Just how many clearing firms are there? asks Mr. E. Only about one hundred, says Mr. T. But there are more than fifteen hundred members and associates of the exchange! Mr. E. remembers. Doesn't every trader who's a member handle his or her own account directly with the clearinghouse? No, Mr. T. answers. Only a small portion of the traders are able or willing to participate in the complicated clearing activities, which are really a business unto themselves—and therefore, of course, bring in fees for services rendered, so that individual traders who care to undertake this responsibility may, like many brokerages, become incorporated. The clearing corporations require a separate staff of clerks, accountants, computer operators, and legal advisers. And, says Mr. T., his primary job here is to supervise these functions for his firm's clearing division.

This big accounting room next to them, Mr. T. explains, is where all the brokerage's money transactions on the CBT are rectified. Each brokerage branch is ultimately held responsible for its customers' trades. If for some reason an individual has failed to provide necessary margin maintenance funds, which must be turned over to the clearing corporation at the end of each trading day if the contract position has declined in value, the brokerage firm itself must come up with the money. Thus the exchange and its clearinghouse are always protected from any losses, large or small. Sometimes Mr. T. and his associates in the clearing corporation or in the clearing firm must make decisions disallowing particular traders from trading further if there is an indication of impending insolvency. The many different levels of supervision, from the top management down to the brokers in the many commission, or "wire," houses throughout the country, usually guarantee good performance. If speculators fail to fulfill their contractual obligations, they can be legally prosecuted to obtain financial compensation to cover losses that are owed their opposite parties—which, in fact, are then no longer individual traders who took the other side of the contract but the clearinghouse itself.

But how can that be? Mr. E. asks. Surely the clearinghouse does not speculate. Of course not, says Mr. T. But the whole complex business with futures contracts is made much simpler by removing the opposite parties. Once assured that a secure trade has been made by two individuals or firms, for the same amount of goods in the same delivery month at the identical prearranged price, the clearinghouse actually interposes itself as the opposite party to each of them. In other words, it becomes the buyer to each seller and the seller to each buyer. In that way, each trader owes margin maintenance to the clearinghouse if his position declines in value because of a price change. Or else the clearinghouse itself is obligated to come forward with the profit money when a position has increased in value, depositing it with the clearing firm or commission house with which the contract holder is associated.

Just as Mr. T. is finishing his presentation of the exchange clearinghouses' fail-safe features, here, coming through the doorway with briefcase in hand and clutching a bunch of papers obviously picked up on the trading floor below, walks a figure that looks familiar to Mr. E. Having shaken his hand, Mr. T. introduces Hedging Harry to his fledgling speculator friend, Mr. E. The recent arrival, who's come to present his trading records to the clearing firm, is identified by Mr. T. as a big-deal farmers' hedger, who today has doubtlessly been selling contracts for great carloads of corn and wheat and oats that haven't even been grown yet. True enough, Hedging Harry counters, but they've been sown, anyway. Why doesn't Mr. T. take a few days off, as he did last year, and come out to Kansas and Iowa and watch them grow?

Mr. T. just might. This time, though, he says, maybe he could persuade Mr. E. here to join him there for a tour of the farmlands, which he'd find highly instructive. And they'd probably do it in July, when he could see the ears of corn filling out on the tall stalks—mile after mile of them, millions of them, Mr. E. can't possibly imagine how many! . . . Or maybe they could wait for a while, till harvest time, when Mr. E. could see them picked and piled into the boxcars along the town depot's railroad siding, waiting to be carted off the marketplace or some grain elevator.

Mr. E., Mr. T. whispers to Hedging Harry, doesn't really believe that the corn exists at all. He believes that all the speculators do at the exchanges is trade pieces of paper back and forth: in fact, paper that they don't even see or touch! He doesn't believe in the reality of hedgers probably because he hasn't met one until now. And he hasn't seen a real commodity contract either.

Well, says Hedging Harry, isn't it time for him to see both? And here he is, visible, audible, and tangible, having just completed his business for the day on the trading floor. Altogether, he has sold some fifty contracts of corn futures for July and September, thirty-five of oats, and forty-four of wheat. That's a lot of grain, Mr. E. comments as he mentally multiplies each number by 5,000 bushels. Is that Harry's entire crop? Nope, says this new acquaintance; it's only part of the total crop that his firm hopes to produce this summer.

But isn't he taking a big risk by not hedging all of it? Mr. E. wonders. The other two men laugh good-naturedly. This is only one day's business, they assure him. Mr. T. explains that Hedging Harry represents a huge cooperative agribusiness that grows a wide variety of crops in vast quantities and in different locations over six states. Seven now, says Harry.

Today's contract-selling transactions, he explains, involved hedges for only several divisions for which acreage, yield, and probable cash prices have already been prefigured rather precisely. When Harry isn't here in Chicago working out hedges on the exchange, he's traveling around the country, visiting separate areas and checking over the farm managers' programs preparatory to any hedging action.

Hedging Harry would never *not* hedge, he asserts. He hedges to the best of his abilities, since his job would be on the line if he miscalculated and failed to hedge well. The big farmers, the farm businesses, he says, are the ones most apt to hedge their entire crops on the exchanges. For the grain farmers, the CBT is, of course, the primary place to do it. And that's why he represents his firm as a trader-member here at the exchange. To do otherwise—to seek higher profits by not hedging crops—also risks the possibility of price drops and would be speculating. That is what many small farms do, deliberately or unknowingly. No, Hedging Harry prefers to leave speculating up to the traders like Mr. T. here and the brokerage customers who can take chances that may result in both profits *and* losses. His own corporation expects the guarantee of a reasonable return for producing those many carloads of grains, which will take care of operating expenses and then provide a small margin of profits that makes the whole enterprise worth doing. Farmers can grow their crops having the surety that, once the crops are on their way to market, they will earn back exactly what the crops are worth to them—whether the price is higher or lower than anticipated. And this is possible thanks to the nationwide network of speculators who put up money backing their trading positions and are willing to lose margin money if they guess wrong.

And speaking of margin money, Hedging Harry has come in now to transfer funds from the corporation's bank account to its hedging account, which Mr. T.'s firm handles for the exchange clearinghouse. Oh, says Mr. E., does this mean that hedgers have to pay in margin deposits too? Sure, says Harry. Just as all speculators must maintain percentages of the contract values with the clearinghouse, so do all hedgers who sell or buy futures on an exchange. Any price change that moves against their positions requires that additional margin money be added to their accounts. All traders and hedgers, whether purchasing or selling commodity contracts, whether speculating or seeking insurance against adverse price changes, must put earnest money behind their transactions. Selling hedgers, of course, won't end up losing anything if they have hedged properly. Even if they lose the margin maintenance fund through an increase in value of the contracts they have sold, they'll make up for it when they sell the commodity on the cash market because the price will be higher by about the same amount they have lost on the futures contracts. In that situation, though, the short speculators will lose if the commodity price increases, since they have no actual goods to sell. After all, they were entering into a *contract* to sell, not selling the goods themselves.

Speaking of contracts . . . Mr. E. says. Oh yes, says Mr. T. He has promised to show Mr. E. one. Well, now that Hedging Harry is going off to tend to his business, why don't they go into Mr. T.'s office and get a sample copy of a corn futures contract? They walk together into the office, and Mr. T. leads his friend to the window providing a partial view of Lake Michigan. The winter ice has been breaking up, he says, freeing the waterway for shipping all the way to the Atlantic. They stand for a while at the window, with Mr. T. pointing out the cityscape and waterfront sights to his bedazzled friend. Each season, Mr. T. declares, has its wonders in Chicago; but to him spring—with the reawakening of the land, of commerce—is the best.

But now . . . he reaches into his desk and pulls out a formidable-looking document several pages long, in fine print. He hands the form to Mr. E. This, he says, is one of those papers on which all the traders down there on the floor and all the commercial hedgers and all the customers in commission houses around the nation base their trading. But although these forms do exist, as Mr. E. can see for himself, only privileged or very interested people ever see them. Why? Because it isn't necessary for traders to do so. Brokerages and clearing firms handle the paperwork and legalities for them, as if by proxy. But the account holder is ultimately responsible for fulfilling the contract's terms or else closing out the contract before the delivery month.

Read! Mr. T. commands. And Mr. E. does read a few paragraphs that pertain to the grade of the corn, its precise measurement, its moisture content, the necessity for inspecting it, the details of transporting and storing and insuring it, and the methods of delivering it to the purchaser. Of course he finds it very dull reading. And there's much more of the same stuff written in the same legalistic terminology. No wonder people don't ask to see contracts! he comments, handing this one back to Mr. T.

His friend laughs. No, he didn't think Mr. E. would want to read it through. Speculators aren't concerned about such things—though commercials who intend to make or take delivery certainly are. And commercials also want to know that the commodities they deal in and are hedging on the exchange are considered in exacting ways and have a contractual existence to protect them. The important aspects of the contract for the speculators themselves, says Mr. T., are that it is based on real goods and is a legal document enforceable in court, if necessary. Contract holders who have not canceled out their positions by delivery time are legally bound to deliver goods or to receive them, receiving or paying in exchange the previously agreed-upon sum. And no longer is the financial outlay an approximate 10% of the contract value for the purchaser: purchasers must arrange to pay completely for the goods when they are received. And contract sellers may be in an even worse or more awkward situation. They have promised contractually to make delivery of goods, and so if they don't actually have the goods at that time, they must then somehow secure the goods by payment so that they can make delivery—to earn the price they agreed to receive for the goods. If the commodity itself is scarce and expensive, they may succeed at last in liquidating their legal obligations by belatedly offsetting their contracts with goods commercials are willing to provide because they intend to sell them through the exchange. But they will do so at a loss—perhaps a considerable one —besides having the nuisance and worry. And if they fail to honor the terms of the contracts, the brokerage or clearing firm becomes responsible to the clearinghouse for their debts, and they can be sued for default of payment.

Such predicaments seldom happen, though, says Mr. T. Mostly they come about through inattention or irresponsibility on the part of speculators. If speculators, however, neglect to heed approaching delivery dates, their brokers should remind them of the dates. Also, the clearing firm will send out notices of delivery a few days before due dates, at which time speculators must initiate moves to liquidate their positions—unless they deliberately choose to become involved with the actual commodities.

Just how closely does the clearinghouse follow what's happening with the futures contracts? asks Mr. E. Very closely indeed, Mr. T. replies. From its knowledge of the various futures contracts that are still being held *open*—that is, without an offsetting trade that closes out a position—it keeps a constant tab on what is called *open interest* in each particular future. This figure, Mr. T. explains, can be of great concern and help to speculators, partly as an indicator of other speculators' activities. As the delivery month approaches, traders begin to close out their positions, and the futures price commences to correspond with the current spot, or cash price, as the "true" or most reasonable value on each contract is being settled in the marketplace. The open-interest figures can be further broken down by the exchange to indicate how many hedgers' contracts have also been bought or sold, to establish the solid basis for the speculating that takes place over the commodities.

A low open-interest figure usually indicates a thin market, says Mr. T. Neither traders nor hedgers seem very involved. A high-open interest figure, conversely, shows there is a lot of active hedging and speculating, in which the speculators help provide liquidity by their buying and selling, so that prices do not jump around with large gaps as much as they might in a thin market. And of course by hedging on the exchanges, producers and processors can be assured of the necessary protection against price fluctuations caused by supply and demand variations. The year's speculation activities also serve as spurs to produce more of a particular crop in the following year or as reasons to produce less of it and plant more of something else. Now that speculators are looked upon more as insurance underwriters than as irresponsible meddlers, their function as risk bearers is replacing the older, somewhat sinister image.

Mr. E. should keep in mind, says Mr. T., that just as all speculators are not buying contracts, not all hedgers are selling them. In reality, thousands of hedgers are buying while thousands are selling, all in different quantities and in different months, depending on their commercial needs. Speculators take both sides also. Yet new speculators tend to think in bullish terms, of buying contracts—as one buys stocks or real estate—instead of selling them as well.

What happens to the open interest when a contract holder cancels out his position? Mr. E. wonders. When two speculators close out their contract obligations by an opposite transaction, the open-interest figure decreases by one—or however many contracts they sell or buy back, Mr. T. replies. And each time there is a new contract created by a new buyer and a new seller, the open-interest figure increases by one. Though each is involved in an opposite trade, their positions as buyer and seller remain "open." However, if one cancels out and his position is picked up by a *new* buyer or seller, the open interest does not decline.

But how is the money owed to or due from the clearinghouse itself figured at the close of each trading day, as Mr. T. says is always done? Mr. E. asks. It isn't easy, Mr. T. answers, but it was ever so much harder in the days before computers and lightning-speed calculators, when people mostly had to do all the figuring instead of machines. While he's talking, Mr. T. gets up and gestures to Mr. E. to follow him into the large room where the accounting work is done. It is filled with all sorts of electronic and mechanical devices at which operators are busily engaged.

In the case of any one firm, such as Hedging Harry's, says Mr. T., what they have to do is calculate the net losses on contracts against the net gains and then rectify any deficit immediately by depositing funds with the clearing corporation. The same totaling up of gains versus losses is done in the various branches of the brokerage firm itself, with each unit responsible for its own customers' profits and debits. If an individual speculator needs to add more money to his account in order to cover losses, he gets a "margin call" from his broker.

This daily clearance of accounts, for the whole system's protection, requires close attention to the current value of each contract, the margin required, and the daily limit. As a rule of thumb, says Mr. T., you can estimate that the margin requirement would be 10% of the contract value, while the daily limit would be less, perhaps just 5%. That way, a maximum price move against a position would be about half of what a trader initially deposited to buy or sell the contract. Brokerage firms *mark to market* all their customers' active trading accounts each day, withdrawing funds if they are on the losing side in a price move. These funds would have already been deposited by the responsible clearing firm with the exchange clearinghouse.

But what about those great quantities of grains that Hedging Harry's corporation produces and then hedges? says Mr. E. Don't those require a lot of money in securing the futures contracts to begin with? And then to maintain margins on top of it? . . . Oh yes, Mr. T. agrees, there is much money involved. But then Hedging Harry's company has large financial assets to advance in the cause of insuring the value of its crops —knowing that a good harvest will get the money back.

And what happens if a commercial needs a buying or selling hedge and nobody wants to take the opposite position? Mr. E. wonders. That rarely happens, says Mr. T. Almost all the time somebody is willing to buy or sell almost anything for the chance of profiting, as long as there is a safeguard factor in the trade and the price is mutually agreeable. Speculators thereby help the economic situation by their willingness to take chances—and in the process provide the essential liquidity needed by commercials. If somebody had contracts to buy or sell griffins, he'd probably find opposite traders—who are dealing in contracts, anyway, and their value fluctuations, so that it may not matter at all to them what the contracts themselves are concerned with.

But an accredited commodity exchange, Mr. T. goes on, does have its contracts based on realities. There are no mythical creatures traded on them. Yet what if one of these existing markets has only speculators buying and selling thousands of contracts with one another, without any hedgers involved at all? Mr. E. wonders. Such a situation may be possible, Mr. T. replies, but it is highly improbable, since sooner or later what is happening out in the real world of commodity producing is bound to affect the contracts and prices in the marketplace. The commodity exchanges aren't just big casinos where speculators buy and sell among themselves. The whole mechanism is tied into reality by the fact that real goods—wheat, copper, live hogs, foreign currency—must be delivered against contracts that are not closed out—and must be paid for.

Many commercials, in any case, Mr. T. continues, choose to hedge their positions well in advance of the real need to buy or sell. But what if in the meantime some large-scale speculator has managed to corner the market by selling or buying all the available contracts on an exchange? asks Mr. E. Of course this tactic has been tried in the past, Mr. T. admits, but usually it doesn't end up working well. Just how many thousands of tons of potatoes can one man eat—or want to try to sell? Greed takes a lot of work. And anyway, nowadays there are a great many rules and mechanisms that prohibit such schemes. For example, any time traders buy or sell a certain minimum number of commodity contracts they become classified separately as *large traders* and as such are disallowed from acquiring or selling more than a specified amount on that exchange. If they attempt to do so by subterfuge, using intermediaries, they can be expelled if they are members or prevented from trading further on that exchange if they are not.

But are hedgers similarly limited on how much they can buy or sell? Mr. E. wants to know. No, says Mr. T., farmers can sell as many grain contracts as they need to, since their trading is based on real commodities. Hedging Harry's corporation is seeking insurance, not profit, and thereby gives speculators something to speculate upon by selling many contracts. And Mr. T.'s baker client, the fellow who purchased the corn contracts today through Mr. T.'s trading, can buy as many corn contracts as he needs—backing them up, after all, with cash, just as speculators do.

However, says Mr. T., if a quantity being hedged through contracts seems unduly large or if the exchange supervisors question what is going on for any reason, an investigation will be made to determine a hedger's ability to produce or acquire the commodities themselves. Strict rules and constant supervision are made and maintained by exchanges not just to prevent unethical conduct among traders and to settle any disputes among them. They are also there to protect the great majority of traders who are consistently ethical in their dealings and whose livelihoods depend on the fair workings of the speculating mechanisms as well as on the sustained good reputation of the commodity market itself.

By now the two friends have migrated back to the reception room, where they encounter Hedging Harry on his way out after finishing up his business with the clearing firm. Now, gentlemen, says Mr. T., it is definitely time for lunch! Would Harry wish to join him and Mr. E. today? No thanks, he must decline because he's got an engagement elsewhere. But he shakes Mr. E.'s hand, invites him to come to the farmlands and look around one of these days—with or without his friend Mr. T.—and cheerily wishes him success in the future as a speculator. They can always use one more in the marketplace, so long may he prosper there!

Mr. T. has gathered up a folder of papers that have to be delivered to the office of the clearing corporation itself. The two men walk to the elevator and take it to the fifteenth floor, emerging close to their destination. Mr. T. walks in, greets the receptionist, and hands her the folder. He's being the delivery boy just now, he says, because he's taking his friend here to various places around the premises, to reassure him of the solid and very busy reality of the commodity market! He then gives Mr. E. a quick look at the clearinghouse quarters—which resembles most other business offices, Mr. E. decides. The contract trades and the financial accounts for which his clearing firm is responsible have been recorded here in computer coding for quick access and compact storage, only to be removed when a customer or trader closes out a position. There is small chance for error or oversight once the cleared transactions are programmed into the information network of this wondrous electronic system. The entire experience has been most reassuring to Mr. E.

As they take the elevator down now, Mr. E. asks Mr. T. whether he ever does much trading on other exchanges. Yes, of course he does! Mr. T. answers. He doesn't just confine himself to the CBT out of loyalty because he's a member there. Whenever he gets interested in any commodity that isn't carried on the CBT, he quite easily buys or sells futures contracts. Though of course the transaction can't be done by himself on a trading floor. Like other speculators, he gives his order to the brokerage, which then transmits it to the proper place and person and later confirms its execution if what he wanted was done. That reminds him that when they're at lunch he wants to discuss two topics with Mr. E.: the relationship between speculators and their brokers and some basic information about giving orders.

By now they are out on the street. Mr. E. looks up again at the large building appreciatively. No longer will what goes on within it seem so impersonal and strange or chaotic and threatening to him. The sky is blue and an early spring breeze is blowing off the lake, bringing the fresh smell of open water and green forests and faraway sunlit fields being planted with grains for summer and autumn harvesting.

Mr. T. sniffs the air and gazes around him at the towers of his city. Chicago lies at the very center of the human universe, he proclaims as he strides vigorously upon the pavements toward the restaurant nearby. And at the very center of Chicago, unquestionably, sits the Board of Trade! And, adds his friend Mr. E., at the very center of the Board of Trade will be found Mr. T. himself—and he is glad that he has seen Mr. T. there today.

They enter the restaurant, a small and intimate one whose majordomo at once conducts Mr. T. to a table next to a window. Surely Mr. E. is hungry after a long morning spent at the brokerage, in the pits and among computing machinery, says Mr. T. He himself is ravenous. Studying the manu, he chooses items as he might choose commodity contracts: beefsteak, potatoes, wheat and soyflour biscuits, corn pudding made with eggs and sugar—and whiskey made from rye. All are nutritious and delicious. Why not eat, whenever one can, small symbolic portions of commodities, he declares—the futures contracts for which he is buying and selling, for himself and others? Doing so creates a demand, which furnishes a supply, and when that demand is oversupplied, the price goes down, and afterward so does the future supply, which means that in time, with more demand in a time of scarcity, the price will rise again. . . . And so the market goes, eternally fluctuating as it is meant to do, always to be guessed at because nothing is ever certain—or should be in the eternally changing universe and human society. And everything, he adds, can be ever so slightly affected because today he has ordered a luncheon mainly consisting of basic commodities!

But don't many people find this very unpredictability of supply and demand, this price wavering, exasperating and time-consuming? asks Mr. E. Can't the commodities markets eventually learn so much about all the variables that they can fine tune themselves and take out all the guesswork? Then all the data could be fed into giant computers. The government would be able to tell the farmers exactly how to plant: what, how much and where, for whom and at what price. They could do the same with the processors, instructing them in what to make and how much they could sell it for. Then since all things would be known to everybody, the speculators would become a vanished breed, an extinct species of economic activity.

Since Mr. E. keeps a solemn and intense expression on his face, Mr. T. reacts hotly to his proposals. Hasn't he seen what happens when governments tell their citizens exactly what to produce and how much they should be paid for their efforts? he argues. Surely Mr. E. has read of the angry frustration of consumers who cannot purchase what they like because the supply is controlled and the price in any case becomes prohibitively high because of the lack of competition? Or the price may be kept nice and low, but then there is none of the product in the first place that the ordinary person might obtain. Besides, no government in the world can tell wheat to grow or order storms and blights to go away! Free enterprise and free trade are the very cornerstones of American democracy, and the commodity marketplace . . .

But he can see now that Mr. E. is grinning at his vehement eloquence. He deliberately and cleverly aroused it, just as he used to do in their fraternity years together! he recalls now. And it is good to know, says Mr. E., that some things and some people remain constant, even while prices fluctuate, governments fall, and the value of the dollar plummets at home and abroad. Mr. E. assures his friend that since he already enjoys trying to predict the unpredictable, even when he's wrong, he is almost certain to want to keep the speculating breed alive and thriving by joining them himself.

And yet he wonders, Mr. E. goes on, about how the "little guys," the small, part-time speculators, can successfully fit into the trading scheme he has just seen today. They're simply too far away from the action and confined by modest assets to be able to compete effectively with the big professional traders. If they know the field well and trade wisely, says Mr. T., by their very removal from the rapid, big-money trading going on upon the exchange floors they can operate in a very different arena. They should be minimally affected by the power ploys of the large traders, whose day-to-day or hour-to-hour tactics—something akin, really, to the moves and bluffs of professional gamblers—may or may not assist their own chosen contract positions at the time. They are in a far less precarious post, risking far less comparatively—and also rarely needing to give concentrated daily attention to speculating, as the big guys must. For them it is a sideline business, not a full-time profession, and if they choose their contracts well, much of the time they can ride through the ups and downs of price fluctuations essentially as "position" traders, who operate as insurance underwriters rather than as gamblers.

But what protects people from speculators who try to manipulate the market, perhaps in subtle ways, so they can gain great profits? Mr. E. wants to know. The small speculators' best strategy, says Mr. T., is knowing how to move in order to prevent other traders' actions from manipulating *them* and their money. And this, of course, takes time, study, and practice. Yet he can feel assured that nowadays it's very difficult indeed to try to "corner the market," let alone to succeed at it—or to get away with other dubious or unethical tactics that affect other traders.

The exchanges aim to be self-regulating and self-policing, Mr. T. goes on. But they cannot at all times know what is going on among a few unscrupulous traders or be able to right every wrong. That's why something like the CFTC is a necessary watchdog. What's that? asks Mr. E., who often has trouble with names with initials. It's the Commodity Futures Trading Commission, his friend tells him. The rather new federal regulatory agency that replaced the CEA, or the Commodity Exchange Authority. The older organization lacked funds, staff, and enough muscle to crack down on trading practices that were suspect, whether involving frauds and attempted manipulations, or possibly causing harmful effects on the American economy as a whole or to one part of it, such as the farmers. The CFTC even has the power to close down trading at certain crisis times, when the markets have been affected by international events or fiscal problems that bring on panicky buying or selling before a situation can be reasoned through.

Sometimes, then, Mr. T. goes on, the exchanges may need some assistance from an impartial source, which happens to be the government. So he himself would far rather have the CFTC people watching over the exchanges and trading than not at all. The CFTC has representatives on all of the commodity exchange trading floors, at all times. If as a trader he is behaving himself, he personally has nothing to fear. And as a trader he greatly objects to another trader's doing something that may turn his own potential profits into decided losses—whether there in the pit or in the outside world—such as deliberately spreading rumors that create buying sprees or selling panics and using other illegal manipulative techniques to cause price changes that benefit the unscrupulous speculators. A few bad traders can taint the reputation of the entire commodity marketplace, which is basically legitimate and respectable. Commodity trading, Mr. T. says emphatically, all along the way has an admirable system of checks and balances that can usually eliminate both errors and cheating. Mr. E. has already seen a number of them today. And he might keep in mind that the CFTC has offices around the country with "hot lines" to receive any complaints from commodity speculators about particular trading practices or unfortunate experiences with brokers.

Mr. T. sounds as if he respects this CFTC instead of resenting it, as surely some traders might, Mr. E. observes. Mr. T. agrees. He's not all that happy about a Big Brother who watches one's every move. But what he really doesn't like are those people who cheat and steal and harm because nobody's watching them and they know it or because they are allowed to get away with wrongdoing since they're more powerful than others. That is no way to run a democracy, Mr. T. declares, *or* the commodity exchanges, which through the free interplay of supply and demand, of hedgers and speculators taking up buying and selling positions, should arrive at the fairest and most reasonable price for the time and place.

But now, says Mr. E., what was Mr. T. going to tell him about choosing a broker? For the small, at-home speculator, which Mr. E. will be, Mr. T. begins, the relationship with a broker is crucial. There are other ways of entering speculation of course, like "pools," partnerships, and commodity services that manage accounts. But somebody who wants to make personal decisions and trade individually, as Mr. E. will surely want to do, must deal directly and frequently with an *account executive*, or *broker*, who handles the transactions for the speculator on the various commodity exchanges. And of course the broker will be working for a brokerage firm that in turn has memberships in the exchanges and their clearinghouses around the United States and probably around the world.

But pity the poor brokers! says Mr. T. Or at least take their situation into account when expecting certain things from them. They're in a predicament that most people try to avoid. They must present an aura of extreme omniscience because they feel obligated to impress their clients with their market acumen, implying perhaps that they can accurately predict price changes in various commodities. But they can't with any degree of reliability because nobody can, not even the specialists themselves—some of whom work for brokerages as advisers.

Now, says Mr. T., your average brokers, or "registered commodity representatives," are intelligent. They have extensite backgrounds in commodities and have had to pass muster by several organizations to get where they are. But it's tough for them, as it's tough for everyone in the business, to know exactly what the market is going to do. But can brokers level with their clients? Can they say to a customer, "Gee, I really don't know which way corn is going," or "To be honest, I don't have the slightest notion what platinum will be doing next June"? No, of course they can't. And that's the other side of the vise they're caught in. On one side they must appear to be all-knowing, full of sage advice; but on the other they're as fallible as the rest of us. If they really *knew* all the secrets of trading, do you suppose they would remain brokers? Hardly. They would be the richest traders in all the world's commodity exchanges.

Then there's another thing, Mr. T. goes on. It's called *churning*. Beware of it! It means stirring up business all the time—getting customers to sell or buy, just because doing so generates commissions for the brokers, which in commodity trading are paid only after a *round turn,* that is, when a position is closed out. Since brokers may be expected to produce sizable amounts in commissions each month in order to keep their positions in brokerage firms, they may try to churn their own clients by giving them advice or opinions or "tips" that perhaps weren't even asked for. Customers who follow their brokers' leads without understanding what they're doing may soon come to grief because they relied on somebody else's judgment and not their own. Brokers can supply useful information about a variety of things, whether from their own knowledge and experience or because their firms receive a lot of current market news and statistics. But brokers should not make clients' decisions for them. And clients are not ready to enter the commodities field until they are extremely well informed about it, so that they know exactly what they want to do and why and can set definite limits within these transactions, which can be incorporated into the orders themselves.

And how does one do that? asks Mr. E. Well, his friend explains, he saw several examples upstairs in the brokerage office when the customers' orders came in. Remember the stop, limit, good till canceled, and so on? The speculators who sent in those orders had gone to some trouble to decide in advance precisely how to approach the market: they determined which commodity they wished to trade in, the quantity involved, and whether to buy or sell the futures contracts, of course. But they also decided time limitations on the orders, whether to accept the market price or to try to come in under it or be willing to go over it, and whether to impose a built-in safety device—the stop loss—that would automatically move to close out a position if the price reached a certain "trigger" figure that the speculator had predetermined.

Yes, Mr. E. is beginning to comprehend how commodity speculation involves much more than simply buying—or selling—futures contracts. Maybe one should go to school to learn how do to it properly, he suggests. And certainly his broker, Mr. B., indicated that he expected him to undergo a strenuous learning period before he would be willing to take him on as a client! At this news Mr. T. perks up. He likes the sound of this Mr. B., he says. If Mr. E. has a personal rapport with him, which Mr. T. considers important in a broker-client relationship, as well as respect for his intelligence and integrity, he may be in very good hands indeed—*if* he himself is willing to serve that apprenticeship period before he actually enters into real trading, which, as he knows, is going to be risky no matter how knowledgeable he becomes.

But isn't there some school for novice speculators? asks Mr. E. Oh, a few exchanges—including the CBT—sometimes have brief introductory courses, and there may occasionally be some seminars given around the country, Mr. T. answers. But as far as he knows, no college as yet actually offers a straight course in commodity speculation, though the subject is talked about often enough in schools of business and financial investments. It's a good idea . . . but what he thinks might be even better would be an apprenticeship training program, say, where the novice would be gradually introduced to the practical aspects and details of commodity trading by a person who's a past master at it, an accomplished and highly experienced trader already. It could be an educational experience that would first combine guidance with do-it-yourself learning before the real and risky doing was undertaken. Mr. E. might ask his broker friend Mr. B. about such a thing, Mr. T. suggests. Maybe he'll know of something or somebody. Doing it that way would be better and, well, more companionable than doing it wholly on one's own.

Their luncheon is over now. The two friends, well fed and filled with a long morning of conversation, leave the restaurant to go their separate ways. Gratefully, Mr. E. thanks Mr. T. for all his time and trouble taken up in introducing him to the commodity exchange. Trouble? asks Mr. T. No indeed; with him it's always a pleasure to welcome a new speculator into the society. Keep in touch! he says as he goes running off toward his home at the Chicago Board of Trade, where the trading day has ended and the clearing process has begun.

A few days later, as Mr. E.'s airplane takes off from Midway Airport and banks northeast as it climbs high above the great American city of commerce, he gets a glimpse of the characteristic shape of the CBT building. He pictures to himself the scene taking place this morning on the trading floor, with Mr. T. perhaps engaged again in some action in the soybean pit. Or will it be wheat or iced broilers now, or Ginnie Maes?

Commodity speculation has acquired the necessary reality it lacked for him before Mr. T. took him on his trading rounds. Mr. E. is ready now to learn in earnest how to become a speculator.

PART THREE

A Short Course in Speculating

CHAPTER NINE

Starting with Fundamentals

Our novice speculator, Mr. E., has just settled down in the study of Mr. S., the past master of commodity trading, with whom he hopes to serve an apprenticeship period. Mr. B., the broker, had introduced him to the silver-haired man after Mr. E. expressed the desire to learn about the techniques of speculating directly from a practitioner of it.

Before he takes on a private pupil, Mr. S. is saying, he wants to make sure that he won't be wasting his time as a guide to someone who really isn't right for following the speculator's road. Even though Mr. E. has agreed to pay a standard consultation fee for this professionally conducted yet informal course in speculating, Mr. S. explains, he must understand that time and energy are more precious to him than money, and so he dislikes squandering them. It is ill advised, he has discovered through experience, for those who are psychologically unfit for trading to attempt to alter themselves in order to make a few bucks. Therefore he'd like this to be at first a get-acquainted session, and if Mr. E. seems right for speculating—and Mr. B., who judges him to be so, is rarely if ever wrong in his assessments—they'll just move ahead to some basics in trading.

While Mr. S. has been talking, Mr. E. couldn't resist occasionally glancing around at his surroundings, which are both comfortable and luxurious. In the oak-paneled office a tall bookcase is filled with books on finance, economics, and the history of money and a whole row of large

yearbooks about commodity trading. He admires a few antique prints—
are they woodcuts?—of cereal grains in harvest perfection. Also on the
wall is a large handsome chart giving pictures, code letters, and trading
months for the various commodities on different exchanges. And through
a large window above Mr. S.'s desk he can see a portion of his lush
estate. Knowing that his host is a retired banker, Mr. E. wonders how
much of this apparent affluence has come from commodity trading. He
decides to ask Mr. S. outright.

Oh, through the years he has probably doubled, even tripled, his
income by speculating, Mr. S. replies, not at all offended by the question.
And now that he has officially retired, he can devote even more time to
it. He is glad that he has an occupation that keeps him busy and in touch
with the outside world and also provides added income at this inflationary
time, when set pension payments decline in value.

But doesn't Mr. S. find commodity speculation a rather nerve-
racking activity at this period in his life, when he should be taking it easy
and enjoying his "leisure years"? Mr. E. inquires. At this Mr. S. laughs
resoundingly. He has always thrived by confronting challenges and taking
risks and making innumerable decisions: he wouldn't want things otherwise. Occasionally he'll take a vacation from it all, close out all his trading
positions and go off on a long trip somewhere, for a respite now and then
is advisable. But mostly he feels content just to keep his hand in the pits
and rings of the commodity exchanges by sitting here in his study, receiving reports, making charts, and frequently phoning his broker, Mr. B.,
with his latest orders. But his activity is not nerve-racking to him. In
trading, of course, one expects to lose part of the time. After all, no one
has yet discovered a way to make guesses about future price changes that
are even 50% accurate, at least that he knows of. Trading techniques and
plans make all the difference in net profits or losses. This is why beginning
speculators must undergo some sort of learning period if they want to
survive as traders. So Mr. E.'s willingness to do so is already a strong
point in his favor.

Mr. S. is asked to sketch a profile of the failed speculator in order for
Mr. E. to judge whether he too has personality drawbacks. Well, Mr. S.
starts in, if speculators are indecisive and fret too much over everything,
they shortly become insomniacs and nervous wrecks and who knows
what else. Or if they are headstrong and impulsive, they may come to bad
ends quickly through a few misguided and poorly conducted trades. If
they are gullible, they are easy prey for other people's schemes for getting
rich that make them think they'll get rich the quick-and-easy way. If they
are incapable of making or unwilling to make simple calculations, disinclined to learn some fairly detailed matters, unable to remain calm and
patient in trying times, and uncomprehending of the intrinsic workings of

the commodity market, then they'd better move along elsewhere. All these types, says Mr. S., are usually the ones whose unfortunate experiences are recounted and remembered by their acquaintances, giving commodity speculation its tainted reputation among potential traders. And Mr. S. refuses to take part in assisting them to their doom!

But now it's Mr. E.'s turn to talk about himself, so that Mr. S. can learn about *him*. How much does he know already about the commodity field? What attracted him to it to begin with? What does he hope to accomplish by speculating? And what aspects of his character seem to indicate that he may be successful in this fast-moving, high-risk form of financial activity? These questions must be asked and answered before Mr. S. can feel assured about tutoring Mr. E.

First of all, Mr. E. tells the hoped-for mentor about the succession of events, from Dr. M. the mathematician on to real-estate involvement, that led him to Mr. B., who suggested the possibility of commodity speculation as a suitable form of financial betterment for him. And what Mr. S. has just said about himself—about liking challenges and decision making and risk taking—makes strong sense to him because these are built-in characteristics of his own. He is willing to expend time and effort learning something that interests him and can eventually reward him. In fact, he wants to realize practical results—like money—from his dedication and actions.

Perhaps Mr. S. recalls hearing Mr. B. say how Mr. E. recently visited the Chicago Board of Trade? Yes, he was given an insider's tour of the place by his trader friend, Mr. T., who took him to the brokerage's order-receiving office, the trading floor, and even to the clearinghouse. Much about commodities that had seemed to him baffling and unreal or untrustworthy was dispelled by this visit to the marketplace itself. So Mr. E. returned home quite convinced that he wished to become a speculator. But he wants to go at it properly—which is why he's sitting here in Mr. S.'s study, desirous of benefiting from a highly experienced trader's knowledge, advice, and instructions, which will prepare him for sensible trading.

Mr. E. believes that he has a certain amount of stick-to-itiveness but confesses that he likes to keep things rolling along, to change vistas, to make decisions if only to clear the agenda so that he can proceed to the position of making more. Ah, that sounds good to Mr. S. because, he declares, commodity speculation is a perpetual decision-making exercise. It is for decision makers, not for procrastinators, who look for the ideal situation or perfect solution before making a move—and then may be too late to do anything worth doing or else have become so convinced of their rightness that they fail to spot the pitfalls ahead.

Successful traders, Mr. S. avows, are rarely fearful of taking reasonable risks or of making irreparable mistakes. They base their moves on rationally determined programs—perhaps led there first by sheer instinct for potential reward—and make sure that safeguards and exit zones exist. Their risks are affordable: they know what they'll lose if they lose. They also know what they are doing and what they hope to accomplish, and these aims are moderate, possible and geared to reality. Since they have clear-cut objectives and aim to succeed, they realize that achievement only comes by acting and risk taking. If the positions chosen turn out to appear wrong, then they'll move out of them as deftly and quickly as they can to avoid more severe punishments. These traders are also philosophical about any negative experience that their guesswork brings to them. At least they can turn financial losses into the profits of new wisdom. Past frustrations and mistakes concern them only as far as they bear upon what they are doing now or will do in the future. "He who never makes mistakes never accomplishes anything" is a Chinese proverb that has long been a guiding principle in Mr. S.'s own life, not just in speculating.

Nothing teaches you faster and better about your own inherent character than commodity speculation! Mr. S. concludes. But what about this important patience factor? Mr. E. wonders, since he tends toward *im*patience with many things. His unhappy experience with real estate was a good example. When he's putting his money into something, he wants to have some fairly immediate action. Perhaps that's why poker and some other lightweight forms of gambling appeal to him. He also doesn't like to make commitments that get him bogged down in boring details and niggling responsibilities. He tends to move from one thing to another too, once he has explored the possibilities and payoffs. It isn't that he's flighty or fidgety, he guesses. It's more that his interests are so varied and wide-ranging that he doesn't want to be held down by one particular project. (At this he notices Mr. S. smiling at him rather approvingly.) As for doing simple calculations and other paperwork, he supposes he'd do them all right if he saw the necessity. But arithmetic was never his best or favorite subject in school—probably because it wasn't made relevant to the world beyond the classroom with which he expected to concern himself after being graduated.

Well! exclaims Mr. S. His visitor does indeed appear to be an excellent prospect for speculating. Not only does he know himself rather thoroughly, but the character "defects" he mentions may actually even be assets in a trader. Also he is already directly acquainted with many basic mechanisms in the market, and so he'll comprehend his place within it as a speculator. Yes, Mr. S. declares himself quite satisfied with his pupil's qualifications. Apprenticeship will be a highly useful experience for him, Mr. S. promises. He'll learn many things that will serve him well later on, after he acquires enough information, practice, and self-confidence to begin speculating on his own. By the end of this intensive-study method, which shouldn't take more than a few weeks, Mr. E. will already be formulating his own particular approach to trading. It probably won't be either the fundamentalist-trader's or the chartist-trader's methodology. And it won't be Mr. S.'s or Mr. T.'s or Mr. B.'s way—or that of a textbook or some get-rich-quick author. He'll blend aspects of other people's techniques and advice with a growing knowledge of the markets, adjusting them to his own interests and personal style of thinking and doing. And Mr. E. can learn a great deal too, if he wants, from Mr. S.'s experience. Oh, he'll have some tales to tell, besides just giving Mr. E. problems to work out here! And he'll launch Mr. E. into doing his own "paper trading" in advance of actual trading, so that Mr. E. will be exposed to some trial situations in speculation before actually confronting the realities of money risks in the real marketplace.

Their sessions together, Mr. S. goes on, will be stepping-stones toward the real trading that Mr. E. will learn to do on his own. Since it's good to know in advance where one is going, he'll just outline the course ahead. Today they'll discuss some fundamental matters connected with commodities; later they can move on to the "fundamental" approach to trading itself. That will lead into the second main approach—the "technical," or "charting," one—and Mr. S. will show his student how to make and read bar charts and point-and-figure charts, the price charts most often used in trading. Then they will investigate chart patterns, basis, spreads, and anything else Mr. E. may wish to know about. And in the last sessions Mr. S. will attempt to impart some of his own accrued wisdom to his graduating apprentice, emphasizing his own personal approach to trading. Calling it "actuarial" because it combines prudent money management with the shifting realities of the market, he thinks Mr. E. will find it quite useful in assisting his own decision-making process regarding commodity speculation.

Is that term *fundamental,* applied to a trading approach, which Mr. S. mentioned, more inclined toward the basics? asks Mr. E. He hopes so, since he admits to a certain aversion to all those charts he has seen reproduced in books and booklets on commodities. He actually avoids reading such things whenever possible; he'd rather have somebody else reduce them all down and tell him what they mean, as in a magazine article, and let him make his own interpretations. So if this is the technical way of trading, can't he somehow avoid it? He can't visualize himself sitting around all the time fiddling with charts and graphs in order to decide what to do!

Mr. S. sees, of course, that Mr. E. has said this good-humoredly. But there's enough truth in his objections to merit a straight answer. All traders have to use charts of one kind or another, he says, in order to know what's going on now with prices and what went on in the past if they are looking for patterns of behavior that may indicate what can happen in the future. They can rely on other people's interpretations if they want to, but many of the best speculators wish to make their own independent evaluations of a given situation. Mr. E. doesn't have to be the kind of trader who can't make a move without consulting a hundred charts and maybe making some of his own, but he'll probably find them invaluable once he understands what they can show in both short-range and long-range price movements.

Why, even the fundamentalists make and use charts, Mr. S. goes on. They also contrive all sorts of interesting mathematical equations, which they call *models*. Mr. E. may get something out of these too, once he knows what he's looking for in a particular trade. But it's true that the fundamentalists don't use charting so religiously. Yet there's nothing like a good, simple graph to show certain basic concepts and phenomena clearly and concisely. Take, for example, the perpetual interplay between supply and demand—which is what the fundamental approach is primarily concerned with.

At this, Mr. S. shifts his swivel chair a few feet over to the wall next to his desk. Mr. E. realizes that in his initial survey of the room's furnishings he had not noticed the small chalkboard. Perhaps the latent professor in him, says Mr. S., prefers using this board for doing calculations. One can always erase miscalculations, and paper is saved. Also, a point that needs to be demonstrated, as now, somehow seems more impressive. It's as if he were lecturing to a whole classroom of eager students—who may only be eager, he adds, because they know that if they learn their lessons well, they'll have a good chance of making money!

And while Mr. S. is talking he is roughly drawing his version of the interaction of supply and demand in society for a representative commodity—like wheat or cotton, he suggests:

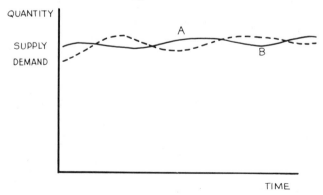

Of course this is not a precise rendition of any particular phase in economic history, Mr. S. admits. The graph is only intended to show how supply and demand continuously attempt to meet each other in the middle. Whether or not any government is consciously trying to control either element, the forces in human production and consumption are such that a shift in one causes a change in the other, aiming for some optimal state wherein supply exactly equals demand.

But neither Mother Nature nor human nature can be dictated to, Mr. S. now declares. The factors that alter supply and affect demand are prodigious in number and complexity. And of course many—like next month's weather—can be predicted, and are forever being predicted, but not necessarily with great accuracy. They can be guessed at, but they won't be absolutely known until the future becomes the present.

Mr. S. now points out that even a small oversupply, like that at point *A,* can result in a relatively large decrease in price. And now he sketches a separate graph, right below the supply and demand curves, that represents price movements corresponding in time with what goes on with the two other variables:

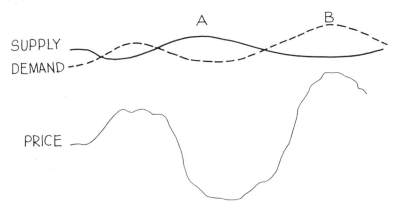

After all, he says, if no one wants to buy the excess in a commodity, then in a sense it becomes valueless. This is especially true for something that cannot be stored. Likewise, an insufficient supply, like that at point *B,* can result in a relatively large price increase—particularly if an essential foodstuff is involved.

Notice, Mr. S. tells Mr. E., how supply and demand are amazingly in step. But you can't expect things to come out perfectly in any commodity, after all, since so many conditions can affect supply and since sometimes even demand is subject to human whims and adjustments. Small discrepancies between them usually result in comparatively large fluctuations in price, which are reflected, magnified really, on the commodity exchanges. Consider *A*, where supply exceeds demand: the value is very low, and so the price declines substantially. At *B*, however, with an excess of demand, the price rises because people are quite anxious to get the commodity and are willing to pay more for it.

Yet observe, Mr. S. continues, how the supply and demand curves never really get far from each other. This is due to the feedback system inherent in the interconnections of supply, demand, and price. Mr. E. has surely heard it before, but Mr. S. will go over it again because it's the ruling principle in the production of commodities and therefore is a prime concern of commodity speculators. If demand exceeds supply, the price rises. As the price rises two things happen. The consumers will decrease the demand, but meanwhile the producers are increasing production in order to sell the commodity at the higher price. In this case production increases the supply to match the demand, yet the demand will lessen in order to accommodate the decreased supply.

When the supply exceeds demand, Mr. S. goes on, the price drops. As the price drops two things happen. Demand increases, but there is a decrease in production because of the prevailing low price. The drop in production will eventually cause the supply to come back down to match the demand.

The futures markets enter into all this constant fluctuation in production, Mr. S. explains, because they allow a producer or consumer to sell or buy the commodity in the future. He is aware that Mr. E. already knows about hedging. By selling high-priced wheat futures the farmer feels confident in going out to grow that wheat. If the price declines in the actual commodity, he won't get hurt. And by buying sugar futures at a low price, the candy manufacturer can securely go ahead and make his confection and sell it at a predetermined price. If the sugar price rises, he need not take a loss.

The entire production-marketing mechanism, Mr. S. now asserts, is really nothing more than a means of allocating resources. The scarce, high-priced commodity has its production increased. The abundant, low-priced commodity has its production decreased. No other socioeconomic force has been found to be as efficient as this self-perpetuating device linked up with prices. Although a dictator can threaten citizens in various drastic ways if they fail to do the prescribed things, no totalitarian government has yet found a way to force wheat to grow or copper ingots to shake themselves loose from the ground and gather in warehouses. The commodity-pricing mechanisms of the free world, which work within the well-regulated commodity exchanges, recognize that you can't tell Mother Nature how to behave or ultimately control the results of human work in production. Nor can you dictate for long how people will choose to use or consume that production. And this is why the fundamentalist traders watch supply and demand very closely.

Even the concept of supply and demand changing with price is further complicated, Mr. S. goes on, by what economists call *elastic* and *inelastic* demands. Elastic means that as the price rises the demand decreases, as one normally expects. With inelastic demand, though, the price may rise but the demand may maintain its same level because the commodity itself is essential to industry or to consumers, and to increase significantly the present supply may be difficult, even impossible. For instance, take silver, Mr. S. proposes. Apart from its other important uses, it is used in camera film. Kodak can make about two thousand average rolls of film with one ounce of silver. Though the price goes up to affect the company and ultimately the consumer, the demand does not slacken from this quarter, for there is no substitute yet for silver. Yet so little of the metal is used in one roll of film that the slight increase in price may hardly be noticed by the consumer. Fundamentalists understandably then distinguish between commodities that tend to have elastic or inelastic demands, which are reflected in price trends.

Mr. E. remarks that the term *fundamental* sounds like a form of religious persuasion. He is naturally reminded of the interesting parallel in use by fundamentalist Christians. They both have an orientation toward the most basic ingredients in their fields of interest, Mr. S. agrees; but that may be all. Or is it? The human mind abhors a vacuum; it also gets uneasy at the prospects of infinity and the eternal flux. Fundamentalist religions populate the empty spaces with knowns and explain change and eternity. Fundamentals-attentive speculators take into account and label every conceivable factor that enters into supply and demand in commodity trading. Then they try to make a science, not a religion, out of their efforts. In the process they discover laws of both nature and human nature. But many of these earnest and diligent traders fail to recognize that commodity speculation may be essentially an art, not a science! Mr. S. exclaims. When laws and rules and firm beliefs are applied in the marketplace, reality may simply refuse to be obliging and conform to expectations.

And that, says Mr. S., may be a large drawback to the strictly fundamental approach to trading. Sometimes you can get to thinking that you have to know all history and all current events, no matter how obscure, in order to make any decision regarding taking a trading position or removing yourself from one. Each fact and figure sought or just encountered begins to assume some significance that then must be weighed and measured against other facts and figures. You may feel you really need the world's biggest computer just to keep track of everything and maybe even make all decisions for you. (Though that won't necessarily improve your guesswork either, Mr. S. remarks parenthetically.)

So fundamentalists don't suffer from an undersupply of information, Mr. S. tells Mr. E. It's the oversupply that gets them! National and state governments, at speculators' requests, could deluge them with bounteous bulletins regarding crop forecasts and harvests, weather and animal diseases, plant genetics and new farm machinery—and how each may affect production and futures prices. Commission houses and subscribed commodity advisory services will provide a steady stream of reports and charts. A brokerage handling commodity accounts has constant electronic contacts with news specialists and experts. The information is indeed staggering in sheer bulk and intricacy. But how can one speculator assimilate it, let alone correctly interpret it? Mr. S. asks Mr. E., who looks startled indeed.

To give an example of the sort of literature that inundates a trader, Mr. S. picks up a Crop Reporting Bulletin kindly provided by the U.S. Department of Agriculture. He hands it to his student and asks him to appraise it. Mr. E.'s head reels when his eyes confront page after page of statistical charts regarding acreage planted and harvest yields in particular crops in different sections of the nation. He moves on to a prose section dealing with planting progress thus far in the calendar year. Having breezed over the detailed coverage of winter and early spring weather and its effects upon soil conditions and temperatures throughout the agrarian portions of the country, he cannot resist reading a paragraph to Mr. S.:

> Snow accumulations and subnormal temperatures held most outside activity to a minimum during February. Snow in the North and above normal precipitation in the Southeast and Pacific Coast area prevented an early start for spring land preparations. Deep snow blanketed the Nation from the northern Great Plains, across the Corn Belt and into the Northeast. Adverse weather and wet, cold soils delayed cotton planting in southern Texas. A few early corn fields were planted across the South on lighter well-drained soils near the end of February. Plowing in the South was underway but lagged the average pace. Frequent rainfall and melting snows kept soils saturated in many parts of the Nation during March. Near-normal to above-normal temperatures melted the snowcover rather quickly, causing some flooding and standing water in low-lying fields. Soggy fields slowed land preparations throughout most of the month. However, land preparations surpassed a year earlier when the spring season was particularly wet.

Now what, asks Mr. S., can Mr. E. make of all this? If he wanted to take a trading position on a new crop of cotton, corn, or soybeans, he might want to digest the entire bulletin and even wait for more. And isn't that what Mr. S. was talking about before? asks Mr. E. Naturally, says

Mr. S. If the fundamentalist trader is considering acquiring contracts in soybeans, for instance, he will want to know a great deal about them as a crop: exactly how and where it is grown; under what conditions and when it is harvested; what its supply history has been; which nations use it, when, and how much; what domestic usages it is put to; how prices have gone in the past twenty years; which factors can suddenly change its price. So one could study soybeans for months, for years even, and still not know enough to feel sufficiently expert to commit to the precarious position of either purchasing or selling a futures contract! *If,* adds Mr. S., one wished to be absolutely sure of being right, which nobody, even the commodity specialists, can be. No matter how much experts know, they still take risks when they take contract positions—though they do increase their chances of being right if they are familiar with the most important factors controlling supply and demand.

Why, the commodity information that is spewed forth daily is utterly fantastic! Mr. S. exclaims. Walking over to a device that Mr. E. hadn't noticed before, he flips a switch. Immediately the machine starts to click. A roll of paper covered with purple printing emerges and coils onto the floor. Is that a ticker tape? Mr. E. inquires. No, Mr. S. replies, this is known as a *broad tape*. A ticker tape is a very narrow paper tape that only carries price information for either stocks or commodities. Ticker tapes are what one sees displayed on the walls of brokerage firms. A broad tape is broad in two senses of the word. It is physically wider. And the information it shows is decidedly broader in scope.

Mr. S. tears off a piece of emerging tape and hands it to Mr. E. to have a look:

SOYACROP 5 RIO
   WORKING OUT THE CRUSH ON AN AVERAGE OIL YIELD
OF 18.5 PCT, APPROXIMATELY THE RATE SO FAR THIS
YEAR, GIVES ABOUT 1.6 MLN TONNES OF SOYABEANOIL,
THE MINISTRY SOURCES SAID.
   THEY SAID THERE WOULD BE A CERTAIN AMOUNT OF
BUYING BACK OF OIL EXPORT COMMITMENTS BY
CRUSHERS AND THIS WOULD RESULT IN FINAL OIL
EXPORTS IN THE CURRENT MARKETING YEAR OF ABOUT
250,000 TONNES. THIS LEAVES 1.15 MLN TONNES OF OIL
FOR THE INTERNAL MARKET AND INTERNAL
CONSUMPTION OVER THE CROP YEAR IS ESTIMATED AT 1.1
MLN TONNES.

MORE 1759.

Now, be honest, Mr. S. urges, what course of action would you take, based upon this data? Would you be able to interpret it correctly and know all the other pertinent data before other traders caught on, if you felt there was something significant here? Mr. E. seems overwhelmed and admits it. You see, says Mr. S., there is just too much to know and the markets are too complicated for any one small speculator to approach them with a know-it-all confidence!

Mr. S. now switches off the Teletype machine. This rented device, he comments, is hooked into the Reuters news network, and so it is often referred to as "Reuters." There are other services, such as the one Dow Jones provides, but some don't specialize in information relating to commodities and may be more oriented toward securities. And by the way, he adds, it is an education just to see the huge amount of specific news pouring out from such machines and then compare it to the general information one receives when watching the 6:00 television news!

Yes, virtually everything can become grist for the fundamentalist's brain mill, Mr. S. continues on, because it is always on the lookout for new elements that may well alter the relationship between supply and demand in a variety of commodities. For instance, he says, suppose a trader receives the morning newspaper and notices on a back page a small report quoting Peruvian fishermen's complaints that their anchovy catch is way down. So what? somebody else may ask. But our fundamentalist trader jumps. So plenty! He knows that anchovies make an important livestock feed. And although anchovies aren't traded on American exchanges, other commodities that are used in feeds—most significantly, soybeans and soybean meal, which match anchovies in protein content —*are*.

So now, says Mr. S., let Mr. E. become that speculator and decide what his move should be right now. With a glint in his eye Mr. E. accepts the challenge. Why of course he would buy contracts for soybeans or soybean meal, he declares almost at once. Because here or elsewhere in the world, if anchovies are in short supply, there will be a strong demand for a substitute, a different but equally nutritious type of livestock feed. Soybeans will surely go up in price, and so the trader would want to go "long" on them, having anticipated the price rise.

Ha! says Mr. S., happy with his apprentice's response. But what would the small, at-home speculator do to compete effectively against the large traders? Many of them are right there in the pit now, able to execute their own moves without having to call a broker to do it for them. And they can also afford to purchase many more contracts than he, before a great buying spree begins.

And perhaps on the same day, Mr. S. suggests, Mr. E. the speculator is listening to a radio report on financial news. He hears that the Soviet Union is forecasting a bumper crop in wheat, the largest in its history. Since this nation is the biggest producer of world wheat, the amount should be impressive. Now how will Mr. E., the small speculator, handle this news? Well, he would phone his broker right away, says Mr. E., and tell him to sell wheat contracts for him—whatever he could afford. Why? pursues Mr. S. Because the impending great surplus of Russian wheat will make American wheat less valuable, Mr. E. responds. Thus he could profit from being in a short position as the price plummets.

Okay, very good! Mr. S. compliments him. These are two examples of fundamental data that must be handled immediately by any speculator interested in taking the best position in a futures trade. However, he cautions, one must realize that invariably by the time small speculators —you and I—receive the news, the large traders have known it ahead of us because they are located closer to news sources. So by the time small speculators act, the price has already been affected by the large traders' taking positions. You'd be riding along on their coattails—or should one say hides?—because they will be surging off like bulls or bears in one direction or the other. That means that no matter how early and fast you give your order, the market will already be heading in the direction you chose to go, taking the price up or down with it. The futures prices in these commodities would already be discounted.

Discounted? Does that mean that a contract can be bought at a discount? asks Mr. E., puzzled. Mr. S. laughs. No, it's not a retailing come-on, he says. In commodity trading the word refers to a price's immediate response to some new factor affecting supply and demand, added to the ones already known and accounted for in the current futures price. And this, Mr. S. goes on, is why the commodity market itself is considered a *price-discovery mechanism.* By their actions in the market-place traders and hedgers have together arrived at a realistic price *for now,* after examining trends and statistics of all kinds, and have then gone forth to bargain with one another on trading floors. But what isn't known, of course, is what the futures price will be tomorrow or a month from now, since it will continually respond to new variables over which no one can have any control or foreknowledge.

But isn't that rather unsettling? ventures Mr. E. If all known factors are built into the current price and only the unknown will change the price, how can one predict a price change accurately and consistently?

It can't be done, of course, replies Mr. S. But that is really to the advantage of the small speculator. If future prices were even reasonably predictable, the futures market would no longer need to exist in order to provide price-change insurance for commercials. Therefore one more arena for financial betterment would be denied to the average person, who now at least has as good a chance as anyone to profit by guessing at future price changes.

Now fundamentals-oriented traders, Mr. S. continues, won't necessarily accept the current price for a futures contract as what it *should* be at a particular time. They are always inclined to probe deeper into the supply and demand factors and their variables, as though looking for an indication that the present price may be higher or lower than it ought to be—given the extra knowledge that they have of the total situation.

Well, Mr. E. ventures to say, fundamentalists must have to know a lot about a lot of things! Indeed they do, Mr. S. agrees. They work awfully hard at acquiring their information and then sorting it and selecting the data they need to design a particular trading program. And above all, Mr. S. concludes, they must have an excellent acquaintance with the commodities themselves that they're speculating upon.

Mr. S. looks at his desk clock, gets up, and goes to his bookcase. From it he takes several books about commodities—in general and in particular—and hands them to Mr. E. This will be his homework over the weekend, Mr. S. says. He wants Mr. E. to be able to discuss the commodities on the American exchanges with at least a degree of familiarity the next time he comes. Because, don't forget, they are what all the speculating is about!

Mr. E. follows his guide through the doorway of the study. At the main door the two men shake hands—each is pleased with the meeting and ready to resume the next step of their journey together.

CHAPTER TEN

About the Commodities

Part of his weekend was devoted to reading several of the books that Mr. S. lent him, says Mr. E. He read them in a rather cursory way, to be sure, because he was avoiding any close study of charts and tables. Mainly what he wished to do was acquire a smattering of knowledge about the commodities carried on the American exchanges.

And that's exactly what Mr. S. hoped he would do, Mr. E. is told. Now Mr. S. expects him to tell some of the things he has learned. For example, did Mr. E. discover any one common thread that binds all the commodities together? Mr. E. ponders the question for a moment. Well, it's easy enough to group many of them in units, like the metals and grains and meats. But it's hard to determine what could link them all. Except that they all have futures contracts traded on the commodity exchanges.

Why are they there, does Mr. E. suppose? Well, is it just the habit of history? Mr. E. wonders. For obviously there are many other commodities produced in large quantities, raw or otherwise, that could be added to them. But why should any more be added? Mr. S. pursues. Mr. E. guesses that since the commodity markets exist for the purpose of putting hedging commercials together with risk-assuming speculators, surely there must be other products of the land whose prices fluctuate unpredictably.

Ah, says Mr. S., has his pupil then proposed the thread that binds? What? asks Mr. E., looking surprised. Changes—unpredictable ones—in prices? Mr. S. nods his assent while Mr. E. says he thought there might be some material characteristic they possessed in common. No, says Mr. S., only an economic one. Their futures prices fluctuate greatly because of the impossibility of correctly determining in advance either supply or demand, or both, of each commodity. In wheat growing, for instance, unreliable weather and disease factors make harvest figures unpredictable, and, thus, are important price-altering variables.

Remember, too, Mr. S. says, that there are some very important commodities for which futures contracts are not traded on an exchange. Take salt, surely a major commodity. Yet its supply and demand factors are so well known that it is not suitable for trading on an exchange because its price varies minimally.

Then Mr. E. should also realize, says Mr. S., that through the years a number of commodities have been tried out on one exchange or another, but often commercial or speculator interest proved insufficient to make them worth keeping there. With other commodities the producers and merchants aren't ready yet to relinquish their controls. And with still others, the market mechanisms are not yet developed or innovative enough to accommodate them, or even to consider them yet in some cases.

Economists and financial experts, Mr. S. explains, have always been far ahead of the public in comprehending commodity speculation's insurance aspects as well as in approving its function as a rational means of price determination. The possibilities for putting new commodities on the exchanges depend upon working out the various details involved in handling futures contracts for them. All too often tradition—yes, the very habit of history that Mr. E. mentions—dictates what is considered and done, in spite of the technological progress that makes new market methods useful in handling commodities *and* contracts. A most striking example, Mr. S. goes on, is the introduction of *live*stock futures in the early 1960s. It was fought by some large commercial interests, but the Chicago Mercantile Exchange went ahead and tried it anyway. The commotion and complications anticipated failed to materialize. Instead, the CME— seemingly on its last legs at the time—got a reprieve, then a swift prosperity. Equally dramatic was the introduction in the early seventies of those "soft commodities" that Mr. E. has doubtless heard and read about: the various financial instruments that hardly seem to fit into the traditional classification of commodities until one examines them closely —as they will do later today.

So having a troublesome, unpredictable price fluctuation is the primary requisite of a tradable commodity, concludes Mr. S. What other characteristics would Mr. E. care to propose generally? Well, says Mr. E. alertly (for he was well prepared to answer this question), there must be a wide demand for them because people need them or industry uses them. They are often seasonally produced—or at least were in the past, before new growing and storage methods and year-round world markets changed things. They can be reduced to units of a particular size or weight or number. They can be classified according to quality or kind. They can be transported in bulk. In most cases they must be converted into another form in order to be consumed or used by the public. And most of them are not highly perishable or else can be kept in a form—dried or frozen, say—that prevents rapid deterioration.

Bravo! says Mr. S. Now he wants to hear about the main types of commodities, from Mr. E.'s perspective. Well, first are the grains, of course, he says, which inspired the whole commodity exchange mechanism. In this country there are mainly wheat, corn, and oats—plus soybeans, of course (but even if they are legumes, they are mostly used like grains). And grouped with them are "oil seeds"—like rapeseed and flaxseed. He hadn't known until now, he adds, that linseed oil comes from the latter, and he's pondering whether the new acrylic-based paints have cut way down on the demand for it. He also surmises that if sunflowers get on the commodity market, they'll be classified as a grain too, though obviously they are not, since a real cereal grain comes only from members of the grass family.

Having now read some introductory materials about the grains, Mr. E. admits that he learned much he didn't realize. He had not known, for example, that about 90% of the corn processed in the United States goes into livestock feed, for domestic or export use. He noted too that world wheat production comes to about 11 billion bushels annually, grown on more than half a billion acres—frequently in places he'd never have thought suitable for wheat, such as India. He didn't even know that the Soviet Union is the world's largest wheat producer by far, normally contributing about 100 million metric tons to the total supply. The United States generally comes in with about half that amount, a fact that surprised him indeed. Mr. E. also wasn't aware that there are so many different varieties of wheat—hundreds of them, with new ones being developed all the time by plant breeders—or that the type of wheat used for pastry making is quite different in makeup—gluten content especially —than that used in baking bread or manufacturing pasta. Yet for futures trading purposes all this wheat in the United States can be reduced rather simply to contracts on exchanges in Chicago, Kansas City, and Minneapolis!

Yes, says Mr. S., since wheat is a living organism, scientists can continually improve it genetically in order to build in protections against particular diseases by developing disease-resistant strains. And they can also create new strains for specific wheat usages. He now picks up a pamphlet for his "grain shelf" on the bookcase. Showing Mr. E. a few photographs of sick-looking wheat stems and heads, he almost chants a succession of afflictions that beset wheat: stem rust, orange leaf rust, stripe rust, mildew, steptoria blotches, streak mosaic, soilborne mosaic, false-stripe, barley yellow, root and foot rots. . . . And then he moves on to the pests that strike at wheat: wheat stem sawfly, wheat midge, pale western cutworm, green bug, cinch bug—and don't forget the grasshoppers, those horrible locust swarms dating back to ancient history! Then once the crop is harvested, he goes on, there are other types of insects that love to get at stored wheat: the flat grain beetle, sawtoothed grain beetle, lesser grain borer (Mr. S. hopes that he himself isn't becoming a grain borer!), red flour beetle, long-headed flour beetle, Angoumois moth, cadelle, and rice weevil. Agricultural chemists and biologists laboriously search for new, improved insecticides and even other pests that will prey upon wheat pests—and hope that neither solution will pose worse threats to human producers and consumers. They look too for harmless chemicals that will readily eradicate weeds: the unwanted companion plants to crops, which steal space, sunlight, water, and nourishment.

Mr. E. is fascinated with this recitation. Agriculture is certainly much more complicated than scratching holes and sticking seeds in the ground! Farming is a business that increasingly requires a lot of knowledge and know-how, says Mr. S. And need he say that some of this must also be absorbed by the speculator who trades in a particular commodity? Of course, the fundamentalist traders specialize in this form of wisdom, he points out. In order to weigh the factors affecting a future harvest, for instance, they must consider the results of acreage surveys and the weather reports conducted both on the ground and in the air—from high-flying satellites now. And then there are the tricky matters of weighing the effects of old and newly announced agricultural policies of the Soviet Union, the United States, China, India, France, and so on; the effects of the U.S. government's price-support programs; and the effects of export-import prohibitions or quotas, balance of payments, exchanges of goods, outright handouts to needy underdeveloped or famine-stricken nations. It turns out that no speculator can consider his own position or that of his nation an "island" isolated from the rest of the world of humanity. Through commerce, through the workings of supply and demand brought on by several billion producers and consumers, everything and everybody are linked in a complex network of associations. And the grains display this interdependency better than all other commodities—for aren't they the "staff of life"?

It's intriguing, Mr. E. now breaks in to say, that in spite of their uncertainty in price, the grains always tend to move together in price movement, whether up or down, though frequently one will lag behind another. Yes, Mr. S. agrees. If wheat, corn, and barley are all going up, oats should soon follow. There's no guarantee, but still it's a safe bet. So when you're thinking about buying one kind of grain, it's wise to look at the recent price patterns of all the other major grains to get some indication of where they're going.

Is it safer to buy grain contracts than to sell them? asks Mr. E. He has heard that somewhere, but then he read in another place that a speculator should be as willing to consider the short position as much as the long. Mr. S. does have his own opinion on the matter, based on both experience and logic. He draws two long, firm horizontal lines across his chalkboard and labels the top one *resistance* and the bottom one *support:*

In the price behavior of commodities, Mr. S. now explains, one notices that in times when extreme inflation or economic depression are not operative, highs and lows tend to move within the bounds of these two price lines—unless some extraordinary supply or demand factor comes into effect. The minimal price for grains would be close to the production costs. Can you imagine it ever falling close to zero? People have to eat, and so there is always some demand for the grains, whereas in periods of severe financial stress people can do without many products that use metal, wood, and fibers. They can cut way down on sugar, coffee, and cocoa consumption. They will limit their use of meats. They should have little money to expend directly or indirectly on precious metals (though some may hoard them as a secure storable and transportable asset, to be sold only as a last resort in staying alive).

In shortages, then, says Mr. S., the grains could conceivably move higher and higher toward infinity, having no price limitations, whereas in surplus years the price could never fall absolutely to zero. The grains, after all, can be stored for future need if nobody wants them now. So probably, concludes Mr. S., a speculator—particularly a beginner—*is* safer buying a grain contract instead of selling it, since although there is a minimum price, usually hovering around the government's loan support, if there is one, in essence there can be no maximum price. A long trader would have less distance to fall than a short trader might have to rise in an adverse price move that goes on before he can safely exit. Thus if one buys wheat at, say, $4 per bushel, he could conceivably lose close to $4 a bushel on it. But if he *sold* wheat at $4 per bushel, the price might jump to $8 or even $10, who knows? And if as a short seller he had

119

stubbornly stayed on for the long ride to the delivery month, maintaining a margin all the while, his initial outlay might have doubled or quadrupled (or more) in losses.

Certainly speculators often earn profits by short selling, Mr. S. agrees. He himself has done so on perhaps half the trades in which he has taken positions. But when speculators go short, they should know quite clearly what they are doing and have a trading plan they stick to, which could even be built into the order they give to their brokers, limiting losses. Price reversals can happen fast and unexpectedly. And somehow, psychologically perhaps, novice speculators tend to think of price rises as being beneficial to them, which would hardly be so if they had taken a short position. Thus they must be extra wary if they wish to be bears.

Apart from supplying food for humans, Mr. S. goes on, the grains have great importance, as Mr. E. has now learned, for animal food. They also have numerous industrial uses, soybeans especially. The oil that is removed from them in processing is converted into an amazing assortment of products, edible and nonedible. As a speculator, Mr. S. is strongly prejudiced in favor of the grains, considering them probably the safest investment of all, since they are more vital to people and society than other classes of commodities. As a short-term investment of last resort in a period of rapidly rising inflation and the diminished productivity and corporate earnings that mark a business recession or an oncoming depression, one might do better with wheat or corn than with stocks and bank accounts—even, he ventures to say, than with silver and gold. Because what could be more current and affordable and "real" than an essential foodstuff—for which there must always be available money?

Now, since they have been talking about commodities one can eat, Mr. S. suggests that Mr. E. take over the discussion for a while and tell him what he knows about the meats. Well, says Mr. E., the main meat-supplying animals traded on the exchanges are cattle, hogs, and chickens. The first two have contracts for live animals, but chickens—called "iced broilers" at the CBT—are slaughtered and packed in ice. Cattle are either "live," which means they are ready for butchering, or "feeder," which means they have to be fed and allowed to grow some more before they can be slaughtered. He didn't realize that overseeing the birth and growth of a calf for about a year and a half is an entirely different business than taking this animal and feeding him until it achieves prime weight. Another surprise to Mr. E. was learning that the cattle business is larger than the corn and wheat businesses combined! The value of livestock in the United States is close to $50 billion. A further surprise to him was that there are five sex classifications for cattle: bulls, cows, heifers, stags, steers. No wonder there is so much confusion on the market!

The animals themselves probably get confused too, Mr. S. comments. But now, what other kinds of livestock are there? Well, live hogs, or course, says Mr. E. And then there are all those pork bellies that people like to talk and joke about. Somehow the words sum up the speculating in commodities so far as the American population is concerned! He was interested to find out that each live hog actually has *two* pork bellies, which go into making bacon. Eggs, he comments, are often classified with the meats because they come from chickens, though some traders consider both broilers and eggs in a separate classification called "poultry." In the past, lard—animal fat—used to be an important tradable commodity because it was used in soap making, cooking, and various industrial ways, but now it has been mostly overtaken by the vegetable oils because of their polyunsaturated fats and has also declined in demand since the invention of detergents.

Meats are an important part of the American diet and are likely to remain so, asserts Mr. S., unless they become permanently so overpriced that few consumers can regularly afford them. Ranchers watch the futures markets closely because they must take in a profit that is above their considerable expenses in producing livestock; which of course partially depend on the current cost of feed, much of which is geared to the commodity exchanges. Many ranchers hedge in order to guarantee a fair price for their efforts and expenditures. But cattle raisers are famous for engaging in the infamous "Texas Hedge"—that is, instead of selling contracts that cover so many head of cattle that they are raising, they *buy* them, figuring that a rise in price will then double their profits. This, of course, is really speculation and doesn't always work out, because panic can grip "longs" who have to sell back devalued contracts before delivery time. So beware the Texas Hedge, my son! Mr. S. declares.

Mr. E. now breaks in with a question as to the future of meats in an overpopulated world that depends on protein sources for sustenance but may increasingly have to find them at a more basic level in the food chain, in the plant realm. Making meat is more time-consuming, more expensive, and less efficient. Having a certain interest in nutrition and the "politics of hunger" around the world, Mr. E. is wondering whether many Americans will in time have to change their eating habits. And also waste less! for he has often heard foreigners complain about the large amounts of meat served in restaurants, with much of it thrown away. When meat prices become high enough and income can't keep pace with them, says Mr. S., the public will consume less and begin a firm line of resistance—he underscores the top horizon on his chart—which will affect both demand and future supply. And then let us all eat soybeans, wheat, and sunflowers! he exclaims. Personally, though, he would miss his steak.

But yes, Mr. S. goes on to say, food supply—from producer to consumer—is far more complex than most people imagine. A speculator gains some unexpected insight into the multitude of variables that contribute to the costs in the exchange marketplace and the public marketplaces, the local supermarkets. It is an educational experience to study the fundamental problems that beset farmers and ranchers in raising food: bad weather, diseases, surpluses elsewhere, government restrictions and rules—plus cash problems, personal and local calamities, labor strikes affecting both production and transportation. Why, the costs alone in using fossil fuels—oil and its derivatives, mainly—for farm machinery and agricultural chemicals (fertilizers and toxins) and then for processing, transporting, and preparing the food for consumer use are astounding! And, Mr. S. ponders, inevitably, how much of that energy—as with meats—is habitually wasted? The new shortage of and skyrocketing price in fuel oil and gasoline, he predicts, may end up changing many ways of doing things. And this is bound to affect the commodity market in numerous ways, not all of which are yet foreseen by fundamentalists.

And yet the buying public visiting the supermarkets, says Mr. E., mostly seems under the impression that bread loaves grow on racks and that beef or chicken enters their world wrapped in clear plastic and set serenely on white plastic trays and that the expensive canned ham never needed care and feeding! But he does admit that he hasn't thought much about such matters until now. Except to complain about high prices.

Then what about those other commodities classified as foods? Mr. S. asks. Has Mr. E. found out much about them? Well, says Mr. E., they're a mixed bunch, really. There's sugar, and that's important. He notes that all No. 11 contracts carried on the New York Coffee, Sugar and Cocoa Exchange are for sugar grown around the world, whereas those for No. 12 are for domestic consumption. And he has learned that much of American-produced sugar comes from the white sugar beet—which surprised him. This is because land in Hawaii and a few places in the South are the only suitable subtropical areas for sugarcane growing. Actually, the United States is one of the leading importers of sugar. It interests him too that sugarcane, like bamboo and grains, belongs to the grass family.

But now, says Mr. E., he's not sure he approves of so much acreage in the world being given over to sugar growing. Sugar, especially refined sugar, isn't really *good* for people. They should be getting their energy-producing sucrose elsewhere, he asserts, making Mr. S. laugh. Tell that to the world! he says. And when Mr. E. finishes his crusade, we'll see whether the demand for sugar declines on the exchanges. The commodity market reflects a society's needs and interests in acquiring certain goods. Whether or not these goods are *good* for them is a very different issue indeed. Speculators who aren't favorably inclined toward a particular commodity aren't forced to trade in it, after all. And in fact if they disapprove of it for some reason, they can easily shun it, the way some groups decline to advertise tobacco and even coffee. But who knows? If he studied more about sugar's many beneficial uses—or about almost anything, in fact, just as he's doing now about commodity speculation—he might find some strong opinions mellowing and then even recognize virtues and uses he never knew about before.

How about coffee? Mr. S. now proposes. Well, says Mr. E., it does get a lot of static from nutritionists, especially about its caffeine content. But he likes it anyway, he admits, so he drinks it—and buys it. Perhaps he likes it essentially because of the caffeine, which after all is a useful stimulant in a number of drugs. Coffee, like tea, is a beverage with a long and fascinating history that speculators might wish to explore in order to acquaint themselves with the particulars and peculiarities in growing and marketing it, says Mr. S., the better to comprehend supply and demand. In the United States, commodity futures are mainly traded in "C" coffee, grown in Colombia and the Central American area. Several foreign exchanges—notably London—deal with the varieties of coffee beans grown elsewhere, many of which may end up in American-consumed blends.

Speaking of tea, Mr. E. interrupts, why isn't it carried on some exchange? Tea is a tough commodity to regularize, Mr. S. answers, because there are three main kinds of it—black, green, oolong—and each has its own types and grades and blends. So although tea is the most widely consumed beverage in the world, it doesn't lend itself well to the normal commodity market. Americans had enough trouble over tea, anyway, in Boston, didn't they?

Well, there's cocoa, says Mr. E., which originated in the New World from the cacao bean—to give us chocolate. But now the African countries of Ghana and Nigeria are the largest producers. Cocoa, adds Mr. S., is an interesting but risky commodity to trade in because its growing requirements make it slow in responding to supply and demand situations. Therefore it can have very wide and wild swings in prices, which can't necessarily be predicted by the experts in fundamental factors.

And then there's orange juice, Mr. E. proposes. He realizes now that frozen concentrated orange juice (otherwise known as OJ or FCOJ) was surely one of the great inventions of the post–World War II era. Yet almost every household in the United States by now probably assumes that it has always been with us. We've forgotten how to squeeze oranges. He hadn't known that Florida takes the lead in supplying it, though. Why, sometimes the 10% of the oranges from California that contribute to the main supply are referred to as "imported"!

Anything else? asks Mr. S. Ah, Mr. E. doesn't want to forget potatoes—Idaho ones (the russets) and Maine ones, carried on separate exchanges. They rank as an American favorite, along with steak, milk, corn on the cob, and mother's apple pie. And like cocoa and corn, says Mr. E., he's pleased to be reminded that potatoes originated in the New World, among the Incas in South America. Potatoes are surprisingly loaded with nutrients, and one could almost live on them alone. He read that they are even good for conversion into a substitute milk for malnourished infants! Most people connect potatoes with Ireland because they grew well there for the poor people. And when a blight hit this depended-upon crop in the 1840s, the Irish began heading for America in an odd reversal of migration begun by a commodity! The potato, adds Mr. S., is still a mainstay. The New York Mercantile Exchange offers a contract of 50,000 pounds, and computed at a price of around 10¢ per pound, this is one of the cheapest contracts to trade in. Though a speculator must beware, because potatoes can be highly volatile in price moves, bringing on a touch of financial blight.

So many of the food commodities are possible to trade on the exchanges now, asserts Mr. S., because methods for packaging, transporting, and selling them in bulk have become systematized and because improvements in storing and efficiently handling them have allowed them to qualify in the same terms as the traditional commodities, the grains. One wonders, Mr. S. speculates, how many new food commodities grown, processed, and used in great quantities by Americans might find their way to the exchanges in the future, perhaps pushing out some of the traditionals?

And now what does Mr. E. wish to present as commodities? Well, he says, there are three kinds that are somewhat similar to foods because they have provided elements for three other basic needs of humanity: clothing, fuel, and shelter. There are the fibers—cotton and wool; the energy-supplying products; and the forest products—lumber and plywood.

Mr. E. remarks that the natural textile fibers don't have the supply or demand of the past, since they are being replaced in many uses by fabrics of man-made synthetics. Synthetics frequently cost less to produce, since many of them are made from petroleum derivatives. Mr. E. wonders now whether the rapidly increasing cost of oil will cause a swing back to the naturals. But wait! Mr. S. warns. The production of cotton takes fuel energy too. It's possible that a rise in petroleum prices will affect cotton even more than the synthetics made from oil. Who knows? People will speculate, but nothing is ever certain in commodity trading except speculation itself.

And speaking of petroleum! says Mr. E. He has noticed that it too has various futures contracts on commodity exchanges. Energy contracts have been around for some while, Mr. S. remarks. Liquified propane on the New York Cotton Exchange is a good example. The whole field is becoming newly energized for speculators, of course, because of the terrific instability in supplies and prices. Sort of an "If you can't beat 'em, join 'em?" asks Mr. E. That's right, Mr. S. agrees. So there are now several different heating oil and industrial fuel oil contracts available. But they are bound to be volatile and risky, whatever the promise in potential profits to lucky speculators. Only skilled speculators should get into them. The fundamental factors alone in considering such contracts, geared as they are to international tensions, oil companies' complex profit taking, and government controls and taxations, are rather mind boggling! But then a lot of speculators are bound to find such situations challenging.

Now, asks Mr. S., continuing his interrogation, what about some other natural products of the land? Well, there's wood, Mr. E. says. And he has read that all wood products have continued to rise in price in recent years, though the supply itself, at least in potentiality, has remained somewhat constant because of reforestation and other tree-farming and wood-conserving techniques practiced by a number of lumber companies. As commodities, lumber and plywood are closely connected with the overall national economy, Mr. S. adds. When the construction business goes into a decline, perhaps because of a business recession or higher interest rates in mortgages, the demand for wood products declines, affecting then their supply and ultimately their prices. For how many commodities is the well-being or ill health of the general economy a barometer, supply-and-demand affecter, *and* price determinant! And yet can't it be possible that business recessions and inflations may cause some beneficial effects? asks Mr. E. Americans are fortunate to live in a land so well supplied with agricultural areas, forests, and minerals. Taking them for granted, they have often mistreated and exhausted them. When it costs them more and more to consume the land's products, maybe attitudes and ways of doing things will change. Perhaps that's so; he hopes so, says Mr. S. And what better way to look at the connections among production, consumption, and prices than by examining the commodity market?

What's next on the agenda? he asks. The metals, says Mr. E., admitting that he liked reading up on them. He found it interesting that all metals on the exchanges—copper, gold, silver, platinum, palladium—have both precious and industrial aspects, though with varying proportions. Copper, for example, is extremely useful as an excellent conductor of electricity, but it also has some value as an ingredient in decorative items. Gold is rare and difficult to extract and purify. Since it is beautiful, malleable, and noncorrodable, it has had a long career as the most precious metal—which causes civilized people seeking it to become barbarians. And yet it too has practical uses, as in electronics and dentistry.

One thing, though, he wonders about, says Mr. E. Why are most of the precious metal prices quoted in troy ounces? What is this "troy," anyway? A troy ounce is actually heavier than the regular, or avoirdupois, ounce, Mr. S. explains. There are twelve, not sixteen, ounces to the pound. This weight designation originated in the medieval French town of Troyes; it is used in weighing coins and precious metals. Mr. E. will notice other weight differences, such as that between the regular, or "short," ton, which has two thousand pounds, and the metric ton, which is heavier by some two hundred pounds.

Mr. E. says he's fascinated with the valuation connection between gold and silver, which people are watching so much lately. Is there any formula that determines the value proportion? Well, generally speaking, Mr. S. replies, it's about sixteen to one, which means that sixteen ounces of silver would have roughly the same value as one ounce of gold. And now, would Mr. E. want to say some things about silver?

Silver is less rare and less valuable than gold, Mr. E. begins, but it makes up for this by being highly important in certain industrial uses, such as photography, and by being both handsome and useful in domestic goods, such as silverware. Also, it can be recovered by melting down silver coins and other silver objects; in the sixties, this practice gave impetus to the exchange in silver coins, which is still going strong. Mr. E. adds that he didn't know that platinum, either as ingot or jewelry, was a popular "collectible" in Japan, much as diamonds and gold are in the Western world, offering inflation hedges besides being used in glass manufacturing and oil refining. And palladium, a metal within the platinum group, is widely used in the chemical industry and in communications systems.

In the past, says Mr. S., nations attempted to base their currencies on precious metals; these metals would be stored away, out of usage, but ready to be brought forward if necessary to back important transactions with foreign governments or with private corporations or individuals who declined to take paper money or paper credits as receipts for debts incurred. When new sources for precious metals were located, as happened when Spain discovered the Americas and swiftly moved in to harvest their storehouses of gold and silver, the value of money of all kinds declined because of the relative abundance of precious metals in coins and ingots and other forms. Thus the basis for money systems themselves was devalued because of increased supply. In the past century, however, Mr. S. goes on, the production of precious metals has scarcely been able to keep up with the urgent, growing need for them, as population and production have increased.

Perhaps Mr. E. has already noticed that they have finished talking about the "hard commodities" now? asks Mr. S. Those are the ones you can touch or even kick if you have to; the ones that have substance. And now they can move on to the "soft commodities." He means the international currencies and the financial instruments, of course? asks Mr. E. Well, he hopes that Mr. S. will be able to clear up his absolute confusion over them. First of all, why are they so "soft"? It seems to him that lately the hardest trading takes place over them! Maybe the term got started, Mr. S. proposes, to parallel the "hardware" and "software" in the computer business, with the hardware being the machinery itself and the software the less tangible programming that it holds.

To launch this part of their talk, Mr. S. wants to know whether Mr. E. is acquainted with the two basics in human economic life. Oh, says Mr. E., production and consumption? Sure enough, Mr. S. replies. Sooner or later everything seems to get reduced to one or the other. Generally, in order to accomplish the second one, you've got to do the first one first, which involves *direct labor,* or work for which you're paid money so that you can purchase what you need or wish to consume— unless, of course, you can work out a straight barter deal. We might admit that it is always enjoyable to consume and generally unpleasant but necessary to produce. The catch is that every item must somehow be produced before it can be consumed. You can't eat an apple before it is grown and picked, whether by you or somebody else. Some modern-day production and consumption can be extremely abstract. Woody Allen, for example, produces entertainment when he writes and performs a script, and the public consumes this entertainment when it attends his films.

Because of the complexity and abstraction of producing and consuming, Mr. S. continues, society had to devise a method of keeping track. Of course we could go back to the barter system: "I'll give you one hundred apples if you put a roof on my house." That sort of direct trading of goods and/or labor. But how would this work in everyday practice nowadays? Consider a musician walking into a McDonald's, saying, "I'll trade you three minutes of guitar playing for one of your Big Macs." None too practical.

So how, then, does one tally the value of goods and labor? It's done with agreed-upon slips of paper—money—that people receive for their production and can then take around to others and trade for consumable items or for a form of labor that they themselves can't perform in the process of consuming. Fine. But this process can be abused by counterfeiters, who print money and then use it to call upon someone else's production and consume it. Yet the counterfeiter himself has not produced the equivalent amount of value for society.

Now! says Mr. S., there are two kinds of counterfeiters: illegal ones and legal ones. (Mr. E. discerns that Mr. S. is clearly enjoying himself.) The illegal kind are those shady fellows who have printing presses in their cellars. Does Mr. E. wish to hazard a guess as to who the legal ones are? Mr. E. thinks a bit and then grins, having caught Mr. S.'s drift. Governments! he proposes. Exactly, his mentor agrees. All nations have legal counterfeiters, usually called something like the Treasury Department. They can print as much money as they are told to or that they think is needed by the people or the government itself.

Sometimes it helps to demonstrate complex arrangements by reducing them to simple diagrams, says Mr. S., going to his chalkboard. This is how things should be, ideally. A, B, and C produce and then exchange different items for consumption, using $1 to keep track:

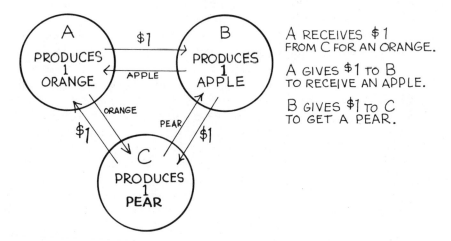

See how neatly and fairly it works out! Mr. S. proclaims. Production and consumption are exactly equal, with $1—the agreed-upon receipt between them—passing from one to the other as payment for the commodity each had separately produced.

In more complex societies, the government determines just what that agreed-upon receipt will be. It declares that a coin or its equivalent in paper money is "legal tender for all debts," meaning that if you're in debt for having received goods or services, you can tender, or offer, this token of value, which must then be accepted as payment. Theoretically, a government should manufacture only the amount of money equivalent to what a nation produces. It follows, then, that the more a nation produces, the more money it should have in circulation. This, by the way, Mr. S. says, is a concept quite appealing to classical economists, who have talked about the "commodity dollar" as the best way to stabilize a nation's—and the whole world's—monetary system; it would attach valuation totally to forms of production.

But what happens in reality in our nation and others? asks Mr. S., going back to his chalkboard, erasing the old C and putting in a new one —the government:

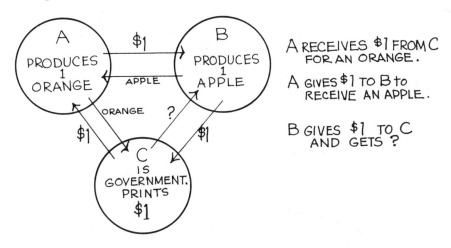

The whole scheme gets fouled up, says Mr. S., because the government pays $1 to A for an orange and consumes it. Meanwhile, A has gone to B with that $1 and bought an apple, which B produced. But when B goes to C with the $1, he can't buy anything of value with it—because C has not produced anything except paper money. And B may be hungry; he wants a pear, not another piece of paper! In other words, the calls upon production—namely dollars—have been increased, while the actual production has not increased. Therefore there are more dollars chasing fewer goods. This means inflation.

If money gets "tight" as demand for it increases, Mr. S. continues, a government can respond by printing more money—but without seeing to it that productivity increases by an equivalent amount. And so the inflation spirals on upward. A greater supply of money causes a decrease in its value. Since the money is worth less, people need still more of it in order to purchase what they must consume. And since the demand for money increases again, the government prints still more—without, again, any evidence that production itself has gone up at all. *Hyperinflation* might well be defined as the situation in which the paper money loses its value faster than the government can print it. It has been known to happen, as in Germany between world wars.

There is always the danger, Mr. S. remarks, that as inflation continues, production and consumption—those two essentials in human society —will get increasingly detached from any solid basis in the monetary system of a nation. Nations, like individuals, must be measured by what they *produce*, not just by what they consume!

So now, says Mr. S., let us move into the realm of international currencies. If one nation's money system is inflated, meaning that the nation's currency has been printed in a supply that exceeds its productivity, what happens to that currency vis-à-vis the currency of another nation in which, for the time being anyway, the government has a better control over its money supply? Well, the value of the dollar will go up or down according to the equivalent purchasing power of the British pound, the Canadian dollar, the Japanese yen, the German deutschemark, the French franc, the Swiss franc, the Dutch guilder, the Mexican peso. And this market can move around exceedingly fast, since sometimes it seems as if there's a race among nations to see who can print money the fastest! And yet, ironically, the faster printer does not necessarily "win" or gain, since its money ends up being worth less because there is more of it.

So let's look at the result in terms of international trading, Mr. S. goes on. If the United States prints faster than Japan while producing no more in valued goods, it will take relatively more dollars to purchase yen. (Just as, if Britain prints faster than Germany, it will take more pounds to buy deutschemarks.) Now suppose an American aircraft manufacturer has just sold airplanes to Japan, which will pay for them in yen. The agreement states that one airplane will be exchanged for so many million yen in ten months' time. But how can the airplane manufacturer know what the yen will be worth in terms of dollars by then? And for that matter, the Japanese buyers will have a similar but opposite concern.

To accommodate problems like this in international trade and the fluctuating currencies, Mr. S. says, the International Monetary Market, a division of the Chicago Mercantile Exchange, came into existence in 1973 with its "floating currencies." It offers both hedgers and speculators a main currency exchange. As the regular commodity exchanges do, it facilitates the transfer of risk in price (or value) change from a commercial to a speculator, giving the one protection and the other the opportunity for profit taking (or, conversely, loss).

Thus, Mr. S. points out, the American airplane manufacturer could hedge his position on the IMM by selling yen contracts to the amount of the Japanese purchase of his products. If the yen went up in value on the exchange, he would lose money there. But—as with other short hedging transactions—he would gain more dollars than originally anticipated. If the value of the yen decreased, he would earn money on the exchange because he had sold yen contracts; yet in the actual transaction he would receive fewer dollars. In either case, the net result would be breaking even in the deal.

And meanwhile, of course, Mr. S. goes on, speculators have accepted the opposite position—buying yen contracts, hoping for a price increase that will profit them. As they do in other commodities, commercials in financial trades occupy both sides, some buying and some selling; and numerous speculators move between them, filling in any price gaps and helping to resolve the proper valuation of the two currencies when the contracts come due.

Mr. E. appreciates this example of a transaction carried on through the "floating currency" exchange, he says. This is the first time he has been able to recognize the usefulness, even the necessity, for this foreign-currency speculation. He thought—as probably most members of the American public still do—that as usual those traders were just wildly buying and selling futures contracts, in this case for paper monies whose values were driven up or down by whims or actions unrelated to actual goods or a nation's production record.

But be cautious! warns Mr. S. The soft commodities are not the proper testing ground for beginning speculators. Nor are they a good place for speculators who have a fundamental approach to trading, since predicting currency prices by the standard methods of studying supply and demand factors is virtually impossible. The economy of one nation in itself is extremely complicated to comprehend, and mixing those' of two nations or more in order to determine what their currency values will do could put a sober fundamentalist in the booby hatch!

As for novices, Mr. S. goes on, they must remember that the hard commodities must all have some lower value limit. There's a price below which wheat or copper or cattle or cotton simply won't go. But since government printing presses can run indefinitely, there is no price below which the dollar or some foreign monetary unit cannot go! A currency can approach zero: remember the Germany currency in the 1920s, when it took a wheelbarrowful of paper money just to buy a loaf of bread? Also, Mr. S. adds, a look at the charts relating to foreign currencies will disclose that some governments occasionally and quite deliberately manipulate the value of their currency—perhaps catching an American speculator quite unaware and administering unwholesome financial losses.

And now, says Mr. S. with a touch of theatricality, they come to the second type of soft commodity and the newest entry on the exchanges— with certainly the promise of more to come, since soft commodities are proving so attractive to speculators and so beneficial to commercial hedgers.

The financial instruments? asks Mr. E. He hopes that they too can be explained by Mr. S. in a way that makes sense to him. He heard about Ginnie Maes and Treasury bills and the like at the Chicago Board of Trade, but his friend Mr. T. couldn't really get into discussing them that day.

Well, so far, says Mr. S., there are Ginnie Maes—the GNMAs, or the Government National Mortgage Association obligations—Treasury bills, Treasury notes, Treasury bonds, and commercial paper. Mr. E. will surely comprehend the situation best if he looks upon speculating in contracts for financial instruments as essentially *speculating in interest rates*.

Commercial paper may be the easiest to understand, he asserts, and so they'll start with that. Mr. E. knows, of course, that corporations often have to borrow money, just as people do. They make agreements with banks, or else they get loans from individuals, acknowledging the debt with a receipt that is called *commercial paper*. When corporations borrow money, they do so at an interest rate that is flexible and depends upon the supply of money available at the time.

The federal government must also borrow money, Mr. S. goes on. It does so by selling Treasury bills, notes, and bonds. The difference between them is basically a matter of how long the debt is for. T-notes are for debts that have maturities longer than bills but shorter than bonds. These financial instruments are usually priced as a "percentage of par." Take T-bills as an example. Rather than lend the Treasury $100 and then receive $107 from it at the end of a year for a 7% rate of interest, you would buy a T-bill for $93 and in about a year's time you'd turn it back in for $100.

In a sense, then, says Mr. S., you're buying the bill at a discount and getting the face value at the end of a specified time. The greater the interest paid, the cheaper the T-bill. In other words, a $100 T-bill selling for $95 would return approximately 5%. One selling for $92 would return about 8%, following the earlier example. So price is an indication of yield, and yield is an indication of price. It is interesting to note, he adds, that these financial instruments have become so acceptable that even states —California is one—allow their treasuries to use futures markets in connection with the state's investments.

The small, at-home speculator, Mr. S. continues, must realize that with these financial instruments there is a minimum interest rate somewhere but really no maximum. Certainly no one is willing anymore to lend money at the low rate of 3%. And some corporations desperate for money may agree to pay 10%, 12%, or 15%—possibly even 25%, since the sky's the limit when commercial paper is given as receipts. And because these interest rates move inversely to the price, there is a maximum price for these financial instruments but essentially no minimum one.

Well, says Mr. E., looking quite alert and interested. Should he think about buying some Ginnie Mae or T-bill futures? he wonders. He can't afford to now, Mr. S. tells him. Apart from the inherent risk in speculating in interest rates, these financial instruments and the foreign currencies deal with very large contracts that have values of up to $3 million, quite a sum compared with the, say, $10,000 to $20,000 values of most commodity futures. Even less for some. He'll need both experience and a lot of capital before he sticks his big toe in that current! warns Mr. S.

Now all this talk has covered the main ground in the U.S. exchanges, says Mr. S. There are surely going to be new commodities, both hard and soft, introduced in the future, since futures contracts are appropriate for many more situations in which price and interest rates vary unpredictably. And then there are options on futures to be considered too. Mr. S. will go into that subject a few sessions from now.

But what about commodity exchanges outside the United States? asks Mr. E. There are many, Mr. S. responds, from London to Hong Kong. Oh, an American speculator can trade on them too through his brokerage firm, just as foreign traders can speculate—or hedge, for that matter—on American exchanges if they choose. Once in a while Mr. S. has bought or sold coffee contracts on the London exchange and entered into other foreign trades over sugar and cocoa. But mostly he has enough to keep him busy here. Besides, he doesn't like figuring the time differential along with everything else. It bothers him to know that in Europe people are trading while he's still asleep, or that when *he* is ready to trade, they have gone home!

He yawns, just thinking of it. Then looking at his clock, he realizes that their session has run overtime, so engrossed have both of them been in the commodity talk!

At their next meeting, says Mr. S., they'll talk in more detail about contracts and prices and other matters. To prepare himself for it, Mr. E. is to look over this list of contract specifications for the major commodities traded on the U.S. exchanges, which his guide now hands him to take home.

A Selective List of Major Commodities Traded on U.S. Commodity Exchanges

GRAINS

COMMODITY AND EXCHANGES	TRADING MONTHS	CONTRACT SIZE	PRICES QUOTED IN	MINIMUM PRICE FLUCTUATION (per unit)	DAILY LIMIT (per contract)	APPROXIMATE PRICE RANGE (1975-79)
Corn						
CBT	Mar/May/July/Sept/Dec	5,000 bu.	¢/bu.	¼¢/bu. ($12.50)	10¢ ($500)	180-380
MID	Same as CBT	1,000 bu.	¢/bu.	⅛¢/bu. ($1.25)	10¢ ($100)	
Oats						
CBT	Mar/May/July/Sept/Dec	5,000 bu.	¢/bu.	¼¢/bu. ($12.50)	6¢ ($300)	100-200
MID	Same as CBT	5,000 bu.	¢/bu.	⅛¢/bu. ($6.25)	6¢ ($300)	
MINN	May/June/July/Sept	5,000 bu.	¢/bu.	⅛¢/bu. ($6.25)	6¢ ($300)	
Soybeans						
CBT	Jan/Mar/May/July/Aug/Sept/Nov	5,000 bu.	¢/bu.	¼¢/bu. ($12.50)	30¢ ($1,500)	450-1050
MID	Same as CBT	1,000 bu.	¢/bu.	⅛¢/bu. ($1.25)	30¢ ($300)	
Soybean Meal						
CBT	Jan/Mar/May/July/Aug/Sept/Oct/Dec	100 tn. (200,000 lb.)	$/tn.	10¢/tn. ($10)	$10 ($1,000)	1-3
Soybean Oil						
CBT	Jan/Mar/May/July/Aug/Sept/Oct/Dec	60,000 lb.	¢/lb.	1/100¢/lb. ($6)	1¢ ($600)	15-50
Wheat						
CBT	Mar/May/July/Sept/Dec	5,000 bu.	¢/bu.	¼¢/bu. ($12.50)	20¢ ($1,000)	100-520
KCBT	Same as CBT	5,000 bu.	¢/bu.	Same as CBT	25¢ ($1,250)	
MID	Same as CBT	1,000 bu.	¢/bu.	⅛¢/bu. ($1.25)	20¢ ($200)	
MINN	Same as CBT	5,000 bu.	¢/bu.	⅛¢/bu. ($6.25)	20¢ ($1,000)	

OTHER FOOD PRODUCTS

COMMODITY AND EXCHANGES	TRADING MONTHS	CONTRACT SIZE	PRICES QUOTED IN	MINIMUM PRICE FLUCTUATION (per unit)	DAILY LIMIT (per contract)	APPROXIMATE PRICE RANGE (1975-79)
Cocoa NYCSC	Mar/May/July/Sept/Dec	30,000 lb.	¢/lb.	1/100¢/lb. ($3.00)	6¢ ($1,800)	50-240
Coffee "C" NYCSC	Mar/May/July/Sept/Dec	37,500 lb.	¢/lb.	1/100¢/lb. ($3.75)	4¢ ($1,500)	50-330
Orange Juice NYCE	Jan/Mar/May/July/Sept/Nov	15,000 lb.	¢/lb.	5/100¢/lb. ($7.50)	3¢ ($450)	45-135
Potatoes (Maine) NYM	Jan/Mar/Apr/May/Nov	50,000 lb.	¢/lb.	1/100¢/lb. ($5)	50¢ ($250)	2½-13
Potatoes (Russet, Burbank) CME	Jan/Mar/Apr/May/Nov	80,000 lb.	¢/100 lb.	1/100¢/lb. ($8)	50¢ ($400)	2-20
Shell Eggs CME	All months	22,500 doz.	¢/doz.	5/100¢/doz. ($11.25)	2¢ ($450)	40-76
Sugar #11 NYCSC	Mar/May/July/Sept/Nov	112,000 lb.	¢/lb.	1/100¢/lb. ($11.20)	1¢ ($1,120)	6-52

Abbreviations: CBT—Chicago Board of Trade, CME—Chicago Mercantile Exchange, COMEX—Commodity Exchange, Inc. (New York), IMM—International Money Mart (Chicago), KCBT—Kansas City Board of Trade, MINN—Minneapolis Grain Exchange, MID—MidAmerica Commodity Exchange (Chicago), NYCE—New York Cotton Exchange, NYCSC—New York Coffee, Sugar and Cocoa Exchange, NYM—New York Mercantile Exchange.

PRODUCTS OF THE LAND

COMMODITY AND EXCHANGES	TRADING MONTHS	CONTRACT SIZE	PRICES QUOTED IN	MINIMUM PRICE FLUCTUATION (per unit)	DAILY LIMIT (per contract)	APPROXIMATE PRICE RANGE (1975-79)
Cotton #2 NYCE	Mar/May/July/ Oct/Dec	50,000 lb.	¢/lb.	1/100¢/lb. ($5)	2¢ ($1,000)	40-92
Oil, Heating #2 NYM	Jan/Mar/May/ July/Sept/Nov	100 metric tn.	$/metric tn.	10¢/ton ($10)	$2 ($200)	40-105
Lumber CME	Jan/Mar/May/ July/Sept/Nov	100,000 bd. ft.	$/1,000 bd. ft.	10¢/1,000 bd. ft. ($10)	$5 ($500)	100-280
Oil, Industrial Fuel #6 NYM	Jan/Mar/May/ July/Sept/Nov	42,000 gal.	¢/gal.	1/100¢/gal. ($4.20)	1¢ ($420)	50-110
Plywood CBT	Jan/Mar/May/ July/Sept/Nov	76,032 sq. ft.	$/1,000 sq. ft.	10¢/1,000 sq. ft. ($7.60)	$7 ($532)	120-230
Propane, Liquified NYCE	Jan/Mar/May/ July/Sept/Dec	100,000 gal.	¢/gal.	1/100¢/gal. ($10)	1¢ ($1,000)	8-50

MEATS

COMMODITY AND EXCHANGES	TRADING MONTHS	CONTRACT SIZE	PRICES QUOTED IN	MINIMUM PRICE FLUCTUATION (per unit)	DAILY LIMIT (per contract)	APPROXIMATE PRICE RANGE (1975-79)
Beef, Boneless CME	Feb/Apr/June/ Aug/Oct/Dec	38,000 lb.	¢/100 lb.	2.5/100¢/lb. ($9.50)	1.5¢ ($570)	90-150
Cattle, Feeder CME	Mar/Apr/May/ Aug/Sept/Oct/Nov	42,000 lb.	$/100 lb.	2.5/100¢/lb. ($10.50)	1.5¢ ($630)	.32-.90
Cattle, Live CME	Feb/Apr/June/ Aug/Oct/Dec	40,000 lb.	$/100 lb.	2.5/100¢/lb. ($10)	1.5¢ ($600)	.35-.80
Hogs, Live CME	Feb/Apr/June/ July/Aug/Oct/Dec	30,000 lb.	$/100 lb.	2.5/100¢/lb. ($7.50)	1.5¢ ($450)	.30-.63
MID	Same as CME	15,000 lb.	¢/lb.	2.5/100¢/lb. ($3.75)	1.5¢ ($225)	
Iced Broilers CBT	Mar/May/June/ July/Aug/Sept/Nov	30,000 lb.	¢/lb.	2.5/100¢/lb. ($7.50)	2¢ ($600)	34-53
Pork Bellies CME	Feb/Mar/May/ July/Aug	38,000 lb.	¢/lb.	2.5/100¢/lb. ($9.50)	2¢ ($760)	28-105

METALS

COMMODITY AND EXCHANGES	TRADING MONTHS	CONTRACT SIZE	PRICES QUOTED IN	MINIMUM PRICE FLUCTUATION (per unit)	DAILY LIMIT (per contract)	APPROXIMATE PRICE RANGE (1975-79)
Copper COMEX	Jan/Mar/May/July/Sept/Dec	25,000 lb.	¢/lb.	10/100¢/lb. ($25)	3¢ ($750)	52-118
IMM	Same as COMEX	12,500 lb.	¢/lb.	10/100¢/lb. ($12.50)	5¢ ($625)	
Gold CBT	Jan/Mar/May/July/Sept/Nov	100 troy oz.	$/oz.	10¢/troy oz. ($10)	$10 ($1,000)	105-550
COMEX	Feb/Apr/June/Aug/Oct/Dec	100 troy oz.	$/oz.	10¢/troy oz. ($10)	$10 ($1,000)	
IMM	All months	100 troy oz.	$/oz.	10¢/troy oz. ($10)	$10 ($1,000)	
MID	Mar/June/Sept	33.2 troy oz.	$/oz.	2.5¢/troy oz. ($.83)	$10 ($332)	
NYM	Mar/June/Sept/Dec	1 kg. (32 troy oz.)	$/oz.	20¢/troy oz. ($6.40)	$10 ($320)	
Platinum NYM	Jan/July/Oct	50 troy oz.	$/oz.	10¢/troy oz. ($5.00)	$10 ($500)	140-700
Silver CBT	Feb/Apr/June/Aug/Oct/Dec	5,000 troy oz.	¢/oz.	1/10¢/troy oz. ($5)	20¢ ($1,000)	4-30
COMEX	Jan/Mar/May/July/Sept/Dec	5,000 troy oz.	¢/oz.	10/100¢/troy oz. ($5)	20¢ ($1,000)	
MID	Feb/Apr/June/Aug/Oct/Dec	1,000 troy oz.	¢/oz.	5/100¢/troy oz. ($.50)	20¢ ($200)	

FINANCIAL

COMMODITY AND EXCHANGES	TRADING MONTHS	CONTRACT SIZE	PRICES QUOTED IN	MINIMUM PRICE FLUCTUATION (per unit)	DAILY LIMIT (per contract)	APPROXIMATE PRICE RANGE (1975-79)
Commercial Paper CBT	Mar/June/Sept Dec	Face value at maturity of $1 million (or yield)	As an annualized discount	1/100 of 1% of $1 million: 1 basis pt. ($25)	25 basis pt. ($625)	6-15% yield
GNMA CBT	Mar/June/Sept Dec	$100,000 principal (or yield)	32nds per basis pt.	1/32 basis pt. ($31.25)	24/32 basis pt. ($750)	7.9-12.23% yield
Treasury Bills (1 year) IMM	Mar/June/Sept Dec	$250,000 (or yield)	Basis pt.	1 basis pt. ($25)	50 pt. ($1,250)	4-12% yield
Treasury Bonds CBT	Mar/June/Sept Dec	Face value at maturity of $100,000 and coupon rate of 8% (or yield)	32nds per basis pt.	1/32 basis pt. ($31.25)	24/32 basis pt. ($750)	7.6-10.6% yield
Foreign Currencies IMM	Mar/June/Sept Dec					
British Pound		25,000 BP	¢/BP	5/100¢/BP ($12.50)	5¢ ($1,250)	157-250
Canadian Dollar		100,000 CD	¢/CD	1/100¢/CD ($10)	3/4¢ ($750)	82.5-102.5
Japanese Yen		12,500,000 JY	¢/JY	1/100¢/JY ($12.50)	3/5¢ ($750)	.33-.57
Swiss Franc		125,000 SF	¢/SF	1/100¢/SF ($12.50)	3/5¢ ($750)	36-68

CHAPTER ELEVEN

Contracts and Prices

Their last, extra-long session, Mr. S. tells Mr. E., covered a collection of miscellaneous information about the main commodities traded on the exchanges. All speculators must have some basic knowledge about them, no matter what their trading orientation is, whether tending toward the fundamental or the technical.

Another type of information equally important to all traders, says Mr. S., is concerned with the futures contracts themselves, which are based on these commodities. These are the real tools for financial advancement and certain details about them will be vital to know. Did Mr. E. study the chart he gave him, to familiarize himself with some of the aspects and details regarding the commodity contracts? Oh yes, he looked it over, Mr. E. replies. But he's not sure how much of the information he has retained. There's an awful lot of facts and figures there!

Mr. E., of course, shouldn't expect to learn everything right off, says Mr. S., because certainly it's too much to absorb at one sitting—or even ten. And much of it one need not try to commit to memory at all. There is always some chart like this one or some other to consult when you need to know something about a specific contract if you're considering trading in it. But he'll find that in time a number of the details will be readily known, through sheer association. For example, what's the size of a grain contract? Oh, 5,000 bushels, of course! Mr. E. responds. Always? asks Mr. S. Well, Mr. E. guesses so. . . .

No, says Mr. S., usually but not always. Has he heard of the Mid-America Commodity Exchange in Chicago? That sounds somewhat familiar to Mr. E. Is that the fairly new exchange there? Yes, says Mr. S., and it handles various popular commodities in contract sizes that are considerably smaller, in most cases, than ones at the Board of Trade or the Chicago Mercantile Exchange or the Commodity Exchange—Comex —in New York. It has 1,000 bushels in its wheat, corn, and soybean contracts. And the gold, silver, silver coins, and live hog contracts are smaller too. Oats, though, does have a 5,000-bushel contract—but then the price of oats remains less than that of most grains. New speculators should keep this exchange in mind for initial trades. Since its contract values are much smaller, dealing in them involves a smaller risk. And trading at this exchange is a good way to try out a few commodities at once, maybe short and long positions too, without running an extreme risk.

Before they do much else, Mr. S. goes on, speculators-in-training should learn to read *and* interpret this basic kind of chart. Now, he says, with the interrogator expression on his face, what are the different categories that are considered for each commodity contract? Mr. E. is prepared for this question. Well, first, he replies, the exchange or exchanges it is traded on. Then, the trading or delivery months. (He noticed that a few commodities are traded in almost every month. Shell eggs at the CME and gold at the IMM can be traded for delivery in virtually all months.) The contract size—very important, Mr. E. adds. How the price is quoted—as in cents per pound, dollars per ounce, cents per bushel, cents per dozen, that sort of thing. The minimum price fluctuation. And the daily limit.

Good! Mr. S. exclaims. The chart Mr. E. has shows price ranges per unit over a five-year period. Some charts have other things, such as *reporting position* and *position limit*. What are these? asks Mr. E. They need not concern the small speculator, says Mr. S., except to be glad that they are there. These tell ambitious speculators who have big assets how many contracts in a specific commodity they can acquire before they get classed as "large traders" and therefore will be watched by the exchange and the CFTC and limited in the future as to how many contracts they can add to this position. The contract valuations in such trading are well beyond the scope of the ordinary citizen-speculator.

That reminds him: did Mr. E. happen to notice a very important figure that's missing in this chart? Contract value? Mr. E. suggests. Sure! says Mr. S. It is not there because the value is always going to fluctuate along with the price. A chart like this, for long-term use, could hardly put down a highly changeable figure. Right! Mr. S. agrees. But still, when talking about contracts, it's good to know more or less what sort of valuation limits one may be dealing with. That's why he likes to keep current figures on the reference chart at his desk, in case he needs reminders of how much a contract would be worth.

How does he do that? Mr. E. wonders. The figures go out of date too fast. He noticed the great variation in price ranges in most commodities for the past five years. Oh, says Mr. S., it doesn't take long to figure current contract values. Mr. E. still looks dubious. Well, Mr. S. proposes, how would he get the value right now of a particular futures contract? From the financial section of a newspaper, of course, says Mr. E. So figure one, says Mr. S., handing him the very page Mr. E. needs to see. "Commodity Markets," the price quotation table reads. Pick a commodity, any commodity, and its delivery month, Mr. S. commands. Okay, December copper, says Mr. E., pleased with his task. He looks under the New York Commodity Exchange to find "Copper, December" and moves across the line to get the settlement price, which he writes down. Conveniently, the section also tells him the contract size: 25,000 pounds. And the price is quoted in cents per pound. So it's easy enough. He just multiplies one figure by the other:

$$\begin{array}{r} \$\ .995 \\ 25{,}000 \\ \hline 4975\,000 \\ 1990 \\ \hline 24{,}875.000 \end{array}$$

So that's December copper's current valuation, he declares. Good, his instructor responds. It would be even easier to do with a calculator. And of course Mr. E. knows how to calculate roughly the margin requirement for this contract, wouldn't he? Well, figuring it at 10% of the contract value, that would put it at $2,487.50, says Mr. E. So any speculator who's considering buying or selling a December copper contract would have to come up with around $2,500, then, Mr. S. concludes. Next week or next month the amount—based, of course, on the current contract value, which in turn is based on the current price—could be rather different.

Okay, moving on now, says Mr. S., please explain to him those other two figures pertaining to contracts: minimum price fluctuation and the daily limit. Mr. E. remembers having discussed them with Mr. T. on the trading floor of the CBT. The first gives the smallest increment by which a new trade can change the current or "market" price within the trading pit, he says. And the second is the largest amount by which the price can be changed during the day's trading. These figures, which are determined by the exchanges whenever tightening or loosening up must be done—as, for example, just before a contract month comes due—do change from time to time. But generally they stay within these bounds, which are obviously both protections and conveniences to speculators if a price is moving against them.

Speculators should be aware, however, Mr. S. cautions, that they can be trapped by these limit moves. For instance, if a trader is short a commodity and the price goes up sharply, he will want to buy back his contract. But with the daily limit, no one may be willing to sell at a price within the daily range imposed by the commodity exchange. In other words, the trading is all one-sided. Everyone wants to buy but nobody wants to sell! Under these conditions trading will be suspended for the day. On a bar chart, the day's entire price range will be recorded simply as a dot—with no high, low, or close. Actually, no trading may even have taken place. These limit moves can continue for days, until the price appreciates enough to induce some traders to sell. So the short trader will have to wait, taking losses all the while, until then.

Now that he's got the newspaper price quotation sheet there, Mr. S. continues, they may as well discuss that and other daily commodity price reports on which many small, at-home speculators depend in watching what is going on at the exchanges, whether or not they have taken particular positions there at the time. He's also going into this price-reading matter now because Mr. E. should know where to get his figures when he starts learning to do his own price charting, at their next session. Charting? Mr. E. repeats, apprehensive. He may love it! Mr. S. tells him. Just wait and see.

But before they go further into price reading, interrupts Mr. E., he'd like to ask something. For some while he has been wondering why the contract sizes are the way they are. Why, for example, is sugar at 112,000 pounds and coffee at 37,500 pounds and cotton at 50,000 pounds? Why is soybean meal at 100 tons (which, if a ton is 2,000 pounds, makes it 200,000 pounds—an awful lot of livestock feed)? Why are there 40,000 pounds for live cattle but 42,000 for feeder cattle?—and only 30,000 for live hogs? (Mr. E. is reading from the newspaper table.) Why are Maine potatoes at 50,000 pounds but Idaho Russets at 80,000? Orange juice at 15,000 pounds? Copper at 25,000 pounds? Plywood at 76,032 square feet? Eggs at 22,500 dozen? And, for that matter, the 5,000 bushels with the grains?

These contract sizes do seem rather arbitrary, Mr. S. agrees. But in most cases these figures were derived from the standard container used by commercials for packing and delivering particular commodities, whether bags, boxes, bins, or railroad cars. The level bushel for grains, with 2,150.42 cubic inches, is a good example. The contract sizes became multiples of the transportable units. In some instances volume (as with grains and lumber) seemed better than weight. And of course dealing with eggs in the traditional dozens makes sense. As for metals, the contract size ranges from the large weight of copper (25,000 pounds), to the small of silver (5,000 troy ounces), to the very small of gold (100 troy ounces) and platinum (50 troy ounces), somewhat depending on how precious the metal is. In the cases of some contracts, the large size might be troublesome to small investors. For instance, trading in potatoes or oats requires far less of a margin than trading in sugar.

Back to price reading now, Mr. S. continues. Mr. E. has seen how the daily price is really *prices,* plural. The day's opening price, the high and the low, and then the settlement prices are given in succession for each month, followed by a "change" figure, in plus or minus, which shows whether the price was above or below the previous day's closing or settlement price and by how much. Perhaps Mr. S. had better explain that each price-reporting service has a different way of giving these figures. So what paper you receive determines whether you'll read the prices quoted in dollars—using decimals—or in cents—given in hundreds. In prices for which there are fractions of a cent, as with grains, these appear as fractions: ¼, ½, ¾. The delivery months are usually shown by abbreviations using the first three letters, but sometimes— especially in price charts—they are given by only the initial letters in proper sequence, as JFMAMJJASOND. The nearest or a nearby delivery month is listed first, and when there are futures contracts given for distant months in the current year or even in the next year (as happens with a few financial instruments), the months appear in succession.

But what do the small *a, b,* and *n* next to the prices mean? asks Mr. E., studying the price-quotation list. Also, why do some commodities have two prices—as 448¼ and 448½? In thinly traded contracts, Mr. S. replies, there might not have been much trading that day, and so the asking price—*a*—or the bid price—*b*—might be given as the most representative price. The *n* means "nominal": the price agreed upon as the settlement price of the day. A *split close,* as in the figures Mr. E. gave, means that sales at both prices were completed in the closing minutes of trading.

Some reporting services carry more information interesting to commodity speculators than others do, Mr. B. goes on. The *Wall Street Journal,* for example, also has a column on cash prices for major commodities, which is valuable as a contrast with the futures prices next to it. That paper also has two other useful sets of figures. One shows the "lifetime high and low" prices for each futures contract since its introduction on the exchange, indicating how little or how much the price has moved during that time period, usually about a year. And the other gives the ''open-interest'' figure, informing the trader of how many contracts are being held by hedgers and speculators and giving some clue as to the overall interest in that commodity and that particular trading month.

Well, with all this talk about reading prices, says Mr. E., he's beginning to think that he may like price charting after all. In fact, his fingers are almost itching to get to it. He can keep busy in the meantime calculating the current contract values and approximate margin requirements in all those commodities, Mr. S. tells him. And that work will prepare him for more calculations to come in a future session, when they will discuss the use of money management techniques while trading. None of the arithmetic is hard. In fact, it could all be done by a fifth-grader using new math or old, figuring by hand or with a pocket calculator. The important thing is to know how to *do* the basic calculations. And since they are based on price, knowing how to read the latest price quotations is vital.

But now, for the rest of their session today, Mr. S. wants to talk some more about the fundamental approach to trading so as to lead into the technical, or charting approach—which will occupy them more in the next few meetings. And the fundamental approach has a lot to do with the main subject of the day: contracts and prices.

Does Mr. E. recall what the fundamentalist trader's aim is? Isn't it to study supply and demand factors concerned with a commodity? Mr. E. suggests. That's his technique, really, Mr. S. replies. His aim is to predict accurately what price changes will occur based on the information at hand. And of course this information is constantly being altered and added to.

Usually, says Mr. S., fundamentalists have to deal with crosscurrents of data that indicate that the price could go up *or* down in the future. They may conclude on the basis of accumulated evidence that the current price has not, in fact, been discounted as yet because traders have failed to notice or react to some relevant factor likely to affect supply and demand. They are ever alert to ''early warning'' signals that suggest the possibility for a price reversal in the future, against the current trend.

Suppose, Mr. S. proposes, that in the midst of vigorous market activity few traders seem to spot in a scientific journal a small article that explores potential ramifications of a new mosaic virus disease transmitted from infected seeds into the soil that may decimate the season's midwestern crop of wheat and be difficult to eradicate in future years? Or suppose that there is little talk as yet about the effect of the new popularity of sunflowers as a crop upon the supply of grains, which are rapidly being displaced in farmland acreage? These sunflowers grow prolifically, require very little care, and produce a high yield of oil and meal. Hundreds of thousands of acres in the United States are being given over to this new crop, which is not yet traded on the exchanges. What will the effect soon be on the soybean and corn markets? one might wonder.

Mr. E. seems startled at having to ponder such new issues, remembering how at their first meeting, when discussing fundamentals, he had been given "news" by Mr. S. that persuaded him to sell wheat contracts and buy soybeans.

To be completely successful, Mr. S. declares, fundamentalists will make their trading decisions by doing these four things: (1) learning all the factors that determine the future futures price, (2) interpreting these factors correctly, (3) making interpretations and acting on them before everyone else does, and (4) managing the trade in such a way that they won't lose their money even if they *are* right. But how could somebody lose unless he's *wrong?* asks Mr. E. and sees Mr. S. grin at him.

They have already talked about the first three steps toward success in the fundamental approach—which, as Mr. E. surely realizes, can never be 100% correct all the time, given the fantastic assortment of information that traders must deal with in order to make trading decisions. But let's say that in a certain situation a speculator is absolutely right: he knows exactly what the price will eventually be when the delivery month comes up. Say that in January he decides that October sugar should really be selling for 10¢ a pound, but it is now 9¢. He takes his $10,000 capital and buys ten contracts of October sugar at 9¢. With 112,000 pounds of sugar in each contract, each cent of change in price means—How much? he asks Mr. E. Well, says Mr. E., multiplying in his head, $1,120 per contract, multiplied by ten contracts, makes $11,200 altogether. So, continues Mr. S., he figures that when sugar goes from 9¢ up to 10¢ he stands to make a profit of about $11,000 on his long contracts. Wow! Mr. E. exclaims.

But hold it! Mr. S. cautions. Does Mr. E. spot where the speculator has made himself vulnerable? Mr. E. ponders for a moment. Prices don't just move in one way—up or down. The price of sugar could go *down* before it goes up, he announces. So if it went down to 8¢, he would have to produce the margin maintenance to cover the decline in contract value, and doing so would cost him the $11,000 he expects to make.

That's exactly right, Mr. S. compliments his student. The speculator has made perhaps a fatal mistake in his logic. He has figured out precisely where sugar will be come October. But he has let his prescience take precedence over his common sense, making him overextend himself in the certainty that he will be right. In that temporary dip in price the speculator must deposit this new money, about equal to the initial margin, with his broker. He can't just assure his broker that sugar is bound to go up again in just a little while and ask the broker to please stand by him and be patient! No, the only way he can persuade the broker of his integrity is to produce the cash needed to maintain the margin. And he cannot do that because he has invested most of his capital in the initial transaction. The brokerage must therefore sell his sugar position to halt further losses. And then what? Well, sugar of course eventually does go clear up to 10¢, just as he had predicted—but without him on board.

And that's just one of the problems with a strictly fundamental approach to trading, Mr. S. says, especially when compounded by ignoring proper money management. Even if a small speculator is a remarkably astute oracle, if he's only a notch behind the big traders in determining the effect of a new item and acting on it, he'll find that the market price is already discounted—adjusted to the change. Or if he's a notch ahead of everyone else, as with this sugar trade, the price may quite possibly move against him substantially before everyone else in the market "catches up" with him, so that finally the contract achieves its "correct" price and valuation.

With that bitter lesson in sugar trading as a forecast, says Mr. S., his apprentice can better understand the importance of wise money management in speculating—which they'll take up far more fully in a later session. If this speculator, for example, had bought only two contracts at 9¢, he would have had the extra capital needed for maintaining the margin when the price dipped down. This is a case of poor judgment combined with the urge to get-rich-quick, resulting in financial ruin for a speculator who might otherwise have been quite competent in determining the direction and dimension of a futures price change.

Remember, says Mr. S., that small speculators also work at a definite disadvantage if they rely too much on the fundamental approach. There are thousands of traders, professional traders, who are constantly analyzing every tidbit of information that may affect the price of a commodity. Of course, not all these traders analyze correctly; but many of them do. The many intelligent, experienced individuals and firms who study the markets constantly and make decisions according to their findings back up these decisions with their hard-won money. It isn't at all just a matter of disinterested scrutiny, with no great personal risks being run by someone sitting in an ivory tower in a government building or a university, surveying the American business scene.

So most of the time small speculators simply must figure that whatever news they receive has already been taken into account, to set the price of the futures contract that it now has. Since the only thing that will change the price is new information that is *not* expected—random information, if you will—small traders do have a chance in sheer probabilities: as much of a chance, perhaps, as anybody if they trade prudently. Therefore, speculators do not try to predict the value of a commodity at some future date, for that has already been done by the market. The best way to estimate the price of a commodity in six months' time is just to pick up the newspaper and see what the latest price for a six-months-out contract is, since that's the consensus of experts. The unforeseen new information that will change the price, though, has *not* been predicted—since it is a random event. And bullish news will cause the price to rise; bearish news will cause it to fall. They'll be talking about this very randomness, Mr. S. promises, in a later meeting, when considering the actuarial approach to trading.

Still, speculators might keep themselves profitably busy some of the time by looking for possible discrepancies between the current futures price and the probable price in the future. Generally, says Mr. S., factors are classified in ways that affect price movements. Turning to his chalk-board, he notes down these categories:

SUPPLY AND DEMAND

KIND OF COMMODITY—SEASONAL

PRODUCTION COSTS

We've seen how the first matter contributes significantly to pricing, Mr. S. goes on. There are plenty of figures available from the government and other sources that anticipate both production and consumption; they are based on past statistics and on projections of supplies and needs, national and international. Included in the supply figures are the *carry-overs*, the stored commodities from the previous season.

Theoretically, many commodities—the agricultural ones in particular—have a regular seasonal price change, which fluctuates according to the probable oversupply at harvest time followed by the rising cost due to shipping and storage costs plus diminished supply. Frequently this seasonal variation is totally discounted or figured into the futures cost, down to the last nickel. The buying or long commercial hedgers are especially good at calculating futures contract prices in order to protect themselves fully during future times of need of a specific commodity. The kind of commodity, then, must always be taken into account when studying futures prices. Many tend to behave in similar ways: the grains are a good example. Others have individual patterns of what one might call "irregularity," when supply and demand get out of kilter enough to cause abnormally high or low prices. Crops like cocoa, coffee, and orange juice are good examples of commodities for which a speculator might anticipate discrepancies to occur.

As for production costs entering into prices, Mr. S. says, it is of course realized that money is always expended in growing or mining or otherwise producing a specific raw commodity. So in theory, anyway, the price should not fall below what the commodity costs to produce. But here is a place where supply and demand come into play again. If there's a huge oversupply of a commodity and hardly anybody wants it right then, the price *can* drop below the production cost. The primary commercial might figure that some income is better than none—unless the commodity can be stored until the price improves. But that is difficult to do with many farm products, the most difficult one just now being shell eggs.

The reverse situation happens, Mr. S. continues, whenever there is a shortage of supply relative to demand. Regardless of the cost of producing a commodity, the market price can reach levels as yet unattained. At such times the speculators who shrewdly or luckily bought contracts make the big profits. On the losing side are the processing commercials who didn't adequately hedge, the speculators who sold contracts and now must buy them back and—guess who? asks Mr. S.

The public itself, Mr. E. answers promptly. Yes, Mr. S. agrees, since increased wholesale costs ultimately get passed along to be absorbed by the consumers themselves. However, he adds, please remember that there is a self-correcting aspect in high prices, regardless of what caused them. High prices encourage more production of a commodity, and increased production brings on an oversupply, which then causes a price drop, which in turn discourages production, leading once more to an undersupply or scarcity. One can depict the economic scene rather like this, says Mr. S., picking up his chalk and starting to draw:

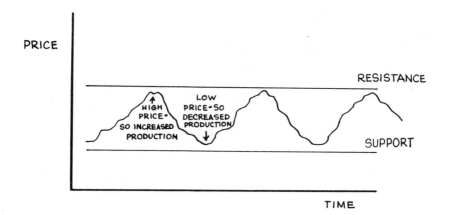

COMMODITY SPECULATION FOR BEGINNERS

Remember our old graph showing supply and demand working in conjunction with price rises and falls? See how the cycles are actually built into the mechanism itself. And if the supply gets too great, the commodity price may actually fall below the "support" line, which is tied into production costs. And if the supply is much too low and the demand remains strong, the price may then rise above the "resistance" line, which is geared to what the consuming public seems willing to pay for a processed product. But the situation rarely lasts for more than a season or so: a farmer will plant the high-priced, scarce crop, not the low-priced, overproduced one. Thus the market allocates resources between producers and consumers.

In some cases, though, says Mr. S., the market price of a raw commodity may not affect the public much at all—evading buyer resistance and protest, as happened with coffee a few seasons ago—*if* it winds up as only a very small part of the final product. Take copper, for instance. It gets into automobiles and electrical equipment, but the amount that is used is minor compared with that of other components, so that manufacturers may not be unduly perturbed over a surge in copper prices, which then must be passed on to customers. Even with bread this can be true, Mr. S. adds. Regular bread consists mostly of wheat, with a few other ingredients added. The costs of processing the wheat and baking the bread and then marketing it make up a large portion of the total retail price of the finished product that the public purchases in the stores. As the cost of a loaf of bread goes above $1, people inevitably remember the good old days when it was 25¢ or less. And most of the time, they loudly blame the wheat speculators at the exchanges for the terrible prices they now have to pay.

But look at the figures! exclaims Mr. S. Even taking inflation into account, the farmer himself earns little more than he used to, whether selling independently or on the exchange. The speculator himself isn't making any more: after all, he makes his profits from price changes in his favor. No, it's the production and processing and marketing costs that occur *after* the trading that are causing the sharp rise in bread prices. And mostly, he comments, these charges are for labor expended on the wheat once it leaves the futures contract stage. Therefore the notorious "middleman" isn't the speculator at all! avows Mr. S. almost heatedly. It's whoever helps that wheat get made into a loaf that is now sitting on the supermarket shelf—including its advertisers. The modern "food chain" from field to supermarket is a far cry indeed from that time when producer and consumer met and bargained directly in the town marketplace. And each step removed from the primary transaction between producer and retail merchant adds another increment of cost. So that, as far as the public is concerned, few commodities it uses actually have prices that directly reflect the age-old workings of supply and demand.

And now, says Mr. S., rising to indicate that their trading-talk session is coming to an end, how does Mr. E. feel about calculating the wide range in contract values, based on the price-per-unit figures in the commodity list he gave him? That way, he'll get a good idea of the great variation in both prices and contract values in each commodity listed.

Fine, says Mr. E. He actually feels eager to see for himself just how much a particular contract might be worth in dollars. Turning to go, he gives a backward glance at the framed antique woodcut of an ear of corn emerging from its sheath of husk. How little he knew only a few weeks ago about what makes the price of corn—and cornbread!

CHAPTER TWELVE
Price Charting

Today is charting day! announces Mr. S. cheerily. Mr. E.'s expression, though, is rather glum. He's still not sure that he'll like making charts or reading them. While looking through the various books about trading that Mr. S. has lent him, he has come to believe that commodity speculators spend most of their time consulting or preparing these boring charts! he declares. Do they ever get around to actual trading?

But Mr. S. just laughs. His pupil will be surprised to find out how much they can actually learn from these charts, he says. But he knows what Mr. E. means. Often these how-to books do resemble textbooks in their great attention to graphs and tables of statistics, and so they are rather offputting to beginners who don't yet understand the need for such close study and who may, in fact, someday manage to trade successfully without being nose-in-the-book scholars. But technicians, or chartists, aren't the only ones who fixate on mapping things as the way to approach trading. Fundamentalists become just as dependent on their "models," their long lists of intricate figures and mathematical calculations that break down supply and demand factors into formulas that the traders hope will guide their position taking in the markets.

And all the charts, says Mr. S., seem to proliferate in kind and number every year, so that there are more and more to keep track of, if one is so inclined. But don't let all these charts and calculations and opinions bother or discourage him! he tells Mr. E. In time he'll learn to pick and choose whatever information he wants from all this activity, for his own purposes. Right now, though, it's highly important to know at least the basic factors with which each trading approach concerns itself. During the past sessions they have generally covered the fundamentals field. Beginning now, Mr. E. is going to get a minimal acquaintance with the technical approach—which, yes, does involve knowing about price charting, and also about a few other kinds of charts that keep track of what the market is doing and has done, as tipoffs for its future behavior.

Technicians, Mr. S. goes on, are not very interested in the workings of supply and demand and their effect on price fluctuations. By studying price movements on charts, they hope to predict effectively the future futures contract prices—and how the prices may change in the process of getting there. Think of fundamental traders, Mr. S. suggests, as people looking at a commodity arena through a telescope, trying to get a long-range view of what the price should be by the time the delivery month comes along. Technical traders, on the other hand, are busily peering through a microscope, examining all sorts of points and wiggles in charts, and anticipating short-range movements and trends in the prices.

Mr. E., though, suspects that neither way of looking at things is right for him. He doesn't have the patience and determined vision of an astronomer or a microbiologist, he says. What *he* likes is the activity and excitement in the trading pits, the overall sense of involvement in the American economic scene. Reality, in other words, not just figures and lines on paper. And that's what he misses when he sees all those charts!

But all those charts, Mr. S. reminds him, attempt to reduce and reproduce this very reality of the marketplace. These compact, graphic ways of conveying information can be greatly useful to traders—depending on what signals they are looking for when practicing their own personal speculating styles. Technicians keep charts on many things: prices, volume of trading, open interest, commitments of traders, basis, spreads, moving averages, market sentiment, warehouse receipts, the difference between ten- and five-day moving averages or between twenty- and ten-day moving averages, oscillators of all kinds, even hog-corn ratios. He wouldn't be surprised if some don't correlate the phases of the moon with swings in prices! (And who knows? says Mr. S. There may be something to it.) Also, far more than fundamentalists, technicians take interest in the psychology of traders, believing that the price movements mostly show human group actions and reactions to a variety of situations that are far more complex than straightforward responses to supply and demand. Chartists are convinced that the current market is displaying a succession of activities that, after being graphed and contrasted with one another, yield a message for astute speculators, who will thereby take new positions or correct old ones already taken. Technicians also often believe that certain commodities' prices have unique behavior patterns that get repeated.

But what happens if several thousand chartists believe the same thing and act on it? asks Mr. E. Then obviously, answers Mr. S., they'll make the very thing happen that they predicted would happen! That, of course, is a most convincing reason why any speculator should know what the chartists are saying and doing at any time in a commodity market that interests him. Because whether or not he agrees with them or wants to go their way (if he can get in adequately in time), he must be aware of their inevitable effect on price changes and trading commitments. Just as, at the same time, he should be alert to changing situations in the fundamentals, in supply and demand, which also have affected trading by the time he gets the news.

Then why should the small speculator bother to do anything, if the know-it-all professional traders have already gotten there ahead of him? Mr. E. naturally wonders. Because, Mr. S. answers, nobody and no approach ever in fact does know everything. As they have discussed before, it's virtually impossible to know everything that needs to be known, including random future events, in order to determine future price changes. Even the big pros are wrong perhaps 50% of the time in position taking, for all their wisdom and experience, their models and charts! But everybody still keeps looking for the magic formula, a wonderful trading secret that will finally extract everything from the myriad facts and figures relating to commodity fundamentals and market behavior.

Then surely mathematicians would be highly successful at speculating if they put their wisdom and skills to work in commodity trading, Mr. E. ventures. At this Mr. S. has to laugh. Some of the *least* successful traders he has ever known or heard of, he says, are in fact mathematicians! This observation initially surprised, but then it began to make sense. Mathematicians tend to get so fixated on finding workable situational equations—having to do with Fourier analysis, wave theories, oscillations, and other abstruse concepts—that they get quite carried away with their abstractions and then fail to notice that plain old reality is refusing to conform to their solutions, on which, perhaps, they invested hard-earned savings.

Well, Mr. E. comments, that actually makes him feel better about his own chances as a speculator notably deficient in mathematical sophistication. Mr. S. assures Mr. E. that he already possesses all the talent he needs for the calculations involved in trading. Some things are more important than mathematical genius—common sense, along with inclinations to doubt and question and to look for the practical, efficient approach in decision making rather than an intellectualized one.

Their conversation, however, has been leading them astray from the principal topic of today's meeting, observes Mr. S. But he is persuaded that the side trip was necessary in order to convince his pupil that there are excellent and valid reasons for learning to use charts. They are not as forbidding and formidable as Mr. E. seems to consider them. And Mr. S.'s own method of teaching chart reading—his pupils learn by actually making them—may be able to arouse and sustain Mr. E.'s interest. Oh! says Mr. E. quite agreeably, he's now quite willing to commence the lesson of the day.

The graphs that speculators primarily use, says Mr. S., are the *commodity price bar charts* and the *point-and-figure charts*. Mr. E., of course, has already seen plenty of both in his perusals of books and booklets about trading. But sometimes not until someone tries to make them personally does the unique usefulness of each kind become apparent.

Mr. S. is now facing the chalkboard. He draws a vertical line and then from the bottom of it a horizontal line toward the right. Upon the first he makes small lines, or gradations, to which he assigns numbers, in increments of five as they go up, beginning with 90. Upon the horizontal line he sets a regular series of downward verticals which, he says, will represent trading days. Price will be charted against time in this bar chart in a line that starts from the lowest price in a day's trading on an exchange and move up to the day's highest price—giving the price range for that day.

For example, says Mr. S., here's a commodity that had a high of $112 and a low of $108. And the closing price was $109: so he puts a small tick in the appropriate spot. He then asks Mr. S. to fill in subsequent prices for nine days and reads off the figures for him:

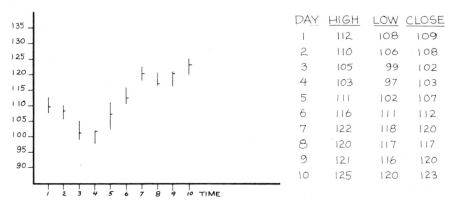

DAY	HIGH	LOW	CLOSE
1	112	108	109
2	110	106	108
3	105	99	102
4	103	97	103
5	111	102	107
6	116	111	112
7	122	118	120
8	120	117	117
9	121	116	120
10	125	120	123

Mr. E., chalk in hand, is enjoying himself. The bar chart, Mr. S. tells him, is the most frequently used price chart. He'll notice that there will be variations on it, such as a line put straight through for the median price or a dot used for the opening price, depending on what the chart maker finds significant. The bar chart can be adapted for other time periods, such as a week or a month of trading, and doing so condenses information better for long-range viewing.

There is another type of chart that many traders find valuable: the point-and-figure or P & F, chart. Oh, Mr. E. remarks, the one with all the *X*s and *O*s. Which aren't shorthand for hugs and kisses, says Mr. S., but stand for rising prices and falling prices.

First, he declares, you need a grid type of graph paper. Having erased the bar chart, he now prepares the chalkboard by roughly drawing a large square and within it a number of regularly spaced horizontal and vertical lines. On the left-hand side he sets down an ascending price scale similar to the previous one. Okay, he tells Mr. E., he needs to have some price figures now. The usual P & F chart is made by looking only at the closing price.

The chartist must make two decisions: (1) What is a "significant" price change in the same direction that the price has been moving in? and (2) What is a "significant" price change in the reverse direction? Mr. S. will assume that five points in the same direction is significant; any less he won't bother to chart. Further, it takes twenty points in the opposite direction to signal a "reverse" in prices, and this starts a new column. This would be a one-to-four.

So here are the closing prices, says Mr. S., for a sequence of days. And he writes them down on his chalkboard:

DAY	CLOSE	COMMENTS
1	499	PRICE UP FROM 480
2	500	PLACE "X" IN 500 NOT UP TO 500 YET
3	504	NO CHANGE
4	505	PLACE "X" IN 505
5	504	NO CHANGE
6	490	NO CHANGE
7	470	A REVERSAL [505-20=485] PLACE "O" IN 470
8	465	PLACE "O" IN 465
9	470	NO CHANGE
10	485	A REVERSAL [465+20=485] PLACE "X" IN 485

And here, says Mr. S., is the chart that accommodates them in a one-to-four P & F chart:

510					
505	X				
START→ 500	X	O			
495	X	O			
490	X	O			
485	X	O	X		
480	X	O	X		
475		O	X		
470		O	X		
465		O			
460					

A chart like this, Mr. S. explains, means that any reversal price change that goes a specified number of points above or below the latest closing price thus far recorded will initiate the starting of a new column to the right. There will be *O*s if the price has dropped, *X*s if the price has risen—with any additional prices in between the reversal *X*'d or *O*'d in the new column too. This will be continued as new prices come in *until* there again is a specified "significant" reversal, which will trigger the next column of opposing *X*s or *O*s.

Now that Mr. E. has seen how several columns were filled in by the price changes he had provided, Mr. S. suggests that he come up with some new random prices of his own, within the same general range, and then do the next charting sequence himself. While Mr. E. is setting down numbers Mr. S. is telling him that he's obviously a participant type, not a spectator. Many decision makers learn far better by doing things than by sitting and pondering theories. That's one reason why his coaching method involves far more activity than book reading. It isn't that speculators are illiterate: far from it! But many are restless types who don't want to pore over scholarly texts. They want to take part in action and see the results of action.

But what is the real purpose of these point-and-figure charts? asks Mr. E., still involved with his assignment at the chalkboard. They are intended to show only the significant price changes over an indefinite period of time—unlike the regular time that is plotted in the bar charts, Mr. S. replies. One column could represent a day's trading and the one next to it a whole week or more of trading. What is shown is a general trend toward rising or falling as well as the price range. P & F charts display overall price movements and filter out ingredients in bar charts that are considered nonessential distractions, such as daily transaction ranges. The various patterns that are made up of filled-in graph squares can have definite meanings for P & F chartists; this is especially true of resistance- or support-breaking new trends that should deliver definite buying or selling signals to the attentive trader.

The more finely tuned these P & F charts are to reversals, Mr. S. continues, the more sensitive they will be to price changes that may be significant. Some chartists make detailed measurements of the column's dimensions in so-called *congestion areas,* as though such calculations could provide magical solutions, adds Mr. S. But much of the time, technicians are searching for, and finding, many of the same price-movement patterns, or formations, that are located and labeled among the price bar charts.

Mr. E. will surely find it interesting to see how a P & F chart can differ considerably from a bar chart, even though both are based on the same daily trading figures. Mr. S. notes down a list of prices for ten days, roughly sketches first a bar chart and then, alongside, a P & F chart with a five-point increment and fifteen-point reversal:

DAY	HIGH	LOW	CLOSE
1	10	5	10
2	18	6	12
3	26	18	25
4	32	25	28
5	45	35	45
6	45	28	31
7	32	25	25
8	27	26	27
9	20	15	17
10	16	10	10

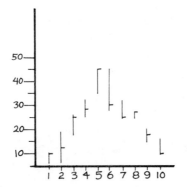

5 × 15

But which kind works best? asks Mr. E. inevitably. Mr. S. shrugs. Each is good in its way, he declares. Which one you use depends on what information or patterns you're looking for, on what your basic trading methods require. He himself uses both but has never felt that it is necessary or indeed wise to rely a great deal on what the charts "tell" a trader to do. More about this later!

And by the way, Mr. S. goes on, these charts can be plotted not only for daily activity but also for weekly or monthly activity. That is, you can plot the high, low, and close for an entire week or the high, low, and close for a month.

Since each contract has a limited life—July 1981 wheat will "go off the board" in July of 1981—these longer-term charts continue plotting from one contract to the next. Such charts are sometimes called *continuation charts*. Each bar, says Mr. S., is marked for the high, low, and close given for a week, with the week's highest and lowest prices graphed along with its closing price. At switchover day, when the contract becomes due and therefore the futures price becomes the cash price, both the old and the new contract prices (for the succeeding month) are plotted, often creating a double-length bar, like so:

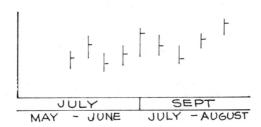

Details like these don't matter much, Mr. S. explains, except in special cases, like potatoes, where bar charts can be misleading. He erases the earlier chart to sketch several new samples—which might record what happens on a switchover day. See how the continuation chart combines the prices for both the October and the December futures contracts, he says:

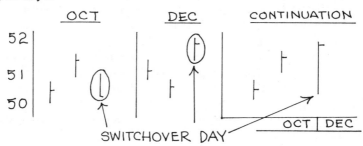

159

And notice, Mr. S. goes on, how the time is divided into the *contract* months, below which are the actual months themselves in which trading has gone on.

Mr. S. is now roughly sketching a horizontal framework for a five-year long-range bar chart for a representative commodity. He has selected cotton somewhat arbitrarily from a book in his bookcase to show Mr. E. the overall effect of recording weekly prices over a lengthy period of time, so that Mr. E. can see the wide shift in highs and lows:

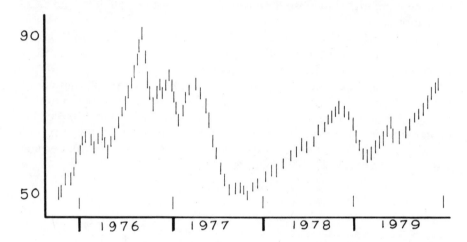

On a published long-range price chart, of course, Mr. S. points out, considerably more detail can be shown, with prices even given in monthly intervals.

Now, proposes Mr. S., let's look at this subject of price charting from the point of view of what *we* are mostly concerned with as speculators. We want to know whether the price of a commodity is going to turn around and head in the other direction, up or down, or if it is going to continue moving in the same direction. We would certainly be very happy to detect chart patterns that will tell us what will happen.

Generally, Mr. S. declares, there are two main pattern groups. The first are called *reversals* and the second *continuations*. As one would expect, the first pattern is supposed to signal a major reversal in price—from down to up or from up to down. The second is supposed to signal where a price trend pauses, or "rests," before continuing in the same direction. And the term *continuation* shouldn't be confused with a continuation chart.

Consider, he says, beginning to draw, the commodity price that is heading down and then abruptly turns back up again, making a pattern like so:

160

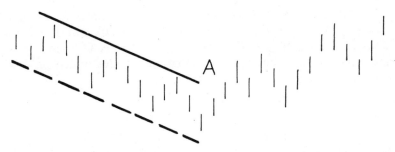

This pattern could very well be spotted as a "V bottom," Mr. S. remarks. Notice that the *downtrend line* was broken at *A*. The trendline for a *downward* sloping price is made by connecting two or more relatively *high* days. An *upward* trendline connects the *low* prices.

But what's the other line, the dotted one, that Mr. S. has just drawn below the trendline? asks Mr. E. Oh, that's the *channel line,* he is told. It parallels the trendline, whether above or below it, more or less connecting the highs or the lows. The space between them is called the *channel,* and prices tend to stay within its limits as long as the trend continues up or down.

And so, says Mr. S. adding another set of price bars to his chalkboard, here is a corresponding *uptrend line* and reversal for a price turning around from up to down:

Now, he tells Mr. E., look at this one:

That, he says, is known as a *double bottom.* Then he adds a third segment that repeats the pattern again:

Does Mr. E. care to name this one? A *triple bottom?* he ventures. Correct! says Mr. S. And how about taking the chalk and drawing what he thinks a *saucer,* or *rounding, bottom* might look like? Mr. E. steps forward and makes a tentative sketch of bars under which he draws a dishlike curve:

Mr. E. is seeing that price charting can be fun! Mr. S. remarks. It's a fine way to exercise one's imagination. For example, here is what technicians call a *head-and-shoulders top;* they often find it a highly significant price-reversal pattern:

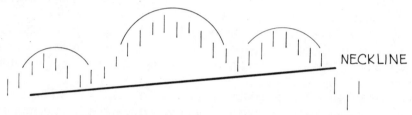

Notice the somewhat horizontal line? It's the "support" here, the neckline. So, says Mr. S., his pupil may now depict a *head-and-shoulders bottom,* complete with a reversed neckline:

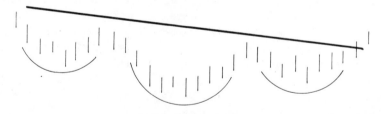

Very good! Mr. S. compliments Mr. E. Now, he'd like to point out that these head-and-shoulders patterns often seem to signal reversals in price. Whether this happens because of natural causes, as a sort of "wave" dynamics, or because traders expect it to happen and therefore *make* it happen through position taking, Mr. S. observes, he and other speculators may never know.

Those were some examples of reversal patterns. Let's consider now some continuation patterns, Mr. S. proposes. This means that the price "rests" a bit before continuing on its same path. He is drawing again, and adding trendlines to the small bars. Now, he says to Mr. E., please label which one looks like a *wedge* and which a *triangle:*

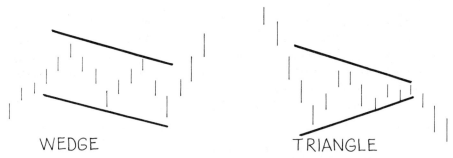

WEDGE   TRIANGLE

Fine, says Mr. S. Actually, the figure at the right is called a *symmetrical triangle*. The direction of *breakout*—going above or below the trendlines—is supposed to indicate which way the price will continue to move. Some chartists claim that with some triangles one can predict the direction of breakout before it occurs, as with these ascending and descending triangles:

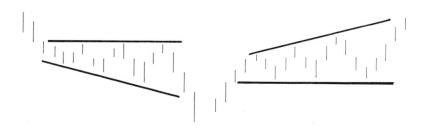

There are many, many other patterns in the technicians' carpetbag, Mr. S. continues, plus some more in the point-and-figure charts. But there's not enough time right now to consider them. And remember that these are just representative patterns that were drawn here. The charts of price variations in a *real* commodity don't turn out so neatly, and discerning patterns in them at all can be very difficult.

But let's take a look at some other tools of the technician, Mr. S. suggests. First of all, there's the *moving average*. Mr. E. knows, of course, how to average five numbers. So let's take the closing prices for the last five days of trading. Well, with a five-day moving average, a technician is always taking the last five days. In other words, he calculates each new closing price into his average and then drops the closing price of six days ago. Like this:

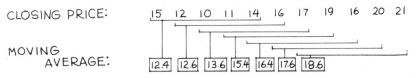

CLOSING PRICE: 15 12 10 11 14 16 17 19 16 20 21

MOVING
    AVERAGE: 12.4 12.6 13.6 15.4 16.4 17.6 18.6

The average moves along with the price chart. The more days that are calculated into the average, the less that any one price change makes a difference. So a five-day moving average would be more "sensitive" than a ten-day one; a twenty-day moving average would be more "sluggish" than a fifteen-day one. It might look a bit like this, says Mr. S., sketching:

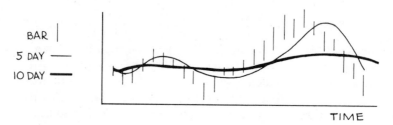

Technicians have developed all sorts of rules to use moving averages, such as "Buy when the five-day line crosses the ten-day, if moving from below to above."

Oscillators can be used in much the same way, Mr. S. declares. A simple oscillator can be developed from just the closing price of the day —merely subtract yesterday's close from today's and plot the results. For example:

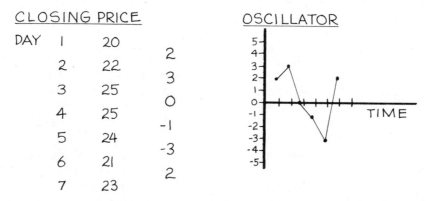

But of course, says Mr. S., such a simple oscillator is not too valuable. The more sophisticated ones take differences between five- and ten-day moving averages, say, or between twenty- and ten-day moving averages. Why are they called "oscillators"? Mr. E. wonders. Because the lines have the tendency to oscillate back and forth, sometimes quite dramatically, around zero, Mr. S. answers.

In any case, Mr. S. asserts, the issue of whether an investigation of past price behavior can determine the future course of the price is still hotly debated. Perhaps all these various patterns come about in a purely random way. Consider an illustration of this, says Mr. S. Suppose you turn on the radio and all you hear is static. That means one of two things: either there is nothing else on that particular channel except static, or there is a signal there that is hidden by the static.

Therefore, he goes on, you can try to tune the station in better. If you then get recognizable sounds—music or human voices—a station is in fact broadcasting at that spot on the dial. But if you continue to get static, the matter is still inconclusive. Perhaps there is music hidden underneath that static. You might then continue to fine tune the radio over and over, hoping eventually to hear some human sounds.

Now this, Mr. S. explains, is the problem involved with the signal-to-noise ratio. If you see or hear something that is jumbled, there may well really be a message hidden in all that noise. The solution in that situation then is to extract the signal from the accompanying static.

What he's getting at, says Mr. S., is that technicians claim that the chart patterns may look random, but that hidden in them somewhere is a design that, when decoded, should allow them to predict the future price swing of a commodity. In other words, they claim that there really are signals under all that noise.

But the truth may be, Mr. S. goes on, that this contention has never been wholly proved. Any further fine tuning of the static may just result in more static. That does not mean that the signal is *not* there. But it also does not mean that the signal *is* there. It's inconclusive. So far no one has found that hidden signal with absolute certainty, though many believe that it can be done.

But what about computers? asks Mr. E. Can't they help speculators? Professionals—traders and brokers—do use them, says Mr. S., but so far they really don't seem to be any more accurate than human minds themselves in locating signals or, more importantly, in predicting future price changes. But, of course, if people or machines could do so with great accuracy, speculators would be soon out of business! And that seems highly unlikely, since the entire commodity network is made up of so many complex and often highly unpredictable variables.

Even with computers, the futures markets are still in existence, obviously, says Mr. S. But that does not mean that computers are worthless in trading. For one thing, they allow a large commodity pool or brokerage house to keep track of their equity and customers' accounts. Computers can also be used to calculate moving averages, oscillators, and the like. These can be used as evidence (circumstantial at that) of a price move, but they are certainly not the crystal balls looking into the future that so many expected. Computers aren't magical, after all. But they are able to manipulate a lot of numbers very rapidly and also contain phenomenal "memories" in their data storage banks so that data can be instantaneously retrieved.

But back to the price charts now, says Mr. S., and their connection with traders' decision-making processes. Has Mr. E. ever heard the expression *technical rally?* Well, he'll hear or read it often enough in years to come when he's trading. What is it? Mr. S. will provide an example. Say the price of a commodity has been doing something like this:

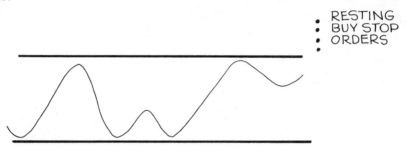

The price has persistently bounced up from the support and then bounced down from the resistance, Mr. S. observes. Probably a lot of people placed a *buy-stop order* right above the resistance; which means that the commodity will be bought when it rises above a certain price.

What kind of traders would place a buy-stop order? asks Mr. E. And what does it mean, anyway? It's an order placed earlier with a broker that will get "triggered" once a specific price has been reached. So mainly two types of traders give them: those who are short the commodity and therefore afraid of a large run-up in price, and so have decided to get out of their contracts if the price breaks above the resistance; and those, mainly technicians, who feel that a breakout above the resistance portends a long-term run-up in price and therefore go running with the bulls.

What can happen consequently, Mr. S. explains, is that almost anything—even a rumor—can cause the price to edge up beyond the resistance, where there are plenty of potential buyers waiting: all the buy-stop orders are touched off, and the price really shoots up. However, it won't necessarily keep going up if there is no underlying fundamental reason for the commodity to continue upward in price. In this case, the only fuel feeding the rise was the batch of buy-stop orders. Then all the buyers will have already bought, there will no buyers left, and so the price will fall backward again, perhaps sinking well below the original resistance line.

The same phenomenon, of course, Mr. S. points out, can happen in reverse with the support line and *sell-stops,* which are used by long traders who are wary of bearish moves and also by technicians looking for the very start of a downtrend. For a time their moves may cause an unnatural flurry of rummaging around below the support line, but the prices may suddenly take an upturn that will make them unusually grumpy.

Mr. S. notices that Mr. E. is beginning to look a bit glassy-eyed, as though he has already taken in too much information. He is staring at the chalkboard while Mr. S. erases it, almost as if he were watching television.

Wake up! Mr. S. urges him, and Mr. E. sits upright from his slouched position. The charts have begun to get to him after all, he admits. Are they over yet? he asks hopefully. Ah, stay a while more, says Mr. S. But only long enough to get his homework assignment. Mr. E. audibly groans. Once he's gotten a good night's sleep, Mr. S. promises, he's bound to love this work. He hands Mr. E. a sheet of paper. On it are prices for forty trading days. What is he supposed to do with them? asks Mr. E. Well, take them home, get out some graph paper, and then construct three charts—a bar chart, a P & F chart, and a five-day moving-average chart—based on these figures.

Not entirely to his surprise, Mr. E. grins. It'll be a challenge, he says as he departs.

CHAPTER THIRTEEN

More Technical Tools

The modern commodity trader, says Mr. S., has a number of other gadgets in his toolbox besides the various price charts to use for profitable endeavors. He has just looked over Mr. E.'s charting homework approvingly and then declared that they are ready to move on today to other forms of charting that assist in decision making and position taking.

Technicians, he continues, are very attentive to how volume and open interest change along with price. *Volume*—the number of contracts traded within a specified time period, as per day or week or month—may be an important indicator of the future trend in prices. But like everything else in commodity speculation, Mr. S. points out, there are no infallible rules; that is, rules that work consistently well all the time.

Now, what would a volume of one thousand contracts mean to Mr. E.? Well, he replies, probably that one thousand people bought a contract for a certain commodity, while an equal number sold. But he realizes, of course, that instead of a thousand buying and a thousand selling, there would actually be fewer participants, since one person can buy or sell many contracts. It is easier, though, to consider just two people per contract, one buyer and one seller, Mr. S. agrees.

But all right, he says, are those one thousand buyers buying new contracts they did not own? Or are they buying back the old contract they had formerly sold? For in the latter case, they would of course be canceling out their previous commitments. Hmmm, says Mr. E. wonderingly. How can one tell the difference?

That is where *open interest* comes in, Mr. S. points out. Ah, this begins to sound familiar to Mr. E., who remembers his discussion with Mr. T. at the clearing firm. Open interest, Mr. S. is saying, is the number of contracts currently in existence, or "open"—that is, a certain number of people have promised to buy a commodity come delivery month and the same number have promised to deliver the commodity. Now, he goes on, if the volume is one thousand contracts and the open interest increases by one thousand contracts, then all of the volume on that trading day, or in that trading week, went into creating new contracts. There are new buyers and sellers coming into the market.

On the other hand, says Mr. S., if the volume is one thousand contracts and the open interest decreases by one thousand contracts, then all ·of those buying that day were buying back what they had previously sold, and all of those selling were selling what they had previously bought. In practice, though, on any one day on an exchange, there is a mixture of new buying and selling that creates new contracts combined with buying and selling to liquidate existing contracts. So the situation can be complicated. Technicians who analyze price, volume, and open-interest data to get some indication of an impending price move likewise have developed some complex charting and interpretive techniques.

A typical clue, Mr. S. continues, might be picked up by a chartist if the commercials are engaging in *selective hedging*. We've seen how a commercial who buys and holds a commodity for future selling—a grain elevator operator, for example—will protect his position by selling the futures in that commodity. In this way he'll break even whether the price goes up or down, if his hedge is perfect. Well, if the price starts to get very low, the commercial may decide that it can't go down much further. Therefore he may not hedge his entire inventory but only part of it. True, he may realize that the price can drop even lower and that he is taking a risk by not being completely hedged. But he feels that this risk is one he can handle. This is very similar to the deductible clause in normal automobile insurance policies, Mr. S. points out. The insured party agrees to pay the first $100 or so of damages, accepting that risk that he can afford in order to decrease slightly his insurance premium.

In commodities, this selective-hedging clue can be picked up by seeing the open interest suddenly plummet. The speculator may then anticipate a price increase in coming months. Conversely, if the open interest remains very high during a period of high prices, commercials may be unloading their commodity onto an unsuspecting horde of speculators, and they will be preparing to deliver it to these unwary long traders, at the agreed-upon high price. But what happens then? asks Mr. E. The speculators, when faced with delivery, will naturally try to sell their contracts, Mr. S. answers. And this will actually bring about a sharp decline in prices, as speculators realize that they have "overbought" the commodity at an inflated price.

However, Mr. S. adds, it is often difficult to say with any certainty what "high" open interest is. One could compare current open interest with that of past years. Even so, there would be distortions, since any commodity might currently have more or less of a "following"—commercials and speculators dealing in futures contracts—than it did in prior years. Many commodities actually tend to experience periods of being popular, which may not necessarily be to anyone's advantage. Also, during times of volatile prices, certain commodities seem to require more hedging among the commercials involved in producing or processing them. In any case, a very rapid change in open interest, or a relatively unusual high or low amount, may portend a price turnaround, which of course is a source of avid concern to profit-seeking speculators, who hope to anticipate such an event.

Volume, says Mr. S., is often recorded as straight bars on a chart, which represent numbers and give a rather jagged appearance. And now he demonstrates by drawing vertical lines on his chalkboard:

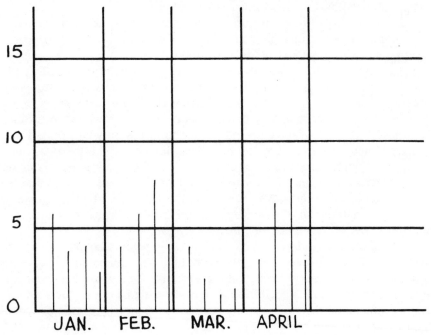

Regarding volume of trading, he says, many books and advisory services make a great to-do over it, open interest, and price action for just one day of trading. But this can be very misleading. Remember, the commodity exchanges are not there basically for the convenience and enrichment of speculators. Their primary function is to allow commercials—those in the real business of handling certain commodities—to hedge their normal activities, through the financial entry of opposite commercials and speculators in futures contracts.

So, Mr. S. points out, much of what happens in one day of trading in the pits on some exchange floor has absolutely nothing to do with the probable course of prices or the ultimate cash price when a delivery month comes due. It may simply reflect the sudden large offer or bid of a commercial hedger, with a speculator—frequently a pit trader or scalper —accommodating that hedge temporarily by buying or selling in an opposite position.

For instance, says Mr. S., a grain elevator operator somewhere might have had a farmer offer him 100,000 bushels of wheat at a certain cash price. The operator will check the futures price, and if there's enough of a difference—or *basis* (they'll talk about that word later, Mr. S. remarks) —to allow him a profit, he will sell futures contracts while buying the cash commodity itself. When the order for the sale of twenty contracts of wheat goes into the trading pit, it's usually a scalper who buys the contracts, often at a price slightly under what wheat was just trading at. Then the scalper will attempt to sell at just a high enough price above what he purchased it at, maybe only 1¢, in order to make a profit for his work in accommodating a hedger.

Yes, Mr. E. agrees, that's exactly what he himself saw happen at the Chicago Board of Trade, with Mr. T.'s friend the corn pit scalper. Ah, so Mr. E. comprehends the function of the scalper! says Mr. S. Well then, would he like to calculate the profit a scalper might make on a 1¢ price difference in this wheat trade? One cent on a contract of 5,000 bushels would be $50, so twenty contracts would make it $1,000, Mr. E. promptly replies. Not bad if one could do that in a morning of trading, he adds.

But Mr. S. would like to point out something: the entire transaction had nothing to do with what the grain elevator operator, the farmer, or the pit trader himself felt would happen to the price of wheat in the months to come! Each was only performing a day of business.

So speculators, Mr. S. amplifies, should keep in mind that a large part of trading activity—maybe even 50%—goes on to take care of hedgers, though that depends on the commodity and the time involved. Hedgers can take out a large number of short or long contracts, retaining their half of the open interest, while a series of individual speculators may

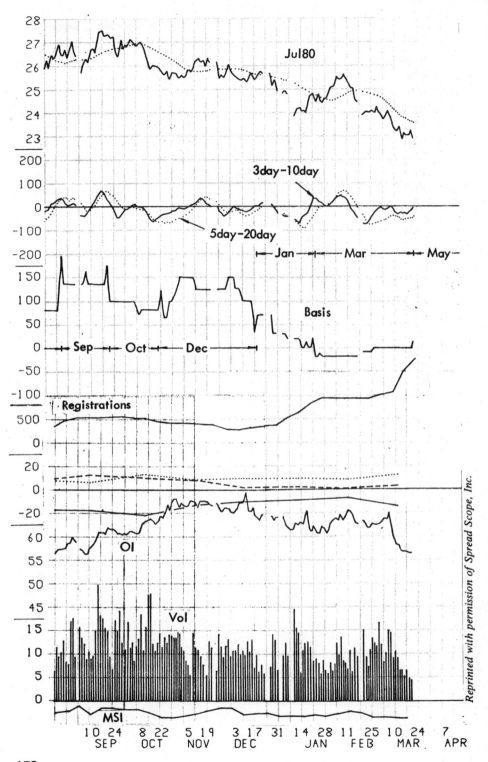

Jul80

3day-10day

5day-20day

Jan — Mar — May

Basis

Sep — Oct — Dec

Registrations

OI

Vol

MSI

10 24   8 22   5 19   3 17 31   14 28   11 25   10 24   7
SEP   OCT   NOV   DEC   JAN   FEB   MAR   APR

trade the contracts on the other side back and forth among themselves as the prices jump up and down. When hedgers occupy the "wrong" side of a contract, they make up for it by being able to sell or buy at an advantageous price in the cash commodity market. Any money they have lost in contracts has been paid almost as premiums to those speculators who virtually "insured" these positions against loss and now have collected profits for their risk taking. These fortunate speculators also collect from the losses of the unfortunate speculators who likewise occupied the losing positions.

Another thing to keep in mind, adds Mr. S., is that a lot of activity in trading at a particular time may involve *spread position taking*. Many of the larger, more sophisticated, professional traders regularly deal in spreads. These traders may be simultaneously buying wheat but selling corn, or selling August pork bellies and buying February ones, and so on. We'll discuss spreads in greater detail later.

In any case, says Mr. S., he doesn't know how some magical patterns of accumulation and distribution can be divined by studying the day-to-day trading charts that track prices, volume, and open interest. But the small, at-home speculator should know how to read them and how technicians interpret them. And there are still more trading factors that change with time and thus can be scrutinized in graph forms by chartists. The main ones, he says, are the commitments of traders, market sentiment index, warehouse receipts, basis, and spreads.

Do speculators have to chart all of those too? asks Mr. E., looking rather overwhelmed. No, says Mr. S. reassuringly. There are services that they can subscribe to that will do the charting for them. *Spread Scope* is one of them. Here on page 172, for example, is a page from that publication, which shows various different trading factors that have been charted week-by-week over a seven-month time period.

These charts aren't very difficult to learn to read, says Mr. S. But the most important thing for part-time speculators to understand is the concepts behind them, which are probably easier than many concepts connected with their regular occupations. Speculators, of course, are always searching for clues that will lead them into the best trading deals. Through the years, technicians have hit upon particular ones as being more dependable or intriguing than others. A highly important indicator to some chartists is the *commitments of traders* lists and charts. These show the percentages of hedgers and speculators involved in contract positions— net long and net short—and whether the speculators themselves are large traders or small speculators.

And here in their conversation Mr. S. sketches a sample chart for traders' commitments:

He explains the three kinds of lines by writing their meanings on his board:

.... % OF SMALL SPECULATORS NET LONG (+) OR NET SHORT (-)
____ " " LARGE " " " " "
____ " " HEDGERS NET LONG (+) OR NET SHORT (-)

But what do these various commitments actually show? asks Mr. E. Well, replies Mr. S., theoretically hedgers are neutral. The contracts they buy or sell cover their own business needs. They are the essential fuel, though, that keeps the market running, and their entry—the number of hedgers' contracts and whether they are short or long—indicates to traders whether the hedging action is being made to avoid price rises more than price drops or vice versa. In other words, hedgers react to a prevailing opinion that the market already seems to be heading in a bullish or bearish direction; new hedgers enter at certain points in response to new situations affecting their own financial positions.

It is vital to understand the hedgers' perspective on another matter besides price-change protection, Mr. S. points out, which is that banks increasingly refuse to lend money to commercials unless they are well or fully hedged. So whether it is the farmer who seeks capital in order to produce this year's crops or the processor who may ultimately buy this produce and will need borrowed capital to do so, hedgers are involved in opposite positions in the commodity market for good reasons. Thus when a large hedger sells or purchases contracts, speculators are given more real substance to trade upon.

As for the traders' positions in contract commitments, says Mr. S., one may well regard them generally with this line of reasoning: large traders are professionals who have more money to commit to particular positions. They probably have a lot of solid information behind their moves. They are usually right—and perhaps that is why many have become large traders. So if large traders are buying, then *you* should be buying too! Small traders, on the other hand, are likely to be wrong—and that is why they have remained small traders; or else they are poorly informed and impulsive novices. Therefore if they are buying, then *you* should be selling!

Mr. E. notices Mr. S. eyeing him. Is this really so? he asks. Are large speculators mainly correct and small traders notoriously wrong? Mr. S. laughs. He had been presenting "theory" in this commitment watching, he admits. Reality of course often proves quite different from the arguments contrived by deductive reasoning such as this. Large traders, it's true, are apt to be close to news sources so that they can make the appropriate moves early. They are often rich enough to devote all their time to pondering what's happening in the commodities—and to pay experts for their sage advice.

But the situation is not nearly as hopeless as it may seem. Conservative, knowledgeable small speculators who have another source of income through their normal jobs probably have just as good a chance of making commensurate profits as the big guys, Mr. S. now maintains. And in fact they may be risking comparatively less, since they may be disinclined to try sudden or unusual commitments, which large traders, after all, can afford to do, thereby sustaining considerable losses whenever prices fail to move in some anticipated way. Large traders can establish a new trend because small speculators watch what they do. But that doesn't necessarily make them right, in the long run, since a price that runs up or down only because of their initiating action will eventually run out of steam and reverse itself.

Speculators are always considering what the experts are saying and doing, Mr. S. goes on, because they are aware that traders of all kinds are apt to respond to new information and advice, by either buying or selling or canceling out on previously taken positions. Thus there is the *Market Sentiment Index,* or *MSI,* which compiles the percentages of reputable market analyists who are bullish or bearish on a particular commodity.

There are dozens of services that supply both information and advice to speculators, as Mr. E. may imagine, Mr. S. says. Some are the brokerage houses themselves, which have their own market experts. They provide forecasts, Teletyped bulletins, and other news that the customer can draw upon directly or through his own commodity representative at the firm. Then there are various professional commodity services that send out newsletters and charge a subscription fee.

But what's the effect of all this advice being given? asks Mr. E. Ah, says Mr. S., that brings up a special approach to trading, which is an offshoot of the technical one. Some speculators—called *contrary-opinion traders*—believe that one should observe what the majority of these advisers are saying about how the market will go and watch what the traders themselves are doing—and then go and do the opposite! They theorize that most speculators, when told that a price will go up, will rush out and buy as soon as they can, thereby creating an *overbought futures* whose price is already high. And since most of those who are bullish will have already bought, or may be selling at an inflated price to overeager buyers in order to take profits out now, soon there will be nobody left to buy. As the delivery time draws closer, buyers will have to cancel out their positions by selling, and since there will be no new buyers left at the high price, the prevailing price must inevitably come down. It is this predominant bullish or bearish attitude that the Market Sentiment Index shows.

Now consider contrary-opinion traders, Mr. S. proposes. Having assumed that this overbought condition would happen, they might have taken their risk much earlier by becoming bearish and selling short while the buying mania was still going on. And the higher the price at which they sold, the greater the profit they now stand to make as the price drops lower and they then make an offsetting contract purchase.

Mr. E. finds this contrary-opinion trading rather reasonable and indeed attractive. Someday Mr. E. may try it, yes, Mr. S. agrees. Now and then he does it himself, occasionally with good success if he reasons it through properly. But Mr. E. should be forewarned that trading *against* the trend, as contrary-opinion traders frequently do, is generally acknowledged to be unwise. However, if such traders are expert technicians, they may have developed certain chart indicators to tell them rather exact points where that trend seems ready to reverse itself. Therefore, with some safety, they can come into the trading at the right place and the right time to earn their profit.

Another item that is regularly charted, Mr. S. points out, are the *delivery registrations*. What are they? Mr. E. wants to know. Most hedgers, Mr. S. explains, just like speculators, intend to cancel out their contracts rather than actually deliver or take delivery on the real commodity when the contract month comes due. However, some commercials do plan to deal directly with the exchanges' cash, or spot, markets rather than cancel out their contracts. This practice is more prevalent among some commodities than others. Which? asks the curious Mr. E. Notably iced broilers, soybean oil and meal, and plywood—all on the Chicago Board of Trade, Mr. S. answers. And to a certain extent silver, gold, and Ginnie Maes too.

If a commercial does intend to deliver, Mr. S. goes on, the firm must do so at a certain delivery point designated by the exchange. The commodity exchange then tabulates the amount of particular commodities that firms are scheduled to deliver and mails this list of registrations to whoever requests it. But what good is that? Mr. E. inquires. Theory tells us, says Mr. S., that if there's an abundance of a certain commodity, a commercial may not be able to do business through its normal channels but instead will deliver the commodity to some exchange delivery point; this will be reflected in an increase in registrations. If a shortage develops, most commercials will not have any goods as yet unspoken for, so that registrations would decrease. The warehouse receipts showing quantities of commodities ready for actual delivery to exchange receiving points therefore confirm whether a surplus or a shortage does indeed exist—and that will have bearing on futures prices in that commodity for months to come.

And now, says Mr. S., they are coming to the "basis" that both hedgers and speculators are always scrutinizing. *Basis,* repeats Mr. E. What's that again? *Basis is the difference between the cash market price and the nearest futures price,* Mr. S. answers. Which would be higher? Mr. E. wants to know. Well, it all depends, says Mr. S. Usually the futures price is higher if the commodity can be stored. But if a harvest month is ahead, the futures price may well be lower than the current cash price.

Since basis is the cash price *minus* the nearest futures price, Mr. S. goes on, the figure often comes out as a negative number. For instance? asks Mr. E. Let's take corn, says Mr. S. In September, right when it's starting to come to market, it may have a cash price of $2.50 a bushel. The nearest futures contract month is December, which may be selling at the same time for, say, $2.60 a bushel. The basis, then, would be $2.50 less $2.60: −10¢, or minus ten cents. Therefore, the cash price would be "10¢ under."

But why are traders so interested in this basis? pursues Mr. E. Basis is especially useful, Mr. S. responds, in reckoning the wisdom of taking a particular long or short position or in undertaking a spread. But how does this work out? Mr. E. wonders. Mr. S. then explains that one must look at the whole hedging process itself in order to comprehend the significance of basis. Professional hedgers—those commercials who specialize in acquiring long or short contracts to protect their companies from financial losses in adverse price changes—look, above all, at the current basis when figuring out how to handle the buying or selling of cash commodities and futures contracts. If a miller buys 5,000 bushels of corn right now, says Mr. S., and then takes delivery of it immediately, he will have the problem of holding the corn until he uses it all up. The costs for doing this will involve such things as storage and paying interest on borrowed money that he used to buy the corn to begin with.

Mr. S. goes on to propose that they roughly estimate that it will cost 8¢ a bushel, including interest, to purchase and store this corn for a month. If the miller needs it in three months' time, he can either buy it now and accept the storage costs of about 24¢ per bushel or else he can contract for it on a commodity exchange. The latter choice of action will mean, in essence, that someone else will accept the cost of storage. Therefore, the corn bought three months away from delivery time will have these storage costs prefigured into the futures price. That's why in the normal *carrying-charge market* the distant or back months—those furthest away from the harvest or production period—will be selling at a higher price, reflecting such costs.

Mr. S. now shows his student how in today's commodity market price report in the newspaper, crops like wheat, corn, soybeans, and oats show prices that are successively higher with each delivery month following the peak of harvest. (And remember, says Mr. S., that wheat's crop year begins on July 1, whereas corn's starts on October 1.)

Commodities' prices, of course, Mr. S. continues, are associated with two different but related markets: the cash markets and the futures markets. The cash market price is what commercials are currently paying for the commodity when they take delivery on it from the producer or dealer so that they can store it or process it in some way. The futures market price is the consensus of what traders believe the price should be in future months.

Futures prices, then, have a lot of hope built into them by speculators, Mr. S. observes. But cash prices are very real and quite definite. The commercials buying the real commodity put up all the money to buy the commodity itself, not just the 10% margin money required of futures traders. This is why it is important to analyze what is currently happening to the actual cash commodity at any time to get some indication as to what will probably happen to its futures prices.

And that, Mr. S. remarks, is the great value of keeping track of basis, which compares cash and nearest futures price. Remember, it is cash price minus the nearest futures price. So if less, it is "under" and therefore a negative number. If it is higher or "over," it is a positive, or plus, figure and considered *at a premium* to the futures. For example, say it's January and March wheat is going for $4.20 per bushel, while the commercial grain elevator operators are paying $4.30 per bushel for the actual wheat. The basis is positive, because $4.30 minus $4.20 is 10¢—or 10¢ "over," making cash at a premium to futures.

Since this price difference, or the basis, changes from day to day, it can be plotted on a chart, Mr. S. explains. And technicians attempt to determine how futures will move by analyzing these charts. If the basis is *normal,* meaning cash is a little below futures, in theory everything is normal, and so you're not being told much, since you'd expect the carrying charge factor to make the futures price somewhat higher.

But if the basis is *positive,* if the cash price is more than the nearest futures, then the situation may be considered unusual. It can mean either that the cash price is temporarily a little high for some reason and will soon come down or that the futures price is momentarily low and should soon rise. The nearest futures price, after all, will quickly enough become the cash price. So if it's now January, it will soon become March, and by then the cash price would be the same as the value of the March futures contract.

Speculators don't buy the cash commodity, of course, Mr. S. goes on. But when using this basis pattern to predict how the futures prices will go, they look for a rapid change as the most significant thing. If the basis increases rapidly, the commercials who must buy the commodity are surely desperate to get it. If the basis decreases suddenly, the short commercials, the producers, are trying to get rid of it. Theoretically, then, says Mr. S., if a shortage develops, commercials will be buying the cash commodity rather madly and at a high price, creating a positive basis until the shortage is somewhat alleviated. In an oversupply situation, commercial sellers may want to unload any excess at reduced cash or spot prices.

So, says Mr. S., when charting services like *Spread Scope* chart the changes in a commodity's basis, they do it according to the positive and negative figures this important trading factor can take. And to conclude his presentation of basis, he does a sample diagram on his chalkboard with a certain flourish:

BASIS

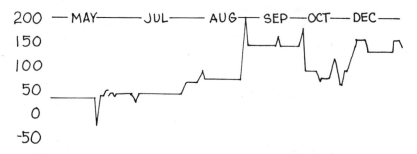

And speaking of *Spread Scope*, says Mr. S., they have now come to the subject of *spreads*, as promised earlier. Mr. E. has surely heard the term often enough by now, here and there, because speculators frequently are involved in this form of commodity trading. Oh yes, spreads! Mr. E. echoes, recalling that Mr. T. undertook one in soybeans at the Chicago Board of Trade. Could Mr. S. please tell him precisely what a spread is? Generally, says Mr. S., a spread involves simultaneously buying one contract of a commodity and selling another, in the hope that the purchased contract will gain in value relative to the sold contract, or, conversely, that the sold contract will lose value relative to the bought one.

The terms *spread, straddle,* and *arbitrage* originally meant slightly different things, Mr. S. goes on, but now have become synonymous in common usage among speculators. Though there are no strict definitions with regard to the types of spread, for the sake of clarity and convenience Mr. S. will fit them into these categories—which he writes down on his chalkboard now:

TIME
LOCATION
SIMILARITIES/SUBSTITUTION
PROCESSING
PSEUDO-SPREADS

In a way, Mr. E. muses, it seems to him that basis and spreads may be somewhat alike, since they both concern the difference between one contract value and another. True enough, Mr. S. agrees. While basis is the cash price of a particular commodity minus the price of the nearby futures contract, a *spread* is the price of a certain futures contract minus that of another futures contract in the same or somehow-related commodity.

The most common spread that speculators use, says Mr. S., is based on a time difference. The same commodity is simultaneously bought and sold in different delivery months. Each *leg*—one side of a spread—is placed on the long or short side of two contracts. Since the spread difference is between these contract months, it is often called *interdelivery*. And since it involves the same commodity, it may sometimes be known as an *intra-commodity spread*.

The concept in making money here, Mr. S. explains, is that as the value of a commodity rises, frequently a *bull spread*—long the near month and short the deferred month—will work favorably. So that if the price of, say, wheat increases as a shortage may be developing, March wheat will rise in price faster than May wheat.

Technicians study spread patterns among traders for clues as to price trends, Mr. S. goes on, so that spreads in particular commodities will be charted just as other trading factors are graphed. For example, if July wheat starts to go up in price faster than December wheat, this movement will show a strong desire to buy the wheat itself, which could foretell a rising trend in price.

Normally, says Mr. S., for corn, a March contract is cheaper than a May contract, which in turn is cheaper than a July contract—because, of course, of the carrying-charge aspect. Both commercials and speculators are sufficiently aware of such regular seasonal factors involved with supply and demand that there are rarely great variations in futures prices from one month to another during normal production years. Also, Mr. S. comments, since commodity trading is now worldwide in scope, during almost every month of the year there are some crops being harvested and some livestock being slaughtered in either the northern or southern hemisphere, so that a deficiency in one area can be made up by supplies imported from the other. Or at least there's the possibility of doing so, which is bound to affect domestic prices. Because of intense attention to the fundamental factors involved in commodities, the futures prices have already been "discounted" by hedgers and traders.

Speculators therefore are on the lookout for discrepancies in prices. If the nearby month starts to gain on a more distant month and actually surpasses it so that the nearby month is at a premium or higher price, then many traders would take this as a bullish sign, a signal perhaps to buy now. Thus the relationship patterns of futures prices among themselves are scrutinized, just as the basis is, in order to determine where to take long or short positions. At the same time traders are aware of the interconnections between certain commodities, such as soybeans and soybean meal, or among the various grains—since they are seeking the best profit-making situations by calculating whether, for example, the price of corn will influence hog farmers to continue feeding and breeding their animals or to slaughter their stock earlier than expected, thereby affecting pork prices.

But aside from being used as a predictive device, spreads can be traded simply for their own sake and doing so can be quite lucrative. But why? asks Mr. E. Since the speculator is not a commercial, Mr. S. answers, he does not handle the actual commodity or trade in the cash price. But he may be able to gain some advantage by buying one futures contract and at the same time selling another, doing some of the precise figuring that goes on with regard to discrepancies in the basis, on which hedging action is usually calculated.

One advantage to spreads, especially to the small speculator, Mr. S. points out, is a lower margin requirement. But how can that be? Mr. E. asks. The transaction seems double the work because it involves two orders, not one. But from the viewpoint of the clearinghouses, Mr. S. explains, there is not as much risk in a spread, and so they do not require as much to cover the positions. Remember, a major problem with speculators is not just in predicting which way prices will go. It's also in having enough money to maintain margins through temporary adversities—part of the money management skills needed in commodity trading.

Consider, Mr. S. says, a contract of 5,000 bushels of wheat at $4 per bushel—for a total value of $20,000. The margin on that will be about

$2,000, which is only about a 10% move in the total value of the commodity. With a spread, though, one can buy July wheat and sell December wheat. In theory, these two wheat contracts will at least move in the same direction, up or down. If July wheat goes up 20¢, then one can expect December wheat to go up 20¢ too. Though of course the spread trader hopes that they won't be exactly in step, with the difference in rate slanted in favor of his particular setup. Now the margin requirement on these two contracts may be only $500. This surprises Mr. E., but then he says he thinks he sees why there is far less risk. What one contract loses in value, the other one may gain. Therefore the speculator and the clearinghouse—his opposite trader, virtually—are risking less on the double deal. That's right! Mr. S. agrees.

But what does this trader hope to get out of the spread? asks Mr. E. Well, let's say he buys July wheat and sells December wheat simultaneously, with July 5¢ under December. Perhaps he buys July at $4.40 and sells December at $4.45. He may put up $500 in margin. After some weeks July gains on December, so that perhaps they are both selling at the same price, say $4.60. Our speculator then gets out of his spread. Since he bought July and sold December, he now liquidates his positions by selling his July contract and buying the December.

Remember now, says Mr. S., that he got in at July 5¢ under December. He gets out when both contracts sell at the same price. He has therefore made 5¢ per bushel multiplied by 5,000 bushels, or $250 on his margin investment of $500. In this case he has received a 50% return in maybe a month or so.

But keep in mind, always, Mr. S. cautions, that the spread can also go against the trader. Perhaps after several months pass, July is selling at 10¢ under December. Then he will lose 5¢ per bushel net. The commission will be another debit. But then he would have figured it as part of the risk he took in making the spread to start with.

What about commissions, anyway? Mr. E. wants to know. Each brokerage has its own rates, Mr. S. replies. There is the normal *round turn commission* in which, in effect, nothing is charged for initiating— either buying or selling—a contract. But later, when the existing contract is offset by an opposite transaction, a commission is charged. A one-day commission, or *intraday commission,* is usually less: this fee is for buying and selling on the same day, a bit like pit scalping, since it involves less paperwork because there is no holdover clearing to be done. And *spread commissions* are less than normal round-turn commissions. Buying and selling wheat and corn simultaneously in a single order will usually cost less than buying wheat and selling corn separately. A typical spread order might read, "Buy July wheat, sell December wheat, 5¢ premium the December or better."

So much for the simple mechanics of the spread, Mr. S. remarks. But Mr. E. surely wonders how the at-home speculator can make a profit from it. Mr. E. nods his head in agreement. Well, says Mr. S., one must remember that one approach of the small speculator is to look for *dislocations* in the price structure. If wheat is "too" low, he buys it. If wheat is "too" high, he sells it. That's the theory, anyway. In practice, "too" high and "too" low are tough to spot. Likewise, the at-home speculator can scan the commodity prices looking for dislocations, or discrepancies, in spreads. In theory, September corn should sell for less than December corn because of the carrying-charge relationship. If the speculator spots them going for the same price, he may reason that this maladjustment is just temporary and that eventually December, the more distant month, will gain relative to September, so that September perhaps "should" be 5¢ under. He might then sell the September corn and buy the December, at the same price, and hope that the spread widens in his favor, so that by the time he closes out—buying the September and selling the December —the December price will be higher than the September one.

Now, Mr. S. remarks, that would be a nice example of a time spread. But some cautionary words are called for here as in all theoretical programs connected with commodity speculation. Not all commodities work out this way even in theory, let alone practice. Consider a live cattle spread. Since the cattle are alive, one can't store them too well. (Though there is some leeway, of course.) Therefore two separate months of cattle will tend to behave virtually like two entirely different contracts. Those difficult-to-store commodities that do not generally follow the usual spread rules are live cattle, feeder cattle, live hogs, iced broilers, and eggs.

Also, Mr. S. goes on, some commodities move in the opposite way, so that in a bull market, the far contract will gain on the near. For instance, the capability for storing potatoes is considerably less than that for wheat or corn. In any one crop year, then, as a shortage develops the distant contract will become relatively more valuable than the near. Therefore a spread may be more safely arranged at a time when a small crop is forecast by selling the early contract and buying the more distant one, since the latter will tend to acquire a disproportionate value.

As limited-risk spreads, Mr. S. would recommend the grains as the best bets. Traditionally, as they have discussed, December wheat will be at a slightly higher price than September wheat because of the carrying charge, which is calculated for speculators in the weekly chart from *Spread Scope*. So if the price of September wheat is 20¢ below that of December wheat and calculations show that the carrying charge is actually 27¢, then going long September and short December exposes the speculator to a risk of only 7¢. How's that? asks Mr. E.

Well, if September gets down to, say, 30¢ under December, then those commercials in the business of storing grains will buy the September wheat and sell the December futures contract, actually taking possession of the grain in September and holding it until December, when it will be delivered at the preset price. The storage cost will be 27¢, while their own gross profit will be 30¢, leaving a net profit of 3¢ per bushel.

Now a small speculator, of course, will not actually want to take delivery of this wheat, says Mr. S., but can go along for the ride, so to speak, using the same action that the commercials take in simultaneously buying and selling futures contracts. Therefore, a spread will be limited on the downside, with the hope that a shortage will develop and the September contract will become much more valuable than the December, allowing the speculator a profit.

But always keep in mind, Mr. S. tells Mr. E., that a lot of other speculators are very likely doing the same thing: buying September wheat and selling December wheat, at maybe a 20¢ difference in price. This means that the spread will have a lot of expectation built into it. As the time of delivery comes due—that is, as September nears—this positive expectation will tend to go out of the spread. The spread will go from the 20¢ down to its calculated 27¢—or whatever the real carrying charge is. Although the risk is limited, this little drop at the end may occur time after time in a commodity, eliminating the profit taking.

Mr. S. has primarily been talking about spreads that involve the same commodity in different months. Now he'd like to mention that the same commodity can be bought in the same delivery month but at a different location or exchange. Thus one can buy Kansas City wheat and sell Chicago wheat. Because this spread is based on location, it is usually called an *intermarket spread*. There are two main reasons for different prices in the same commodity, Mr. S. points out. First, the delivery points are different for different exchanges, and so a commercial taking delivery on K.C. wheat, for example, will pay a different transportation fee than a commercial taking delivery on Chicago wheat. And a second explanation, notably in the grains, is that there are really various kinds of wheat being traded, with different nutrient and gluten contents. Kansas City has hard red winter wheat; Chicago carries soft red winter wheat; Minneapolis has hard red spring wheat.

Professional hedgers are familiar with current transportation charges and the differences in wheat varieties. As far as speculators are concerned, they should be prepared to step in when prices get hugely out of line. If one market's price is temporarily depressed compared to another's, for instance, they would buy at the former and sell at the latter, Mr. S. explains.

Then there are the spreads that involve similar commodities that can be substituted for one another in particular ways by the commercials who use them. One can feed cattle corn or oats, for example. Therefore a spread can be made between them in the same or different months. This type of spread may include most of the grains, or hogs versus cattle. It can occur because the price movement in one commodity tends to affect that of the others in the same classification, even though in some cases the commodities are used differently. Metal prices usually move similarly, but divergent usages disqualify them as regular intercommodity spreads.

It's important to realize, however, Mr. S. asserts, that in the spreads that are contrived between two different commodities, both sides should have a closely equivalent contract value. For instance, it takes about two contracts of oats, for a total of 10,000 bushels, to approximately equal the value of one contract of corn.

Spreads can also be made between two commodities that are interrelated because of processing; that is, one is made from the other. Feeder cattle are fed to become live cattle. Hogs are slaughtered to be made into pork bellies. Wood is made into lumber and plywood. Soybeans are crushed to produce soybean oil and soybean meal.

Here again, says Mr. S., the contract values must be kept more or less equal in order for the spread to work. And that isn't always easy to do. For example, a spread that is long pork bellies and short live hogs is really biased toward the pork bellies, since the contract for pork bellies is 38,000 pounds and the one for hogs is 30,000 pounds. Also, the price of pork bellies almost always runs higher per pound than the price of live hogs.

Mr. S. would now like to emphasize that not all categories that may seem like spreads to traders are officially accepted as such or are unambiguous. Although soybean meal may be substituted for corn as a feed, the two don't combine as a regular spread. Yet one can trade in one month in one commodity (February pork bellies, for example) and another month in a different but related commodity (as July hogs) and still have the trading considered a spread by the Chicago Mercantile Exchange.

Thus there are what one might call *pseudospreads,* which an interested speculator can try even though he will not receive the decreased margin rates customary in conventional spreads, since pseudospreads are not recognized as such by the exchanges. For instance, silver and gold tend to move in the same direction. Yet a speculator who is long gold and short silver will have to put up enough margin money to cover each side of the spread separately. And since corn is fed to hogs, in theory there should be some correlation in price movement. As corn prices go up so should hog prices. Although long hogs and short corn may be considered a bona fide spread to speculators—and in fact the *hog-corn ratio* is closely watched—the trader must expect to cover each margin separately in making up a spread.

Other valuable ones to watch, Mr. S. goes on, are soybeans versus wheat and soybeans versus corn. Even though soybeans are frequently treated by speculators as a grain, technically of course they are not, he points out. And this fact may cause temporary dislocation in the soybean-wheat or soybean-corn spread—which the astute speculator can profit from.

Pseudospreads do not have the advantage of the low margin requirements of normal spreads, remember, Mr. S. points out. They also demand more education and sophistication on the part of traders. There are compensations, though. They give more opportunities to find temporary dislocations in commodity prices. And since they are frequently overlooked by many speculators, some of the competition for possible profits is eliminated.

Well, Mr. S. can see that his apprentice is almost spread-eagled in his chair from sheer fatigue. They have had a long session today, he admits, but they had a lot of territory to cover—and did it. No homework this time! he announces. He wants Mr. E. to rest up and get in shape for their coming session, which will be about managing money when speculating in commodities. So Mr. E. should be ready to do quite a bit of basic arithmetic as part of his final exercises before taking off on his own as a fledgling speculator.

CHAPTER FOURTEEN

The Business of Speculating

Today Mr. E. comes into Mr. S.'s study in a mood that is decidedly excited. Mr. S. notices that he has brought a book with him, and before Mr. S. can ask what it is, Mr. E. is already handing it to him. Has Mr. S. seen it? And if so, what does he think of it? A person in his office, hearing that he had become interested in commodity trading, lent it to him.

Mr. S. considers the title: *How I Made 1.3 Million Dollars in Less Than Two Years in Futures Trading, Starting with Only $5,000!* No, he says, he hasn't seen this book, but he has seen others like it. He knows the type. Well, Mr. E. has been reading it, hasn't finished it quite yet, but is impressed with the possibilities it discloses for making money.

And look at this! Mr. E. hands Mr. S. two ads—one from the local newspaper alerting people to the high profit percentages that can be earned by opening an account with a commodity-investing company, the other a direct-mail brochure revealing all sorts of trading secrets to those who subscribe to a biweekly newsletter for $500 a year.

Well? asks Mr. S., waiting for Mr. E.'s commentary. Well, apparently some people are able to work out systems for making dependable money—and a lot of it—from commodity speculation! says Mr. E. Ah yes, says Mr. S. in a tone of voice that is both cynical and weary. Such people are not, in fact, in the business of speculating in the commodities; they are in the business of speculating in commodity *speculators*. He goes to his desk and takes out a large folder stuffed with papers and hands it to

187

COMMODITY SPECULATION FOR BEGINNERS

Mr. E. In past years, he says, he has been interested in the different approaches and techniques of such entrepreneurs and therefore has collected a good many samples of advertisements and come-on mailing pieces. He also has gathered stories of salespeople who try to solicit customers by phone, using a variety of intriguing gimmicks, such as revealing who tomorrow's winners will be in some contests or races so that the listener will be more attentive and impressed when they call again later—provided, of course, that their predictions were correct! And Mr. S., for Mr. E.'s information, also possesses many newspaper articles that tell of the results—prosecutions and imprisonments—of employing such conning tactics among the gullible public, which is understandably so anxious for quick and easy wealth that it wants to believe that some system exists, the secrets of which can be obtained for a comparatively small outlay of money. And once "hooked," the sucker may sink far more cash into an endeavor than is sensible. But it all looked so safe and so reasonable! he may say afterwards, when trying to explain his moves and financial losses. And of course it did, to *him*.

The essence of developing an attractive new system of gambling or speculating is to make it seem logical, neat, and foolproof. Futures trading lends itself well to this form of money making because its high-profit potential lures a number of people inclined toward pursuing it, who sometimes do so rather recklessly when motivated by desperate greed, Mr. S. goes on. When someone assures them in print or in person that he himself got rich by employing this magic formula, they tend to believe—instead of scrutinizing the facts of the situation, using their rational faculties, and maintaining a healthy suspicion of anyone who's trying to sell them something.

So forget the mathematics for today! Mr. S. tells Mr. E. Before they get into the details of opening a commodity account and deciding how to take positions and phrase orders, they had better discuss the whole matter of predicting the unpredictable—which is what these various systems, services, and con games are based upon. The proponents of these schemes risk a certain initial investment in paper, labor, and advertising in order to reap a large amount of money from speculator types who are willing to "buy" a seemingly guaranteed route to a fortune.

Now this little book here is a good example, says Mr. S., looking at its paper cover with undisguised distaste. It cost somebody $30—which is mainly paying for the revealed secret, since the physical object probably cost no more than $2 to produce. If the author publishes such a book himself, he'll rake in the income. So if fifty thousand people buy the book, he stands to make $1.5 million. And discounting his costs for producing and advertising and mailing, he'll maybe have earned the $1.3 million he *says* he made off commodity speculation!

There's one book, though, that Mr. S. would like to recommend to Mr. E. or anyone who is interested in the possibilities in money-making systems. He takes it from his shelf: *If They're So Smart, How Come You're Not Rich?*, by John L. Springer. The author, says Mr. S., investigated a number of financial advisory services, followed their advice, and concluded that their methods were not profitable.

The new commodity speculator, Mr. S. continues, must be especially wary of the systems salespeople, who sometimes come in subtle forms. Once he gets on a mailing list—maybe by just sending away for information from some place—he may get deluged by literature of all kinds. Phone calls too. He's apt to find a few of the messages convincing and appealing. Who wouldn't like to earn a 2,000% profit in two months by turning his money over to a professional firm that seems reputable and reliable—and without having to exercise his own brain at all? But please note that there is no fixed guarantee involved. In some cases, sure, a sizable profit has been made. But we're told of the occasional dazzling successes, not of the dismal failures.

And why can't there be any certainty in winning? asks Mr. S. Because, says Mr. E., apparently there can be no certainty about the price changes of commodities, on which the futures contracts are based. People can predict what prices will be or how they will change, but they won't necessarily be right. Still, Mr. E. explains, he was quite fascinated with aspects of both the fundamental and the technical approaches to trading, and he has a difficult time believing that in spite of the plethora of contradictory information and speculator behavior, a useful system cannot be devised for making money fairly consistently.

Oh, Mr. S. has his own approach or system, he says. But it's nothing flashy sounding. In fact, it would seem rather dull to many speculators searching for the key to the kingdom of riches. Basically, it involves wise money management combined with attention to the probabilities connected with both insurance and commodity trading. That's why he calls it the *actuarial approach*. And since Mr. E. is surely aware that insurance companies manage to achieve net profits by running a business based on probabilities and risk taking, he'll understand that a conservative trader can do the same, year in and year out.

This perks Mr. E. up. Will Mr. S. show him how? Of course he will, at least in an introductory form and in some detail. But naturally he can't guarantee that Mr. E. or any other apprentice speculator will ultimately succeed, since there's no surefire money-making plan as this little book he brought in today promises. He's only teaching a general method.

For instance—and here Mr. S. begins leafing through the book quickly, glancing at its headings and subheads, its tables and charts—a wary and knowledgeable speculator knows a *pyramid* when he sees one.

And, not being a sphinx provided with all the answers to riddles about the future course of things, he steers away from it, however attractive it may seem to him in theory and set down on paper as here.

Would Mr. S. please explain to him exactly what a pyramid is? Mr. E. requests. It sounds familiar but he's not sure he knows. A pyramid is created by a speculator when he uses his contract winnings to invest in new contracts in the same commodity, Mr. S. answers. It got this name because of its appearance when charted. And he goes to his trusty chalkboard to demonstrate how this happens:

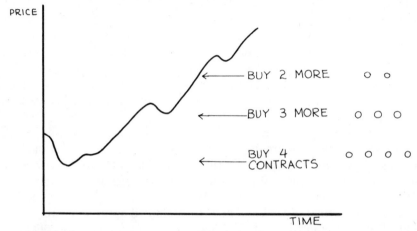

Thus as the price continues to rise, Mr. S. says, the trader keeps stockpiling his holdings, all the time acquiring more and more—which when graphed in terms of contract numbers looks like an upside-down pyramid.

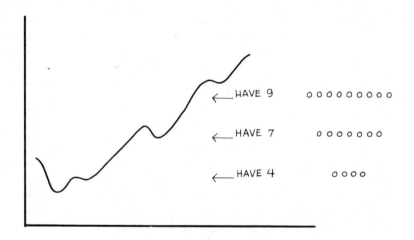

Hey! says Mr. E. That is actually a *parlay,* isn't it? He is remembering his conversation with Dr. M., the actuarial mathematician. And he
knows that a parlay is extremely dangerous to try, even though it looks
terrific. Mr. S. is glad that his student does not have to be shown and
convinced of the perilous predicament of the gambler involved in a parlay. Well, yes, the pyramid is the commodity speculator's parlay. But it's
even more attractive in futures trading than in other speculating vehicles,
such as real estate and stocks. Does Mr. E. care to guess why? He
considers for a moment or two. Because of the leverage factor, he answers. It would make the pyramid so much more attractive, since a 10%
margin would control a value of 100%. But the pyramid will only stay
safe as long as one is winning. Whenever the price reverses itself, the
speculator will have to pay in to maintain the margin. And if the price
continues to move against him, he can get completely wiped out.

And that, says Mr. S., might be called *parlaying to destruction.*
When the winner uses a fortuitous turn of events to finance another turn,
which then goes well, and builds up to larger and larger holdings, he
becomes increasingly dependent on events continuing to go well for him.
But as we know from studying the commodity markets, there is absolutely no guarantee that a price will continue to move in a particular
direction. Even a small, temporary dip can spell disaster if the speculator
has sunk most of his capital into this venture—his "chance of a lifetime"
for fortune—which seems destined to make him extremely well off.

But surely such good fortune can happen to some people sometime,
Mr. E. ventures. Of course it can, Mr. S. agrees. But you should never
count on its happening to *you.* You can hedge your bet sensibly by controlling the risks and come out quite well indeed. In a while, though, he'll
tell Mr. E. of a trade in which, theoretically, a large fortune could have
been made. And he'll show how it could have gone rather differently too.
Since the outcome is never certain in advance, trading involves playing
skillfully in a situation in which both probabilities and sheer random
chance are operative. Knowledge can bias the probabilities in the speculator's favor, but there's always that factor of luck, the unknown and
mysterious element that can suddenly come in to alter the situation in
which expectations had seemed so positive. And luck can come in at
another time in one's favor, just when events might be going badly.

What it comes down to, then, is developing a sensible attitude toward
prediction, Mr. S. says—which the systems sellers fail to teach their
customers because the schemes they are selling allegedly cannot fail. The
irresponsible plans and advice that they dispense, for a price, to the
public depend after all on events going along a predictable pattern. But
the problems inherent in *meaningful* prediction are not explored by the
general public because people don't have to predict much while going

through life in day-to-day routines. And Mr. S. isn't talking about a prediction like "The sun will rise tomorrow"—which is as close to certainty as anything can be but has little profit potential.

Just ponder, Mr. S. suggests, one significant area of prediction that one might expect to be accurate: who will be the next president of the United States? This most important post in the nation is watched continually by hundreds of expert political analysts. Yet could any one of them have predicted the improbable sequence of events and presidential contenders and contests that have given us our presidents in the past two decades? Mr. E., thinking it over, admits that he personally would have been quite unable to foresee the entire succession of personalities.

Well, says Mr. S., the analogy between American presidents and commodity prices may not be as farfetched as it initially seems. There are simply so many known and unknown factors and events that intervene between the expectable and the actual in moving from the present to the future. The past can offer some clues and designs, some helpful information. But it cannot deliver a prognostication that is an absolute certainty —or even necessarily a close one. In both political situations and speculating, predictions are constantly being made; they have to be made, but the outcome may often seem puzzling. One can say there's a 20% chance —or a 50% or a 78% or whatever chance—of something happening and proceed accordingly. But even the probability itself is highly debatable and can only be estimated. Insurance actuaries, of course, have reduced some events to fairly close figures. But they are not dealing with the complexities involved in commodity prices and their constant changes.

Among the traders, fundamentalists and technicians attempt to make close, rational studies of supply and demand and of price behavior to arrive at models or patterns that can be interpreted and applied to future predictions. Computers are also put to work on these problems. And it's important to notice, says Mr. S., that these studies are based on what happened in the past—which may be true for that particular segment of the past they focused on but can readily be contradicted in some other place and which may have a misleading effect on a trader who depends on the studies to guide decisions about future price changes. It's much easier, of course, to be absolutely correct in revealing the past and explaining what happened than to be even moderately correct in predicting the future. The so-called experts are therefore on much safer ground when they tread in history. The present need for wisdom calls forth their sage advice and forecasts of things to come, but too often their version of the future is proven to be science fiction. And one might expect this, since speculation is really more an art than a real science and since it depends upon intuitive actions and improvisational interpretations rather than the mechanics of precise measurements and the discovery of rules and laws of nature.

And yet, Mr. S. continues, moving to his chalkboard, he *is* reminded sometimes, when dealing with price fluctuations, of Professor Einstein's work regarding the essentially random motion of particles within a gas or liquid, which is called the Brownian Movement. And here Mr. S. is depicting small bits of matter moving around in erratic paths, often bouncing against the container walls and frequently colliding:

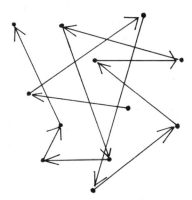

Now, says Mr. S., in speculation on Wall Street and among commodity traders there is a somewhat similar phenomenon with prices and their movements. Some analysts, rather than subscribing to the fundamental or the technical approach wholeheartedly, prefer to consider price changes as occurences to be expected in a *random walk* through a speculators' marketplace. Yes, Mr. E. says, he has sometimes heard that term used in the stock market.

Mr. S. likes to use a somewhat different phrase for commodity speculation's attempt to predetermine price movements. Suppose Mr. E. is in the house, looking out a second-story window, Mr. S. proposes. He sees a drunk leaning up against the lamppost, seemingly about to start off on a staggering journey. He could get a piece of paper and a pencil and sketch features of a street map with houses, a few trees, the lamppost, a parked car, and so on. Then he could record the route that the man takes around the immediate neighborhood. And he could call it a "drunkard's walk," if he liked.

Then, having plotted the whole route, would he be able to see in retrospect some pattern in it? Amazingly enough, he might be able to, since searching for and finding some pattern in even random happenings seems to be human nature. These patterns would, however, be good for only that one past event and not necessarily for future events.

It is always easy for someone touting a book or an advisory service to draw in the correct chart pattern *after the fact*. For example, says Mr. S., suppose this is a price chart of Chicago wheat . . . and he erases the board and draws in some bar chart prices. The novice speculator, he tells Mr. E., may read a book that shows prices and a trendline like so:

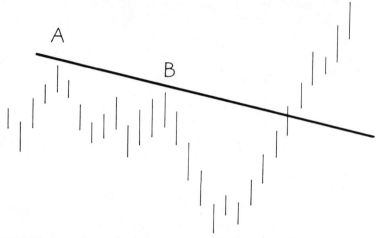

The line connects *A* and *B,* and when it was broken the prices shot upward, Mr. S. comments. A beginner who is impressed after seeing this, and then detects a similar pattern coming up—or has it pointed out to him by an advisory service—might hock his house to buy futures that he expects will make his fortune. But notice, Mr. S. warns, that the trendline in that chart could just as easily connect *A* to *C!* And he demonstrates:

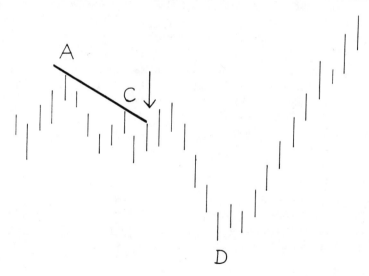

One can always draw the ''correct'' line later, after the price move. But if an unwary speculator had purchased heavily at the arrow, where trendline *AC* is penetrated by the rising price, he might not have the capital reserves necessary to withstand the dip down to *D* and may well have been wiped out.

A chart pattern's developing—such as a trendline's being broken—implies a future course for the price, but it is not a sure thing, Mr. S. goes on. Detecting a pattern may bias the odds in the trader's favor, but there is, after all, no certainty in commodity speculating.

In this example, however, by purchasing fewer contracts the trader could have gotten out with a relatively minor loss if he had felt that the trade was turning sour. Or he might have had enough cash reserves to withstand the dip down to *D* if he had decided to stay with the trade.

Mastering money management techniques can be as important as acquiring expertise in analyzing fundamentals or in chart reading, Mr. S. declares.

Mr. E., he knows, is a poker player, says Mr. S. Therefore he will comprehend the similarity he suggests between a commodity speculator and a good poker player. For both, getting dealt a superior hand of cards or a likely profit-making situation isn't as important—especially over a long period—as ''betting talent.'' An experienced card player will allow his opponents to add in money when he has a good had. If he has a poor hand, he may fold right away or he may bluff the others into folding on the assumption that he has a good hand. The strategy is subtle. A poor poker player who is dealt good hands can still lose money to an experienced and clever player who is dealt poor hands. The ''luck of the draw'' only partly determines who wins.

Being ''right'' about a price move is only part of the successful speculator's strategy. He must also manage his money properly, only taking risks that he can afford to lose. A speculator who is sure that wheat will go up from $3.00 to $4.00 may be right, says Mr. S. But unless he also anticipates a possible dip to $2.50 in between and allows for it in his account, he can still lose.

Does Mr. E. know anything much about *game theory?* asks Mr. S. Not really, he admits, though he's certainly heard of it. Theoretical mathematicians, like Von Neuman and Morgenstern, originated the game concept in decision making, problem solving, and allocation situations, Mr. S. explains. Techniques—some mathematical in design—can be applied to ordinary games of strategy, such as poker, chess, and bridge. They have proven extremely useful to society in situations regarding international relations, distribution of resources, and wartime armament deployment. And of course they can be considered in business competition and in commodity speculation.

Game theory tells us, Mr. S. goes on, that the most important objective of a player is to stay in the game. He should not try to win. Instead, he should try to keep from losing. One can apply this concept to a futures trader. If he wants to survive in the game, he shouldn't concentrate on his winnings, which can take care of themselves as they run along. He should devote his main efforts to avoiding losses in situations in which he has placed his capital. He can do this as a beginner by thinking in terms of how much he may *lose* on a particular trade, in order to minimize his losses. Most novices make the mistake of focusing on what they stand to win if things go well for them. But profits are nothing to worry about; losses are. So as a trading technique, minimizing losses is better than maximizing profits. Every time you try to increase your reward in a winning situation, you also increase your risk—as in a pyramid arrangement. Thus a speculator who gives up aiming for a potential gain of a huge amount, such as a 5,000% return in one year of trading, minimizes his risks and his profits—but very greatly increases his chances for surviving in next year's game.

This reminds him, says Mr. E., of his discussion with Dr. M., who provided the equation for mathematical expectation: the probability of winning multiplied by what is won, minus the probability of losing multiplied by what is lost. And he talked about positive expectation and its importance in insurance. So, Mr. E. goes on, he assumes that this same useful equation would fit well with commodity speculation, since the trader is virtually functioning as an insurance underwriter. That's right! Mr. S. agrees. He should never undertake a trade if after a careful study of the situation, he believes that the financial risk is too great, outweighing the other factors and therefore making the potential gain hardly worth the dangerous entry into the "game."

And to extend the game-playing analogy further, Mr. S. goes on, he might just say that it isn't so much being smart that makes you a successful commodity trader as it is not being dumb! The aim, then, is not to try to be clever or shrewd. It is to keep from doing dumb things.

What is about the worst thing that Mr. E. can imagine happening to him as a trader? asks Mr. S. Probably being heavily short in a bull market with many limit-up days in a row, Mr. E. answers after a moment or two. Why? Well, since everyone would want to buy and no one would want to sell, any short wouldn't have an opportunity to buy back his contracts until the price went maybe sky-high. And where would these limit days most likely occur? asks Mr. S. At whatever markets have few people trading on them and therefore little liquidity, Mr. E. replies. The "thin" markets, Mr. S. adds, naming some: iced broilers, oats, a few of the foreign currencies, and orange juice.

That last one, Mr. S. goes on, might provide a good example for Mr.

E. of how a speculator can throw caution to the wind—can be plain dumb, in other words. Selling OJ from around September on can frequently be a good strategy because the price is artificially inflated due to the hopes of speculators betting on a freeze come January. Doing so can be a prudent move for the experienced speculator, since if there is no freeze the price will naturally decline.

But now consider a fellow who thinks he has learned to analyze the fundamental and technical factors. They are telling him that orange juice will continue to decline further, even though it's December and the price is down to maybe 40¢ or 50¢ a pound. So he goes short in this thinly traded market in which the price is already relatively low and the "freeze scare" season has just begun. And, says Mr. S. rather ominously, it is right at the end of 1976.

Isn't that right before the big citrus freeze in Florida? asks Mr. E. It sure is—or *was*, says Mr. S., since it wiped out our fictitious speculator who had done a very dumb thing. Look! he continues, handing his pupil the bar chart that recorded the precipitous rise in OJ prices. Isn't this the very sort of calamity that Mr. E. had figured was the worst? Good heavens, how much would he have lost? Mr. E. wonders.

They'll figure it out together. Well, says Mr. S., it's a 15,000-pound contract, with a limit move of 3¢ per pound. . . . That would make a short lose $450 per day, adds Mr. E. And there were *ten* limit-up days, Mr. S. says. So that's $4,500 just for one contract. How many OJ contracts did the poor guy have? Oh, let's give him five, Mr. S. decides. So he would have lost $22,500 before he could have gotten out.

Say, Mr. S. didn't get caught in that OJ squeeze, did he? Mr. E. wants to know. No, he was fortunate and had gone long, earlier. But he regrets that he handled his part of the trade ineptly, probably because he sensed the chance for profit, and greed pushed some of his self-discipline aside. He had loaded up rather too much on orange juice at 50¢. When it dropped to 40¢ he couldn't withstand the pressure, and so he had to sell some contracts because he was losing several thousand dollars a week. But he held onto half of them at least, and later on they were bringing in thousands per day. He made a nice profit on the entire move—but how much more he might have made, he sometimes thinks, had he been able to hang in there for a while longer! But of course the wildly inflated price did come from that unexpected and widespread freeze, when it was actually snowing in Florida.

But what about those financial "killings" that people say are possible in the commodities? asks Mr. E. Well, they *are* possible, they *do* happen, says Mr. S., and for him to say they don't would be untruthful. For there's no doubt about it: more money can be made in less time with the least effort in commodity speculating than in any other field of financial endeavor. There are two reasons for this: the great leverage factor made possible by the approximately 10% margins and the tactic of pyramiding, in which profits are immediately converted into margins for more contracts.

But *pyramiding*—says Mr. E. dubiously. Well, it can work for some lucky people who want to risk doing it, Mr. S. admits. And some traders have techniques of pyramiding or parlaying that are more cautious than others, that mainly allow for risking only that capital that has already been won on the trade itself. Yet these aren't the dramatic tales that are told, the once-in-a-lifetime, rags-to-riches stories of speculators who built fortunes almost overnight. So for the purposes of sheer legend, Mr. S.

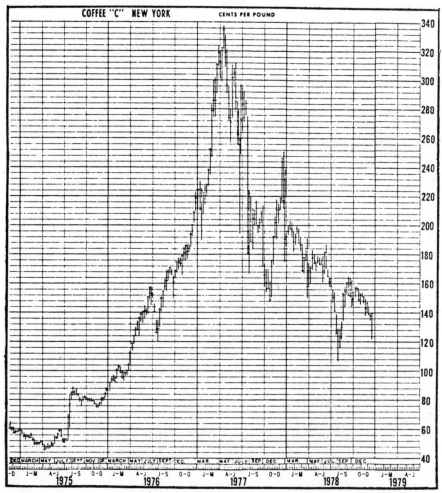

Reprinted with permission of Commodity Research Bureau, Inc.

says, they should construct a mythical trader who gets rich quick, making a pyramid from coffee contracts.

Let's start him out with one contract for Coffee "C" on the New York Coffee, Sugar and Cocoa Exchange, Mr. S. proposes. The contract is for 37,500 pounds. The price is 50¢ per pound, somewhere back in May or June, just where the price has crossed the downtrend line. And it is 1975. Hey, isn't that the year that the coffee shrubs got wiped out in Brazil? Mr. E. asks. Yes, says Mr. S., his student is good on his commodity history. Mr. E. explains that he remembers because almost at once the price of coffee in the markets shot up fantastically, and so for a while a lot of people even refused to buy the stuff. Supply and demand, Mr. S. remarks, simply, as he hands Mr. E. a long-range coffee chart (see p. 198).

Okay, Mr. S. goes on, we'll assume that our dream trader is going to buy as many contracts as he possibly can. If coffee rises 10¢ a pound in value, then the contract has increased its value by $0.10 multiplied by 37,500—or $3,750, a profit that is certainly enough to purchase a second contract with. Therefore, after buying one at 50¢, with a margin of about $2,000, our speculator now has enough profit at 60¢ to buy one more. At 70¢ he has earned enough to buy two more with his profits on the two contracts that went from 60¢ to 70¢. At 70¢ he'll double his holdings in this parlay play and then have four contracts. And so on up. While he's talking Mr. S. is beginning to write figures on the lower left-hand side of his chalkboard, graphically depicting the coffee trader's commitments:

READ FROM BOTTOM UP

300¢ SELL ALL
BUY NO MORE
240¢ - BOUGHT 256 - HAVE 512
200¢ - BOUGHT 128 - HAVE 256
MARGIN CHANGE: EACH 40¢ GAIN = 1 CONTRACT
160¢ - BOUGHT 64 - HAVE 128
140¢ - BOUGHT 32 - HAVE 64
120¢ - BOUGHT 16 - HAVE 32
100¢ - BOUGHT 8 - HAVE 16
MARGIN CHANGE: EACH 20¢ GAIN = 1 CONTRACT
80¢ - BOUGHT 4 - HAVE 8
70¢ - BOUGHT 2 - HAVE 4
60¢ - BOUGHT 1 - HAVE 2
50¢ - BOUGHT 1 - HAVE 1
MARGIN: EACH 10¢ GAIN CAN PURCHASE
ONE ADDITIONAL CONTRACT

Now, he says, at 80¢, each contract is worth $0.80 multiplied by 37,500, or $30,000. Remember that as the total value of a contract increases, the exchange increases the margin requirement. This isn't done on a day-to-day basis, but after a price run-up they will suddenly increase the margin. At 80¢, let's say, the margin requirement was upped so that it now takes a 20¢ rise in price to allow the trader to purchase another contract for each one he already has. So from 80¢ to 100¢ he doubles his contracts, and he doubles them again from 100¢ to 120¢ and from 140¢ to 160¢. And maybe at 160¢ the margin requirement is increased again so that a 40¢ rise is needed to double the number of contracts. And our lucky trader keeps moving along, doubling again from 160¢ to 200¢ and from 200¢ to 240¢. Then he stands pat—and sells when coffee reaches 300¢— that's $3 per pound.

Fantastic! exclaims Mr. E. But how would one calculate his profits? Like so, says Mr. S., already filling in the right-hand side of his chalkboard with figures, starting from the bottom and moving to the top:

PROFITS: READ FROM BOTTOM UP

300					
	60¢	ON 512	CONTRACTS =	$	11,520,000
240					
	40¢	ON 256	" =		3,840,000
200					
	40¢	ON 128	" =		1,920,000
160					
	20¢	ON 64	" =		480,000
140					
	20¢	ON 32	" =		240,000
120					
	20¢	ON 16	" =		120,000
100					
	20¢	ON 8	" =		60,000
80					
	10¢	ON 4	" =		15,000
70					
	10¢	ON 2	" =		7,500
60					
	10¢	ON 1	CONTRACT =		3,750
50					$18,206,250

And when he finishes adding, he points out that there would, after all, be brokers' commissions to deduct. Subtracting a generous amount still leaves about $18 million as a return on an initial investment of about $2,000 in two years' time. That, in theory anyway, was possible for a speculator who relished high risks, back in 1975 to 1977, who kept pyramiding his profits by "rolling over" contracts and buying the same number of new ones in coffee futures.

Mr. E. seems enormously pleased at having been shown how a fortune can be made through commodity speculation. But don't ever forget, says Mr. S., that one can get "killed" just as readily as make a "killing" like this! That was coffee in 1975. But what about coffee in 1973? That chart would show how a plunger could have gone through the same initial sequence, from about 60¢ in January to 80¢ in February, a gain of 33% in a single month. And yet—here Mr. S.'s voice falls—there was a sudden drop from the high. On a chart, dots would now represent the limit days down. If the trader finally managed to get out after the squeeze was on, at 65¢—a loss of 15¢ per pound on four contracts—his total loss would have been close to $20,000! But this is a comparatively modest loss. A plunging novice speculator, starting with $10,000 in his account, might have bought five contracts to start with, then pyramided his winnings, and wound up with a total loss of almost $100,000—in only two months' time. And that, says Mr. S., points out the real dangers in pyramiding. No matter how attractive it looks and sounds, it is always a high-risk venture. The trader who was wiped out in 1973 would not have been around to make any money at all in the big coffee bull of 1975. So as a sheer survival tactic, a pyramid is exceedingly unwise.

Mr. S. has risen from his chair, indicating that it's time for his visitor to depart. Mr. E.'s homework should be of considerable interest to him, he says as he hands back the book Mr. E. brought as well as his bulging folder of literature. Read it all, all of it! he says. And then see if he's still attracted to the variety of commodity con games that are tried on novice speculators. It's a big business unto itself. But as for their next meeting, he will assume that Mr. E. will be ready to apply himself to learning the actual business of commodity speculation. For, like insurance, it *is* a bona fide business and should be conducted as such, using good money management techniques.

And this seems as good a time as any to present Mr. E. with a copy of an interesting statement made on commodity speculation by economist John Maynard Keynes, who was surely the most influential man of his profession in this century:

> In most writings on this subject, great stress is laid on the service performed by the professional speculator in bringing about a harmony between short-period and long-period demand and supply, through his action in stimulating or retarding in *good time* the one or the other. This may be the case. But it presumes that the speculator is better informed on the average than the producers and consumers themselves. Which, speaking generally, is rather a dubious proposition. The most important function of the speculator in the great organized "futures" markets is, I think, somewhat different. He is not so much a prophet (though it may be a belief in his own gifts of prophecy that tempts him into the business), as a risk bearer. . . . Without paying the slightest attention to the prospects of the commodity he deals in

or giving a thought to it, he may, one decade with another, earn substantial remuneration *merely* by running risks and allowing the results of one season to average with those of others: just as an insurance company makes profits.

John Maynard Keynes,
"Some Aspects of Commodity Markets,"
Manchester Guardian Commercial,
29 March 1923, Section 13.

Mr. E., standing in the study's doorway, reads the statement with respectful appreciation. It sounds as if Keynes himself was a part-time commodity speculator, he remarks. Indeed he was! Mr. S. replies. He speculated in currencies. And he was reportedly quite successful at it. After all, professors of economics cannot always make what they consider an adequate living just working at jobs and writing books.

As a matter of fact, Mr. S. continues, Keynes worked for years at the British Treasury. People, seeing him grow wealthy through speculating, accused him of using "inside" information. He told them that this was far from the case: his decisions were made after he read the morning *Times* and executed before he went to work. He even maintained that had he used information available through his job, he might have been ruined financially! Markets, he said, are affected by the public itself and what it knows, not by special information known only to the few. Thus his fortuitous moves could have been done by anyone who read the *Times* with an astute eye for news that would affect prices and monetary values.

And that is something Mr. E. himself might keep in mind. There are definite advantages to being a part-time, small speculator. Since one has a regular job and leads, one supposes, a normal life, one is less apt to get too wrapped up in and psychologically dependent upon what is happening at every instant on the trading floors—as pit traders and scalpers do. Pit scalpers can be right there, in on the action. They pay lower commissions because they are exchange members. But they must *be* there to exercise their privileges. And that, as Mr. E. saw for himself in Chicago, is a highly strenuous job.

Actually, says Mr. S., the successful at-home speculator is much more like the *position trader*. He tends to choose a certain contract position for good reasons, after computing whether he can reasonably afford to keep it. And then he provides and maintains the margin money, riding out this position until close to the delivery month so long as it does not threaten to move drastically against him. He keeps track of the general movement of prices but does not hang on each small jiggle up or down, as if his entire well-being depended upon it.

Oh yes, Mr. E. agrees, being an on-the-sidelines commodity speculator seems like a highly reasonable approach to increasing one's income. And it would allow one to get a good night's sleep too . . . And shaking Mr. S.'s hand, he departs into the dusk.

202

CHAPTER FIFTEEN

Trading the Actuarial Way

It's amazing just how far plain common sense can lead you, Mr. S. begins at his next session with Mr. E. And it can be lucrative too. For instance, he asks his apprentice, what does a commodity speculator try to do in futures contract trading?

To buy low and sell high, of course, Mr. E. replies at once. Or to reverse the order: to sell first and then buy back at a lower price.

That's succinctly phrased, Mr. S. comments. But then where does the big problem lie? Well, nobody can ever know for sure whether the price will go up or turn down from where it is currently, Mr. E. answers. True indeed, says Mr. S., since our predictive powers are generally acknowledged to be decidedly limited where price changes are concerned.

We can get some insight, however, by taking a look at commodity prices over the last few years and then considering what the commodity was worth then versus what it's worth currently. How's that again? asks Mr. E. When buying a commodity, says Mr. S., we trade dollars for it. When selling a commodity, we trade it for dollars. If, for example, wheat once sold for $2 per bushel, at that time thousands of individuals were willing to trade their $2 for a bushel of wheat, while an equal number were willing to trade their wheat for dollars.

We may find it impossible to compute exactly why wheat went for that particular price agreed upon by commercials and traders. We cannot hope to appraise correctly all the factors: planting plans, weather, disease, pests, political happenings, consumer preferences, government price support, foreign agreements to trade wheat. But we *can* make use of the price itself, Mr. S. asserts.

Now look at this long-term wheat chart, Mr. S. requests of Mr. E., and then tell me what you might conclude from what you see here:

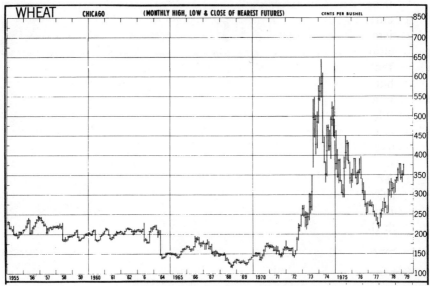

Reprinted with permission of Commodity Research Bureau, Inc.

Well, Mr. E. muses, in 1956 the wheat price was at about $2.50 per bushel. Then for about seven years it oscillated around $2.00. In 1964 it dropped abruptly to $1.50, but it bounced back up to $2.00 in 1966 and then went down to a very low price of about $1.20 in 1968. So that was obviously the lowest it had been in years. (Pity the poor longs! Mr. E. mutters to himself.) Then the price remained near $1.50 until 1972—but shot way up to about $6.50 in 1974. (Pity the poor shorts! he now says.) And just now, as he recalls, the price is hovering between $2.00 and $6.00, somewhere around $4.00—but it certainly could go either way at almost any time.

After analyzing the price history so far, Mr. S. asks, how might we use the information on this chart to guide us in wheat trading? Well, he'd love to be able to buy at that low of $1.20! Mr. E. exclaims. Wouldn't we all? Mr. S. confirms. Anyway, one can see from price charts like this how the prices of all commodities on the exchanges go up and down, continually oscillating between highs and lows. Wheat was destined someday to go down again from its established highs. And it still is. So where will speculators try to buy in now? Should they wait for $1.20 again and then load up?

204

But they may have to wait forever, Mr. E. remarks. Oh? asks Mr. S. Because wheat may never go that low in the future, Mr. E. comments. And why not? Well, the dollar isn't worth what it was then. Ha! says Mr. S. Then Mr. E. has fetched up yet another factor to consider when studying the commodity market situation to look for trading opportunities. *Inflation,* he means then, says Mr. E. Yes, they had talked about how it affects currency and how it makes commodities a good "investment" mechanism in this period of time. But it's true, they haven't discussed how inflation alters the purchasing power of the dollar, which will inevitably affect commodity prices, pushing them up. So that the bushel of wheat that cost $1.20 in 1968 will undoubtedly sell for much more than that now in order to accommodate the devalued dollar.

So what does he have to do in order to figure this out? Mr. E. wants to know, brightening at the prospect of learning something else that is clearly useful. Well, to see what a current price is equivalent to in some past year, says Mr. S., they need to have information about the purchasing power of the dollar now versus what it was then. And fortunately these basic figures are public knowledge, available from many sources. For example, consider this chart in the latest yearbook of the Commodity Research Bureau:

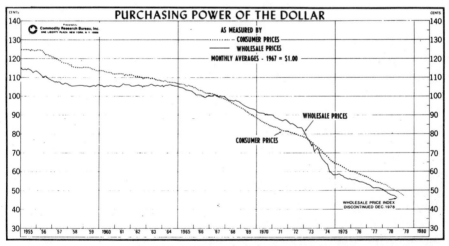

Reprinted with permission of Commodity Research Bureau, Inc.

From this chart one can set up a simple proportion equation to compute the equivalent prices for two different years in terms of what the dollar was or is worth. What's the equation? Mr. E. demands. Wait a moment! says Mr. S. First he wants his pupil to reason it through. If you could once trade a bushel of corn for $1, say, and now that $1 has only half of that former purchasing power, making it worth only 50¢, then how many dollars would it take to purchase that corn now? Well, ventures Mr. E., since it would take twice as many dollars to buy the real goods, corn would go for $2. Correct, Mr. S. says. This is a case of *inverse proportion*.

Now, here's how one can calculate the value of the same amount of goods in terms of what the dollar can purchase—and at this, Mr. S. moves to his chalkboard and writes:

$$P_p \cdot V_p = P_c \cdot V_c$$

P_p : PAST PRICE IN DOLLARS

V_p : PAST VALUE OF THE DOLLAR

P_c : CURRENT PRICE IN DOLLARS

V_c : CURRENT VALUE OF THE DOLLAR

What this means, he explains, is that the past price in dollars multiplied by the past value of the dollar is equivalent to the current price multiplied by the current value of the dollar. It's what Mr. S. calls his *inflation proportion*. So to solve for the current equivalent price, or P_c:

$$P_c = \frac{V_p}{V_c} \cdot P_p$$

Now, would Mr. E. care to use this equation for the corn example? Mr. S. asks invitingly. Mr. E. would. He writes:

$$P_c = \frac{1}{\left(\frac{1}{2}\right)} \cdot {}^\$1 = {}^\$2$$

Good, says Mr. S. And now please calculate the 1968 wheat price of $1.20 for its equivalence in, say, 1977: use the wholesale price curve in the CRB chart—which is based on estimates of the dollar's comparative purchasing power through the years. First, Mr. E. takes a pencil and places it lengthwise against the chart, finding where 1968 intersects with the price horizontal—which he figures at 98. Doing the same then with 1977, he comes up with the figure 51. Then he writes:

$$P_c = \frac{98}{51} \cdot ({}^\$1.20) = {}^\$2.3058$$

So let's round it off to $2.31, says Mr. S. approvingly. And now look again at the wheat chart. Why, in 1977 wheat got down to about $2.20 and then started back up again. So the $1.20 in 1968 was worth approximately

$2.31, and wheat got down to about the same low price in both years, in terms of the purchasing power of the dollar. What a way to make a fortune! Mr. E. exclaims.

But do please remember, Mr. S. hastens to say, that nothing is ever certain in commodity speculation—except uncertainty itself. There are no free lunches, let alone free steak dinners. You always take your chances, your money risks, even with the seemingly sure things. And you must realize all the while that other traders are competing with you, whether taking the same or opposite positions, thereby creating price changes that are bound to affect you somehow.

Yet Mr. E. is sure to find this inflation-proportion equation a highly valuable aid when trading because it helps spot potential bargains. It can be helpful too in a reverse way: you can use the current price as the "known" quantity and calculate what its equivalent price was in the former years that you're studying in order to extrapolate price patterns and histories with what's going on now.

Mr. E. is pleased to have this new calculating tool. Is this the sort of figuring Mr. S. intended to show him when he was talking about the actuarial approach to trading? Yes indeed, says Mr. S. At their last session they spent time considering commodity speculation as a profession, as a business—and specifically as an insurance type of business. The advance figuring is extremely important in arriving at net gains instead of net losses through trading. The inflation proportion is a good example of a trading technique that can bias the probabilities in your favor. You can't know the exact probability of winning on a wheat trade, for example. But by buying lower—close to the equivalent price for wheat in years when there were significant lows—you can certainly improve your chances for success. And you can compute the equivalent wheat prices for perhaps two decades, finding an average price for wheat in any given year, and then buy there, which would be reasonably safe, assuming that the price will tend to rise rather than fall.

All sorts of possibilities abound with the inflation proportion, Mr. S. goes on. We could combine the information with charting: broken trend-lines, V bottoms, and so on. But would this equation work out for a short trade—picking the equivalent highest price for wheat at some future date? asks Mr. E. Sure it would, Mr. S. answers, when you wish to sell rather than buy. But keep in mind that prices can really shoot up if a shortage prevails, and so there is more than just inflation involved in commodity prices. Novice speculators will be better off trading from the long side until they gain experience.

Speaking of inflation still, says Mr. E., does Mr. S. really believe that commodities are the best "hedge" against it? Mr. S. pauses a while before answering. There's no simple hedge against inflation, he answers.

COMMODITY SPECULATION FOR BEGINNERS

The best tactic is to exert effort constantly, partly by keeping your money moving and working in pace with the changing economy. Buying and blindly holding onto something, anything—gold, wheat, Con Edison stock, mutual funds—may not help at all.

Consider gold, if you will, Mr. S. goes on. Is gold a good hedge? It was near $200 in 1975 but then dropped down to about $110. All of those gold bugs who said "Buy gold" were strangely silent until 1978, when gold went to $200 again. Then they wrote more books and said, "I told you so." And since then of course, we've seen it hit more than $800. Many speculators have gotten weary or wounded in the whipsaws going on with gold.

Whipsaws? says Mr. E. Oh, Mr. S. answers, that's the traders' term for the fast up-and-down movements in the price of a commodity that is being overtraded by speculators—where a speculator who has just been hoping for a steady ride to the marketplace gets caught between tugging bulls and bears, who then as delivery date approaches may do panicky contract unloading, creating further havoc in the price action.

While prices may go up and down, Mr. S. continues, a speculator's knowledge should steadily accumulate. The education, experience, and wisdom that he has obtained is his for a lifetime. So good knowledge of the commodity market itself and of the art of speculating itself is the *real* hedge against inflation!

What else must Mr. E. learn before he can safely trade on his own? he is wondering aloud. Many things, his mentor replies, most of which he'll soon be able to pursue by himself through further reading and paper trading. The best way to use the rest of today's session would be to continue on with the calculations basic to trading and with the analysis of trading situations.

Let's start out by going shopping, Mr. S. suggests. Sure, his pupil agrees. But what will they be shopping for? Contracts, says Mr. S. And how much money will Mr. E. be bringing with him? Well, what does it take to get started? his apprentice asks. How much *risk capital* does Mr. E. have? That's the primary consideration. Not his total assets, by any means; only that amount of money that he can safely afford to lose—that he won't sorely miss if it disappears. Money, in other words, that isn't needed for necessities in living, for fulfilling financial responsibilities and obligations. Money that isn't exactly expendable, though, because he would be happy if it could be multiplied by being wisely put to use.

Well, says Mr. E., he has $10,000. Will that be enough? It should be if he trades sensibly, says Mr. S. Some new speculators can manage with $5,000—even less if they combine with a partner. Okay, Mr. S. goes on, what sort of contracts will Mr. E. be shopping for? Something he can afford, obviously, Mr. E. replies. Which means that he puts money down for the margin requirement with enough left over in his commodity account to take care of losses that may occur during several days of trading. Mr. S. adds that he advises him to figure on risking altogether no more than half of his risk capital in any trade, as a precautionary measure, leaving a healthy reserve for some sudden, unfortunate price move from which Mr. E. may not be able to extricate himself for days—remember the orange juice and coffee tales?—and for perhaps, later on, a second, low-risk position to gain more experience.

Now, rather arbitrarily, suggests Mr. S., why doesn't Mr. E. simply choose ten different commodities that might interest him to look into? As Mr. E. reels them off, Mr. S. writes them down on his chalkboard. Then, working together, they fill in the exchange, contract size, and the current price as taken from today's newspaper quotations. The contract months are rather extraneous, they agree, because what they are really looking for is an overall contract value—which will determine, roughly, the margin requirement for each commodity. Their shopping list finally ends up looking like this:

COMMODITY	CONTRACT SIZE	PRICE	CONTRACT VALUE	APPX. MARGIN
CORN	5,000 bu.(CBT) 1,000 bu.(MID)	$3.22/bu.	$16,100 3,220	$1,600 300
POTATOES	50,000 lbs. (NY MERC)	6.26¢/lb.	3,130	350
SOYBEAN OIL	60,000 lbs.(CBT)	26.90¢/lb.	16,140	1,600
COFFEE	37,500 lbs. (NYCSC)	198.39¢/lb.	74,396.25	7,500
ORANGE JUICE	15,000 lbs. (NYCSC)	90.10¢/lb.	17,887.50	1,700
PORK BELLIES	38,000 lbs. (CME)	44.82¢/lb.	17,031.60	1,700
GOLD	100 oz. (COMEX)	614.40$/oz.	61,440	6,000
SILVER	5,000 oz.(CBT)	2762.5¢/oz.	138,125	14,000
COPPER	25,000 lbs. (COMEX)	119.20¢/lb.	29,812.50	3,000
YEN	12,500,000 YEN (IMM of CME)	.4660¢/YEN	58,250	5,800

Ready? asks Mr. S. All right, after looking over this chart, which commodity contract can Mr. E. most easily afford, in terms of initial outlay for the margin? Potatoes, of course, says Mr. E., which is fine with him. He likes potatoes. Okay, how about acquiring two potato contracts at the current price, putting in a margin of about $700 for them. And then suppose the price goes up to the maximum daily limit of 0.5¢ (a half-cent) a pound four days in a row. How will Mr. E. be affected? He begins calculating on a piece of paper:

$$6.26 \frac{\cancel{c}}{LB.} \times 50,000 \ LBS. = \$3,130 \ VALUE$$

ASSUME MARGIN OF $350 PER CONTRACT

LIMIT . $5\frac{\cancel{c}}{LB.}$ OR $\frac{1}{2}$ ¢/LB.

$$.5\frac{\cancel{c}}{LB.} \times 50,000 \ LBS. = 25,000 \ \cancel{c} = \$250$$

2 CONTRACTS FOR 4 DAYS:

$$2 \times \$250 \times 4 = \$2,000$$

And Mr. E. gets excited, almost as if he'd actually *won* that amount. Hold on! says Mr. S. Isn't Mr. E. forgetting something? His apprentice looks taken aback, then sheepish. He had assumed he had bought the contracts, not sold them! he admits. In the short position, he would have lost that $2,000, of course.

Try one long corn contract now, Mr. S. suggests. Dutifully, Mr. E. works out the figures, including four limit days at 20¢ per bushel—with the price dropping down, against him:

$$5,000 \ bu. \times 20 \frac{\cancel{c}}{bu.} \times 4 = \$4,000$$

That's a lot of money to lose! Mr. E. says. Indeed it is, Mr. S. admits. If he felt reasonably confident that the price would go back up to where he purchased it, he could manage to hold on until it does and end up losing nothing, possibly even making a tidy profit on the long haul. But it's the dip down (or up, if you're short) that can do you in, in trading. And often—as they've already discussed—traders tend to forget about providing for the losing times. So not only the initial margin should concern the speculator shopping around for a contract, but also the potential loss. Since the at-home speculator is most likely a position trader, he should always calculate in advance of acquiring a contract position exactly what he may lose—and what he can afford to lose.

And that's an intrinsic part of the money management technique in Mr. S.'s actuarial approach to commodity speculation. He emphasizes this conservative outlook because as a novice speculator he learned the hard way—not having the benefit of a sage trader's advice to the unwary beginner. During his first year of trading he began to do very well. As profits went up he got giddy and cocky. At the same time, and against his better judgment, he started pyramiding on some trades. Oh, nothing very grand, but nonetheless risky. Then the pyramid would collapse and he'd have to start all over again. But rather than get discouraged and leave the arena entirely, he decided to go into it differently from then on. And since then he has done modestly but consistently well.

Unlike many traders who lose, he did not look around for someone —such as his broker—to blame for his own mistakes and poor judgment and bad luck. Blaming others does not contribute to a disappointed speculator's education. Improving one's self-discipline to stick to well-devised trading plans helps considerably. It's a cliché in the business by now, but true nonetheless: a speculator's worst enemies are within him—*greed,* which causes him to take unreasonable risks, such as pyramiding, and *panic*, which brings on precipitous, poorly thought out decisions when things seem to be going wrong for him. To be aware of these tendencies is to be forearmed.

Also, Mr. S. goes on, taking a realistic attitude toward the commodity market's potential offerings cuts down on extreme risk taking. He knows that profits on the order of 2,000% returns on one's money are possible—but not probable. He's known a few people who have earned them on some trade or other. But often these same traders can lose their shirts the next time out. He's content with earnings of, say, 50% in net trading.

How are these earning percentages figured? asks Mr. E. Well, says Mr. S., to make 50% on one's margin money, assuming a 10%-of-the-contract-value margin, the commodity would have to change its value by about 5%. (Minus commissions, of course, Mr. S. adds.) And that 5% would have to be in the right direction! For example, if one buys corn at $2.00, a 5% price rise will put it at $2.10; and the total contract value will then be $10,500 instead of $10,000.

And of course, Mr. S. explains, these profits and losses from trades on the commodity exchanges are reflected in your account's *equity*—that is, how much money is actually in your trading account at any one time. As one would expect, any money placed into the account adds to its value and any taken out is subtracted. It's best to start with enough money to handle any trades being done and not have to bring in more for a margin call. Sending checks takes time for crediting the account. And going in and out depositing and then withdrawing funds from the brokerage creates a nuisance. Any funds in excess of those needed to cover margin commitments should be held in the account until needed or maybe withdrawn just once or twice a year if profits are coming in.

The brokerage firm calculates a customer's equity on a daily basis as part of the "marked to the market" procedure in keeping track of current profits and losses on *uncompleted transactions*—those outstanding contract commitments that have yet to be liquidated by an offsetting sale or purchase. And when a transaction has been completed for a round turn, the brokerage will add or subtract the profit or loss from the trade to the customer's account. At this time, customarily, the brokerage commission is extracted from the speculator's equity. Since the prices and contract values change from day to day on current contracts, a speculator need not be overly concerned about daily changes in his equity, which the brokerage accountants handle routinely. The prudent trader, however, will always be sure that he has enough equity to back up normal margin commitments.

Now, says Mr. S., let's consider the situation of a less-than-novice speculator who's beginning to build up a healthy equity in his commodity account. He is right more than he is wrong. But even that may not save him from a form of folly that can lead to destruction. Mr. S. goes to his chalkboard and begins sketching a graph of this trader's account:

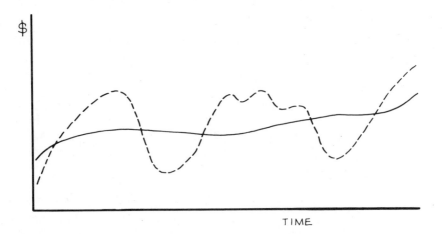

The solid line, he explains, represents the average equity of the account, which is apparently gaining in value. The dotted line portrays the swings in equity as the trader's contracts make or lose money day by day. At first glance it appears as if making and losing in small amounts—say $1,000 give or take in each trade—is essentially the same as winning and losing in larger amounts—like $10,000 in each trade.

But now let's graph how we can still get the same average increase but bet bigger each time—using a large-dot line for this larger commitment:

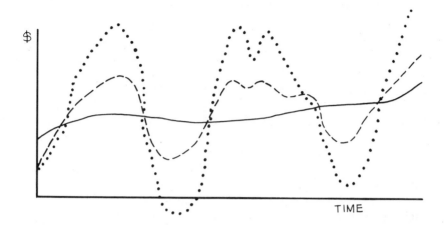

Does Mr. E. spot a significant feature in this graph? Why yes, Mr. E. replies. Although the average stays the same, in this second case the trade-by-trade curve ducks below zero at one point. Indeed it does! Mr. S. stresses. And what happened there? Well, the trader got wiped out, of course. So he's no longer in the game to continue trading to make a profit later on. Yet had he traded in smaller units, he'd still be there maintaining his chance for profit making. It's rather like jumping a one-foot crevice ten times instead of jumping a ten-foot crevice once—and missing!

The lesson to be learned here, Mr. S. goes on, is that a speculator should not overtrade. If he speculates in units too large for his accounts and his risk capital, he's overcommitting them in situations that can readily and quickly move against him. The trader who does this is trying to be smart, trying hard to win. He is not avoiding being dumb or preventing himself from losing the game. Restraint and limited risk are virtues among survival tactics.

So, Mr. S. summarizes, the speculator must always know what he stands to lose in any deal and what he can afford to lose. And by deciding these matters in advance, he can then contrive a particular trading plan for a commodity futures contract that involves placing limits on losses. He will decide how many contracts to enter into initially and of course whether to buy or sell, depending on which way he believes the price will go. He will decide what price he is willing to pay for the contract trade, either specifically or within a certain current range. And there will be other issues too, such as if and when to cancel out on the contract position even though the price is still moving favorably. And these specific decisions that are part of his trading plan, says Mr. S., should be written down and then communicated to the broker at the proper time. Soon they'll discuss the order-giving process itself.

213

He cannot overemphasize the importance of making the initial calculations, Mr. S. goes on. Nor can he make too much about keeping good records of everything involved in a trade. It need not be the sort of paperwork which Mr. E. says he loathes doing. Mr. S. opens a file drawer within his desk to show his student how he himself keeps his current trades in separate folders in the front, which he then retires to the back when the trades have been closed out. But he keeps everything, since he never knows when he may wish to refer to some past experience and since to him there's nothing quite as valuable as his own trading records. No speculator should trust his memory, no matter how perfect he believes it to be, says Mr. S. There are far too many details involved in trading to be able to remember everything, and one can never be sure what information should be kept in the brain for ready access and what can easily be discarded. And even the most important facts and figures may disappear in time, at least in the precision needed for recall when making some new trading decision.

The commodity speculator should also have some basic reference books nearby to consult, Mr. S. maintains. And he should belong to at least one commodity-information subscription service, which can provide price charts and current news relevant to his interests. Mr. S. will give Mr. E. a list of such things before he "graduates" from this trading course and also recommend some books and articles for future reading.

As for opening an account with a brokerage or commission house, it is a relatively simple routine, as Mr. B. surely told Mr. E. The main paperwork involved is to sign a few papers that demonstrate that the new speculator is fully aware that the futures contracts into which he intends to enter are legal contracts enforceable in the federal courts should he fail to come up with funds to support his contractual commitments or to cancel out his position before the delivery date, thereby owing either money or goods.

What about taxes? asks Mr. E. Well, they are very hard to avoid! says Mr. S. In the past, the traditional way to defer paying taxes was to use spreads in various ways. For example, in order to obtain losses for the year, a losing side of a trade would be closed out while the winning side was kept until the next year. Or, to contribute to the year's gains in some tax advantage, the winning side could be closed out instead. The IRS, though, recognized that spreads were being traded frequently just to avoid or defer taxes. So the tax advantages, if any, of spreads have been sufficiently curtailed so as to render spreads practically ineffectual if used for that purpose. Recent rulings also consider short sales as short-term income, not capital gains. A speculating loss can be held against normal income up to $3,000 (currently) on the federal return. A loss exceeding that can be carried over into other years. Practically all subscription fees for chart and advisory services are tax deductible. Since any profit made from commodity speculating is added to a speculator's normal income, he might be advised to go to a professional tax consultant for his own personal situation regarding tax returns.

Now, what else would Mr. E. like to know? How to make up orders for buying or selling contracts, he replies. He recalls that at the Chicago Board of Trade he was quite baffled by some of the phrases used. But his friend Mr. T. explained that a lot of them were just lingo that the brokers and traders use when transmitting orders. So he's not so much concerned about knowing the jargon as he is about giving precise, correct orders—with built-in protections, whenever possible.

Good, says Mr. S. The niceties of expression one's broker can use. The important thing is for the broker to receive and understand exactly what his customer orders. And if anything is unclear or contradictory or wrong, he should be able to question, correct, or clarify the order before it goes out.

Mr. S. stands next to his writing board. Would Mr. E. kindly tell him the main aspects to be considered in giving any order? As his student suggests them, he writes them down:

COMMODITY

AMOUNT OR
    NUMBER OF CONTRACTS

BUY OR SELL

EXCHANGE

Mr. S. wants to add several more:

TIME LIMIT

PRICE SPECIFICS

SPREADS

The points that Mr. E. mentioned are all fairly simple to decide upon, since they are virtually part of the initial trading decision made before the speculator phones the broker. Certain commodities are traded on several exchanges, however, as Mr. E. realizes. And of course he'll keep in mind the MidAmerica Exchange in Chicago, which deals in contract sizes considerably smaller than those in other exchanges. The potato contract in New York is different from the one in Chicago. And the various exchanges that handle wheat do carry different types of wheat at varying prices, as they've already discussed. All the grains are ordered *not* by number of contracts but by number of bushels, in units of thousands, so it would be "Buy fifteen July wheat," say, not "Buy three contracts."

But the order specifics that Mr. S. volunteered are the ones that a speculator must work to comprehend. The *time limit* refers to how long the order should be in force. A *day order* is for just that day. An order that is *good till canceled* is said to be GTC or open, meaning that the floor broker should hold it for execution until the specified price is attainable.

More complex and varied are the order types themselves, which generally are concerned with prices, says Mr. S. The simplest one to execute, of course, is an order to buy or sell *at the market,* which gives the brokerage firm's floor trader instructions to obtain a contract at the price current in the pit when the order is received. An order to buy a March cattle contract at the market, sent in when the price was at 48¢, might be purchased at 48½¢ by the time it is executed. And on 40,000 pounds, that ½¢ difference would amount to $200, Mr. S. points out.

Remember, he says, prices can move rather rapidly during certain days of trading, and by the time the speculator gets an order in, the price may have changed appreciably.

A *limit price order* sets a definite limitation on the price at which a contract should be bought or sold in the customer's behalf, whether the customer is obtaining a new position or closing out an old one. It specifies the highest price that a contract purchaser is willing to pay or the lowest price that a contract seller is willing to receive.

A *stop order* sets a particular price as a "trigger," which will cause the order itself to be executed at the market. A *buy-stop order* must be placed above the current price, while a *sell-stop order* must be placed below the current price. These orders can work to the speculator's advantage because he can determine in advance in some commodity that interests him exactly where he wishes to place a stop order if he wants to go short or long when a price moves in a predetermined way. A stop order can also be placed in advance to protect the speculator from sustaining losses from adverse price moves beyond a certain point. Not all commodity exchanges will accept stop orders for all their commodities, though some require a stop-limit order.

A *stop-limit order,* Mr. S. goes on, gives the floor trader a range in which to execute a customer's transaction. The "stop" part is the trigger price; the "limit" part is the maximum or most extreme price that the customer is willing to accept. Thus, if March wheat is currently trading at $4.80, say, an order that reads "buy at 4.84 stop—4.86 limit" may come in. When the price reaches $4.84, then the floor trader will buy it at the market but only up to $4.86.

Looking at a stop-limit from the short side, says Mr. S., suppose the October cattle contract is at 48¢. An order to "sell at 46 stop—44 limit" tells the floor trader to sell when the price dips down to 46¢, at any price above 44¢. Conceivably, though, he may actually sell at 47¢, because once 46¢ is reached, the next few traders can go back up above that price —which is to the seller's advantage, of course.

One very useful technique is to give two orders at once—one contingent on the other. Say that a trader feels that if December wheat, currently at maybe $4.25, gets up to $4.50, it will then continue on to $6.00. However, if wrong, he will want to limit his loss to just 50¢ per bushel on the contract. He can place the following order to buy and enter an open stop at the same time . . . and here Mr. S. jots down on his chalkboard:

$$B \quad 5 \quad DEC \quad W \quad 450 \quad ST$$
$$EOS \quad 400$$

EOS? asks Mr. E. That's for *enter open stop,* Mr. S. tells him.

Frequently, says Mr. S., an order is given to the brokerage without the word *limit,* yet it is clear enough, since an order to buy is understood to mean below the current market price and an order to sell, above it. It doesn't hurt, however, to use a limit order to buy even when the latest price is below the buy point. For instance, if December copper's last price was 62¢, a trader can specify a buy order at a limit of 63¢. This will prevent him from paying more than 63¢ in case the price rapidly increases during the interval between the time he gives the order and the time it is received on transmitting to the exchange floor.

A *spread order,* Mr. E. should recall, involves two transactions at the same time—buying a contract and selling another contract. Here the trader is not concerned with the prices of the two contracts directly but rather with the difference between them. A spread order might read like this, says Mr. S., writing:

$$BUY \quad MAR \quad COTTON$$
$$SELL \quad MAY \quad COTTON$$
$$150 \quad PREMIUM \quad MAY$$

What does the *premium* mean? Mr. E. asks. That tells the broker that the May price is the higher of the two, Mr. S. replies. Another way of stating the order would be, "Buy a March contract when the March price is 1½¢ under the May price."

And by the way, interjects Mr. S., exchanges don't accept stop orders for spreads.

Well, says Mr. E., he can see how the order itself can be designed by a skillful speculator to protect him in various ways. Yes it can, Mr. S.

agrees. A trader should use whatever devices there are to prevent him from getting into losing circumstances that he would rather not be in. However, he should keep in mind that having an unrealistic order will get him nowhere in a market he may wish to enter right now. He should be able to maintain a certain flexibility, too, when taking a position that may move against him for a while. He cannot always expect to win—though ultimately, of course, in every trade he hopes to do so, virtually by *not* losing. When the losses mount, he cuts them off by clearing out of the trade. And when the winnings come in, he is glad to get them but lets them ride along. He must always beware of the speculator's worst traits: panic and greed, which can ruin his judgment in trades that are going badly or well.

And now Mr. S. would like to see Mr. E. reason through a typical trading problem: which position to take. He would like him to use some calculations he knows, as well as the actuarial principles.

Mr. E.'s analysis has told him that gold, at around $635 per ounce, is at its peak. He is contemplating selling gold. What is a gold contract on Comex currently worth, and what would be an approximate margin requirement?

Mr. E. gets to figuring. He'll round the current prices to $600 per ounce. Multiplied by one hundred ounces, that's $60,000. So the margin might be $6,000.

Okay, says Mr. S., there's $10,000 in his trading account right now. How far can gold move against him before he gets a margin call and then before he gets wiped out entirely? Well, since there's $6,000 already committed to the margin, he has $4,000 left to cover an adverse move, says Mr. E. At one hundred ounces per contract . . . and here he writes:

$$\frac{\$4{,}000}{100 \text{ oz.}} = 40 \frac{\$}{\text{oz.}}$$

So there is enough money in his account to withstand a price move upward of $40 an ounce, for a total price of $640. Above that, he will run out of any reserve funds. What if the margin were less than $6,000: $5,000, say? Mr. S. asks. Well, that would add another $1,000—so that at $650 he would have his entire account committed to that one trade, with no reserve funds. If gold rose above $650, he would have to place new funds into his account or else his broker would have to take him out of the trade.

How much will gold have to move in order for Mr. E. to lose his whole original $10,000? asks Mr. S. Well . . . :

$$\frac{\$10{,}000}{100 \text{ oz.}} = 100 \frac{\$}{\text{oz.}}$$

That means that the price will go from the $600 Mr. E. shorted to $700. Does he know how to figure the percentage move for this gold price? asks Mr. S. Mr. E. will try:

$$\frac{100}{600} = \frac{1}{6} \cong 17\%$$

Good! says Mr. S. Now let's consider another possible trade. Assume that oats are now at $2 per bushel and you think that they are going up. How many contracts of oats will be worth the same value of the one gold contract?

Mr. E. begins figuring:

$$2 \frac{\$}{bu.} \times 5000 \ bu. = \$10,000$$
$$\text{FOR ONE CONTRACT}$$

Since the gold contract is worth $60,000, he can get an equivalent value in 6 contracts of oats. With about the same margin requirement, too. Correct, says Mr. S., though in reality the gold margin may be proportionately more because of its volatility as well as single contract value. But just now they are considering concepts, not fine details.

So, Mr. S. proposes, if Mr. E. buys 30,000 bushels or 6 contracts of oats, how far can oats go down before he loses his entire $10,000? Which is ignoring the fact that he will have had to put in more margin money so that the broker will let him keep the contracts. Mr. S. writes:

$$\frac{10,000 \ \$}{30,000 \ bu.} = \frac{1}{3} \frac{\$}{bu.} \cong \$.33 = 33\cent$$

And that's 33¢, he says. So oats can drop from $2.00 to $1.67, which would be:

$$\frac{33}{200} \cong 17\%$$

About a 17% change, just as the gold price was, only this goes down, not up.

Now, leaving the calculations aside, Mr. S. suggests that his pupil analyze the situation strictly from the standpoint of money management. He can assume that the technical and fundamental considerations suggest an equal probability of making money on the gold short or the oats long.

First, asks Mr. S., what is Mr. E.'s working principle? A belief, Mr. E. says, that one cannot outsmart the market—and the thousands of qualified speculators and hedgers in it—enough to make a huge fortune. Like everybody else, he'd certainly like to do this, but reason and caution must prevail. Therefore, he's interested in withdrawing a fair return on his capital, considering the time, effort, and risk put into trading.

Sticking with the first operating tenet of game theory, he will concentrate on minimizing potential losses, not on maximizing potential profits. That is why he would tend to be leery right away about getting involved in a gold contract. At $600, every 10% move, say from $600 to $660, would be $6,000—or 60% of his working capital. Just a glance at the gold chart shows that it has been bouncing around all over the place for several weeks. The run-ups have been extreme, even though the price may come back down just as precipitously. A mere 10% move is hardly anything in this volatile market.

What is happening with gold, Mr. S. now comments, is that a lot of the short contracts are probably in "weak hands." That is, sad to say, people who don't have the capital to withstand much adversity. And these small speculators, who maybe shorted at $600, take a look upward where gold could go—$650 or $700, who's to say?—and they get very nervous indeed. So no wonder they are also called "scared money." Many longs are equally scared, of course—leading to a lot of volatility.

Well, says Mr. E., he is almost convinced that gold will go down far, maybe to $400, but he just doesn't have the financial resources to absorb price run-ups, temporary though they may be. He would have to set close stops from his initial shorting position, and these would be so close that they would get caught just by the normal price swings.

So he'll turn to oats now, says Mr. E., and consider them. There is no reason why he couldn't do just as well—or just as poorly, it may be—on $60,000 worth of oats as on $60,000 worth of gold. Oats aren't very glamorous, it's true. But then he's not in the business for glamour's sake.

Analysis of the factors involved has told him that theoretically he can make as much shorting gold as he can buying oats. But gold can go up to who knows where, whereas oats can only go down to zero. Although the exact probabilities can't be determined, it seems to him that the probability of oats' going down to zero is less than the probability of gold's going up to $1,200—in equivalent value moves. Since there must be a bottom for oats somewhere, certainly above zero anyway, he'd be buying oats closer to the bottom than he would be shorting gold near the ceilingless top. So his best bet is to buy the oats.

But wait. Mr. E. is studying the oat chart that Mr. S. has handed him. He sees that oats went down to $1 a bushel in 1971. That was a while ago, but if oats do go down again to that price, his 30,000 bushels will hit him with a $30,000 loss—and on an account of $10,000. It's very unlikely that will happen, but still . . .

Considering that, Mr. E. had better not go for six contracts at $2, for he wants to survive for the long haul and be in the business for years. So he'll forego the chance for big profits. But how can he decrease his potential loss? Mr. E. ponders for a few moments, aware of Mr. S.'s watchful eye. He could go into some sort of oat spread, he says, but right now he'd like to stick to a net long position. Or he could buy fewer oat contracts, thereby lessening his risks and also lowering commission costs. He could buy oats not at $2 but wait for a lower price, if one comes along. He could buy all six contracts but set very close stops to limit losses. Or maybe he could in some way combine several of these plans.

That's fine! Mr. S. compliments him. Mr. E. has exhibited a prudent response to a situation typically encountered by a successful commodity speculator. In his analysis, he goes on, a lot will depend on things other than just looking at oats. Such as if he has other margin commitments, how strongly he believes oats will go up, and even if he wants to rest for a while from speculation and take a vacation from it all.

Rest? asks Mr. E., incredulous. But he hasn't even *begun* yet!

But he will, he will, Mr. S. assures him. He's getting ready. So ready, in fact, that he can continue to learn on his own. Because their next meeting will be graduation day. He can expect more questions and answers and general commentary. And maybe a few eloquent speeches too.

As for homework, Mr. S. gives him a little game he has put together to show novice speculators how to *paper trade* on their own, which is an important part of the education process in commodity speculation. There are instructions, charts, and sequential cards with "news reports," as well as sheets for making calculations and keeping records. But this game is based on reality, says Mr. S. It simulates the usual day-to-day paper trading. The decisions that the player makes as he proceeds in his trading course on paper will be affected by a set succession of prices that he cannot know in advance. And these prices derive from particular commodities' actual histories. The advantage of Mr. S.'s game is that it compresses time and duplicates past realities. And as he plays along, Mr. E. will begin to discover what it's like to actually speculate—learning from his mistakes can be a form of profit making.

CHAPTER SIXTEEN

A Commodity Speculator's Guide to Myths and Truths

On this final day of their trading-course sessions, Mr. E. arrives in rather jaunty spirits. Yes, he has been paper trading these past few days, using Mr. S.'s game-style simulated method. And he had a wonderful *and* highly instructive time of it! As Mr. S.'s teaching manual suggests, he made the playing out of positions seem far more real by ":betting" actual money on his trades, making 1¢ stand for $1,000 in value. At first he was disturbed by the preponderance of losses over profits. But the more he played—or *worked* at it, really—the more skillful he got at the whole game. He's pleased to say, in fact, that after a good many hours of application he finally began achieving net profits.

Mr. E. sets the game folder down on Mr. S.'s desk top. He ought to patent that! he remarks. Indeed, Mr. S. is thinking about it, since he is convinced that most novice speculators plunge into the market knowing little, really, about its mechanisms or the various calculations and reasoning processes that must take place before and during a trade. Mr. E. can now proceed by himself, using the current commodity prices for his own ongoing paper trades and watching what happens as he goes along. He'll know when he is ready for the real trading. And in the meantime he can improve his knowledge about many things and perfect his techniques.

But somewhere, says Mr. E., he read that paper trading was senseless, a waste of a new trader's time and efforts. Yes, he's heard that too often enough, Mr. S. remarks, but he can't agree. The "experts" who say that maintain that nothing teaches beginners as well as real experience—by this meaning running the risks of losing, which are highly probable in a net way because of *in*experience. Speculating can be painful enough at times to the battle-hardened veteran without inflicting it unnecessarily upon the untested neophyte. So he argues for as much paper trading as the raw recruit can possibly put in prior to putting real money into the actual marketplace.

And that inevitable tendency of people to believe what somebody tells them, what they see in print or hear, can sometimes create trouble within the commodity speculator's own performance. The put-down of paper trading as merely a frivolous game is only a minor example of the myths that prevail among both the public and commodity traders themselves. Just as Mr. S. collects evidence of the con artists' many ways to gull the unwary and the greedy out of their assets—and, as Mr. E. knows, the commodity market has a somewhat checkered history of both large- and small-scale attempts at this—he also studies a number of the myths that have arisen within the entire field. Many cultural myths do contain elements of truth, of course, but as they get passed along they get elaborated on and changed, and the truth becomes highly distorted or wholly fictionalized.

Now, would Mr. E. want to suggest one of the myths that he has heard for a long time about commodity speculation or speculators? Well, says Mr. E., that a speculator is almost certain to get slaughtered—so it's best to avoid getting involved. Is there some truth to that? asks Mr. S. Obviously there is, Mr. E. replies, if the statistics show that 90% of the *new* speculators get wiped out in their first year of trading. But it has become clear to him that probably most of them were not prepared for the contest to begin with and must have gotten in because they were attracted to the high profit-making potential without realizing that in order to increase their probability of winning, they'd have to do a lot of preparatory studying. Then when they discovered that the market could move as swiftly and ruthlessly against them as it could do rapidly and benevolently *for* them, they felt like live hogs sold off for conversion into pork bellies!—not comprehending their fate until it had happened. And naturally they blamed something or somebody else for what happened at slaughter time. Anything other than themselves, for their failure to be thoroughly armed for the fray.

As a matter of fact, continues Mr. S., an uneducated novice speculator is doomed to failure. If he loses right away on his first few trades, then obviously he will leave the market. But even a first-time winner will probably end up losing. That is because, after his first few winning trades, he will start to think that he has "beaten" the market and will then plow his winnings back into new trades, speculating with more and more. But

223

we have seen that unless one is right 100% of the time, then eventually a loss will occur. And it will be a big loss, taking all of the previous winnings with it—another example of *parlaying to destruction.*

The veteran speculator does not get carried away with his predictive abilities, will be content to withdraw a sensible amount, and will not try for that elusive brass ring of an overnight fortune.

Care to tackle any more popular myths? asks Mr. S. Well, there's the one about how all successful commodity speculators are fabulously wealthy—the implication being that they have gotten rich off the money they have "taken" from the greenhorn speculators and from driving the prices up. Actually, Mr. S. says, that is three myths in one: that all professional traders are millionaires; that they purposely connive and cheat, often among themselves, to bilk the innocent small speculators; and that their activity inevitably causes prices to rise in the commodities they trade in.

Now, will Mr. E. comment about the public's unfortunate image of the Commodity Trader? Willingly, his apprentice starts in. Certainly there are millionaires in the commodities, as there are in all business endeavors. And perhaps there are more, proportionately, among the real professionals, since the money-making potential in the field is admittedly very high for people who know what they are doing. Yet it intrigues him that the public also wants to believe that all speculators, sooner or later, get wiped out by their activities and lose virtually everything, probably even the shirts off their backs. So that in a sense the customary image of the Commodity Trader is contradictory, combining the millionaire with the down-and-out pauper.

And how about that unscrupulous and unsavory reputation of theirs? Mr. S. reminds Mr. E. Well, he wonders about that, he says, and he expects it got started long ago, in what's now far-distant history. He has heard, for example, about the shady deals that went on in back rooms in places like Chicago and New York during the nineteenth century, when the various commodities were transported to the marketplaces where the producers and merchants gathered. And how the commodity exchanges originated, beginning with the Chicago Board of Trade, in order to place these buying and selling transactions above board and in full view of whoever was interested in commercial deals or sheer speculation in futures contracts for forward delivery. But even then some manipulators tried to get rich quick by "cornering the market." And others ran "bucket shops," in which they bought or sold contracts in commodities. In fact, the hopeful speculators never saw these contracts, for their orders were thrown haphazardly into a "bucket," along with others. If they lost, they had to pay in and maybe lose their margin money that secured the contracts. But if they won, they found that their brokers had either absconded with their winnings or had never even gotten contracts.

No wonder, then, that there's a lingering distrust and dislike for the Commodity Trader, Mr. S. comments. No matter how well regulated the exchanges and brokerages may be, no matter that the government has its own impartial agency, the CFTC, to supervise what's going on, in spite of the fact that many federal and state bureaus connected with various commodities actually encourage speculators because of the insurance protection they provide for the commercials involved in them, the public by and large still thinks of the speculator as a shady character involved in dubious and perhaps illicit actions, rather like a hard-bitten gambler. But who, Mr. S. goes on, is this Commodity Trader, in actuality? Why, he may be a she, an accountant or a schoolteacher or a waiter, a lawyer or a banker or a writer—nobody mysterious and threatening at all! In fact, says Mr. S., this Commodity Trader, this "public enemy number one," is . . . *us!*

Mr. E. laughs. Yes, he is personally concerned about telling anybody that he is becoming a commodity speculator because of the strange reactions he has been getting much of the time from others. He finds it difficult even to converse with them on the subject because they seem predisposed to dislike it, even though they often apparently know nothing about it. And they start to treat him as though he were planning to become an embezzler or hold-up man. So it is discouraging to be unable to share this new interest with friends and acquaintances.

Well, he's learning a valuable lesson early, Mr. S. observes. It is one that took him longer, since he kept trying to educate others, to convince them that commodity speculation was a legitimate and intriguing business to get into. He slowly realized that people were mostly bored or annoyed and that he was wasting his time and energy even talking to them about it. Furthermore, he experienced that curious phenomenon well known to traders large and small. People sometimes act envious and even angry if they know you have been winning in some fortuitous trade, in which even the public is aware of sudden price movements. Or, if you're losing badly because you're on the wrong side, they take a certain gleeful pleasure in your sorry predicament, expressing the attitude that "it serves you right" just for being a commodity speculator to begin with.

And that, Mr. S. continues, is just one of the psychological aspects of trading that a speculator must contend with. He'll have plenty of his own emotions to deal with when he trades—for trading, after all, is a highly emotional experience, especially at first. Gradually a speculator, as part of his increasing self-confidence and expertise in exercising self-control, begins to keep in check his strong up and down emotions, which waver inevitably according to how a trade seems to be going. But as for the outsiders, a speculator does best, Mr. S. believes from his own observations, to remain close-mouthed about what he is doing, except with people whose opinions and behavior he can trust not to affect him adversely. In effect, he keeps his own counsel, unless he has a trading partnership with somebody else. That arrangement can sometimes work out well if the associates are like-minded, having similar goals and techniques but perhaps complementary interests and skills, therefore allowing for diversification in trading and entering into several different markets at once to spread the risks.

Now, says Mr. S., there's that last part of Mr. E.'s mythological trinity—that speculators drive the prices up on commodities. What does he have to say about it? Well, Mr. E. answers, it seems as if the public looks around for someone to blame for inflation, for the constant rise in the cost of living. Yet it is clear to him by now that probably as many speculators are involved in selling futures contracts as in buying them— and since their interest is in seeing the price go down rather than up, they are hardly driving up the prices deliberately. Also, he is persuaded that the fundamental interplay of supply and demand, in which the speculators' entry can provide an important liquidity during times of imbalance caused by undersupply that does drive up prices, guarantees that a period of high prices is usually followed by one of lower prices. No, Mr. S. has taught him a great deal about the speculators' good effects on the overall economy. He is reluctant to blame them for inflation and instead looks to the proliferation of paper money that is not based on production—including the production of commodities.

What about some other myths? asks Mr. S. Well, there's the one about commodity speculation being just a large-scale gambling game, Mr. E. volunteers. That, of course, isn't so, since gambling essentially exists for the purpose of gamblers and has no social or economic usefulness. And the action on the commodity exchanges quite decidedly contributes to the social and economic good of the nation and its commodity commercials.

And yet where did the gambling myth come from? Mr. S. wants to know, from his apprentice's perspective. It arises from that fact that both gambling and speculating involve taking risks in order to win or earn more money, Mr. E. responds. Which makes futures trading similar to two aspects of straight gambling in games that combine luck or probabilities with skill. One can never really know in advance how chance will work, but part of the skill comes from an ability to assess probabilities of winning and losing, and another part relates to how one "bets," or manages, his money. The more knowledge and experience one acquires in speculating, the better he can bias the probabilities for winning in his favor.

Mr. E. finds it very helpful indeed to think of commodity speculation in terms of the insurance underwriting function, which is an acknowledged useful profession, unlike gambling. And certainly its centuries-old record as a lucrative but legitimate enterprise that is essentially based on risk taking and on studying probabilities and expectations in order to construct actuarial methods that guarantee steady profits makes it a good model for the serious and responsible speculator. And Mr. E. can see that it's one that Mr. S. follows in his own practice.

Yes, Mr. S. agrees. Successful speculating isn't just straight skill or straight luck: it's a combination of both. And you can never be sure when you enter a trade whether you'll gain or lose. So it is vitally important to develop the right attitude toward what you are doing so that the slightest setbacks don't undo you.

Well, probably the best speculators have nerves of steel, Mr. E. comments. Not so! Mr. S. corrects him. It's good, of course, not to be an extreme worrier, and procrastination is bad. But a good dose of caution is an asset. And so is a tendency to doubt. In a way, the speculator has to contain within himself rather contradictory attitudes: he must make a move believing he is right, yet all the while he must be aware that he may be wrong so that he's ready to protect himself if something goes amiss.

And actually, Mr. S. continues, the sort of person you might think would make an excellent trader—determined, dogged, self-confident, unperturbable—may end up being the worst. He may be locked into the "success syndrome," feeling assured that whatever he does or wants to do he'll succeed at because he always has. Things go easily for him; he has always been a winner because he wanted to win and instinctively knew the way to do it. A winning ingredient in his character is that good, old-fashioned American trait, perseverance. He'll just keep trying something he wants to accomplish, rather stubbornly, and finally succeed. He is positive in his outlook and can't comprehend the word *can't*. He hangs onto something like a bulldog.

But—! Maybe Mr. E. would like to write the scenario now, Mr. S. suggests. Well of course he sees what might happen to such a person now, says Mr. E. Maybe he has overcome all other temporary setbacks he has had in business or in his personal life simply by hanging on and riding it through. But this attitude won't work in trading, especially when you have only limited capital behind you even though your position may ultimately prove right. If this speculator buys pork bellies and they start to decline in price, he may get wiped out if he attempts to hold onto them. And he may not have investigated the "down" side to commodity speculation enough to understand just how far these prices can swing against him. Perhaps he was regarding futures trading as an investment vehicle, not a speculating one, assuming that sooner or later he was bound to

227

receive compensation for having his money used—and not realizing that it could be taken away from him if the contracts lost the value they had when he entered into them.

And then there are the gambler types who are inevitably drawn to commodities, Mr. S. adds. They are willing to take big chances in order to win large profits. Often they haven't studied up at all as to what they are doing there in the marketplace, and then they take too big a chance and get clobbered.

So the people who *seem* best suited, superficially, for commodity speculation may not actually be so, Mr. E. is concluding. Then who is? And here Mr. S. laughs heartily. Sometimes he thinks it's a very cautious, conservative type who is *repelled* by the very thought of commodity trading! he declares. And of course since this kind of person tends to steer clear of the marketplace, commodity futures contracts seldom get into his thinking, let alone his hands. And the new speculators who do go in, to run rather heedlessly among the already battle-scarred but crafty bulls and bears, don't last very long in the arena. More than likely the 10% or so who do survive, to move on to the next year of trading, have learned enough to take a reasonably secure small corner in the constant action. Many small speculators remain so, by their own choice, not wishing to compete with the professional combatants. But some eventually become the large traders one thinks of more as the Commodity Trader.

Mr. E. remarks that commodity trading appears in essence to be a *zero-sum game,* in which all the participants put in money. The winners win by taking money from the losers. So obviously, in order for some traders to make money from commodities, a lot of traders are losing. Well, it isn't exactly a zero-sum situation, Mr. S. answers, as far as the speculators themselves are concerned, because look . . . Now he goes to his bookshelf and takes out the *Review of Economics and Statistics.* Here's a fifteen-year study of who won and who lost in corn, wheat, and cotton, he says. It's called "Can Speculators Forecast Prices?" and was done by H. S. Houthakker. The figures are given in millions of dollars and rounded off:

CORN	WHEAT	COTTON
Large hedgers: −6.09	Large hedgers: −6.28	Large hedgers: −183.45
Small traders: −5.53	Small traders: −20.88	Small traders: +130.88
Large speculators: +11.62	Large speculators: +27.16	Large speculators: +52.58

Look how the numbers add up, Mr. S. points out. The hedgers, in effect, were paying for their insurance. The large speculators would pick this up and also usually take some money from the small traders too. But not always, as cotton shows. Now these minuses, these losses, sustained by the small traders are *net*. Probably a fair percentage of them as individuals secured profits from trading. The ones who lost altogether must have dropped out soon. Others improved and remained small speculators, but still others in that time period surely moved up to become large traders. So it isn't a zero-sum game altogether, since obviously the hedgers on the "losing" side of a trade—as shown notably by cotton here—are not contributing money to "play the game" along with the others. They are securing insurance against adverse price changes, and what they pay out is virtually an insurance premium given to the risk takers who assumed their unwanted risks. And if they hedged adequately, the real losses were minimal.

So commodity speculation *is* indeed a business that is carried on by individuals, says Mr. S., though increasingly, speculators may be collected together in commodity pools. Even though speculating is different from investing, as Mr. E. is aware, it is still helpful to realize that a speculator can benefit by taking an "investment attitude" toward what he is doing, using sensible money management techniques while he operates a small, at-home business in which he keeps careful records of his transactions and thinks through each move carefully. He is better off regarding himself as a businessman than as some mystical predictor of future prices, since essentially he hopes to make money from judiciously buying and selling—with the perennial tactic of buying low and selling high, in whatever order it is done, so far as futures contracts are concerned. And as a matter of fact, if one considers that he can launch an entire enterprise with capital of perhaps only $10,000, the possibilities in commodity speculation seem sensible and indeed promising for someone who is willing to invest initial time in learning the field. That is, after all, what any sane and ambitious person would do if expecting to undertake any other form of business or profession.

Well, says Mr. S., they have mostly been discussing the myths that the general public has about commodity speculation and its practitioners and separating the fables from the facts. He now proposes that they consider certain myths and adages that are passed around among the traders themselves. How about Mr. E. thinking up a few?

The experts know everything, Mr. E. suggests. Well, he recognizes now that they don't. They may be more capable than the general public of foretelling certain price changes, but that doesn't mean that their predictions will prove right. Furthermore, he knows that they usually argue among themselves about what may happen. Should a speculator pay attention to the experts, though? asks Mr. S. He should know what they are saying and what they are doing, Mr. E. answers, because their advice and actions are bound to affect how prices go, if only temporarily, since other traders tend to follow their lead. But still, they may not be at all right ultimately.

Any more? Mr. S. asks. Well, how about computers know everything? Or that someday, anyway, they'll know everything, says Mr. E. That's a good one too, Mr. S. says. They are our twenty-first-century "experts," Mr. E. ventures. And he doubts that they could be as good prognosticators as the human experts. After all, could a computer ever duplicate the uncanny artistry of a great poker player?

Then? Mr. S. urges. Oh, Mr. E. offers that fundamentalists may someday come up with some formulation of patterns that will solve the entire riddle of commodity speculating by telling us exactly what the prices will be, when. At first this secret knowledge will only belong to the privileged few who discovered it or let their friends in. But eventually it would become common knowledge. And then . . . well, either the whole commodity-pricing and allocating system will be turned over to the computerized world, or else people will discover new ways to speculate that react to and rebel against the established patterns!

Well, there's also the rule among speculators that one should just as readily think of selling as of buying, of going short instead of long, Mr. E. proposes. But what Mr. S. has told him convinces him that the new speculator particularly should lean in favor of buying, since there is always a solid base somewhere, even if at zero, whereas there is no sure high beyond which prices cannot go.

And now, Mr. S. interrupts, he would like to suggest several more. Such as, speculators never take deliveries. He knows this is wrong because he himself once actually did so! Inadvertently, of course, for that was not his intention. But it happened, and he's still here to tell the tale. Mr. E. naturally wants to hear more. Well, Mr. S. continues, Mr. E. is aware that when the delivery time approaches, the daily limit is removed on many commodities by the exchanges on which they are traded.

But doesn't that make the prices really shoot up or down uncontrollably? asks Mr. E. And how do the clearing firms and brokerages mark accounts to market? They may do it, Mr. S. responds, on an hour-to-hour basis if necessary. And yes, the prices do tend to move faster, but remember that the majority of the traders are already long gone; mainly the hedgers remain, so that the eventual price is soon going to resolve itself into the current cash price, which is a realistic one. The commercials won't be bothered much by extreme price swings as the contract is approaching its resolution in true value.

And what happened to Mr. S. himself, then? Mr. E. pursues. An error, he says. He was long 100,000 pounds of copper in a bull market and he had a nice profit built up. In the closing days of a contract a *short squeeze* can develop in which the short speculators become desperate to buy back their commitments because, of course, they do not have the actual commodity to deliver and had been hoping that the price would come down in the end. Well, in this particular bull market Mr. S. thought he saw a short squeeze developing. And there he was, a happy little pig, imagining all those short sellers waiting in line to buy his copper. The longer he held on, he reasoned, the higher the price he'd get.

But that's what greed does to a speculator, Mr. S. comments. He held on too long and got a delivery notice! He actually took delivery of real copper? asks Mr. E. in wonderment. Where did he put it all? Well, it wasn't all that bad, Mr. S. replies. The 100,000 pounds of copper didn't arrive in his mailbox. What he did get was a receipt from a warehouse in New York informing him that it had his copper and that he owed money for it and for storage, insurance, and labor. Also an "inspection" fee, though he suspects that somebody makes a nice living out of passing in and out of warehouses with a clipboard, doing nothing much but dubbing a pile of commodities "inspected."

If this happens to a speculator, copper isn't a bad choice. You can easily turn around and *retender* it; that is, offer it for sale. Though that can be expensive and time-consuming, with more fees involved. As it was, he managed to sell the copper to somebody else—to let *them* take delivery. But some commodities, such as shell eggs, cannot be retendered. And when you get delivery, you really have it! So the at-home speculator is advised to be long gone before any chance of delivery comes up.

Then there are various "It can never happen" maxims, Mr. S. goes on, and also some "once-in-a-lifetime opportunities" that they might profitably explore now. Small speculators should always be on the prowl for situations that go against the ordinary run of things, and sometimes they can be spotted early and traded upon.

Consider, Mr. S. now offers, certain events in commodities that have been said to be impossible. Such as grains exceeding government limits. The U.S. Department of Agriculture doesn't have legal limits above which or below which a grain may not be traded, but it does have a program of supporting low grain prices and encouraging storage in time of great surplus. The government normally does this in wheat and corn, and sometimes in soybeans and oats.

Take wheat, says Mr. S. The government has had a loan rate of around $2.35 per bushel for the past few years. In times of surplus a farmer can borrow on the wheat he is growing. If prices remain low, he can default on his loan and the Commodity Credit Corporation assumes control and stores the wheat somewhere, not marketing it right away. In effect, then, this set loan rate is a minimum below which wheat will not go. Except in September of 1977—when wheat momentarily dipped slightly below that theoretically minimum price. So it made a very low-risk trade for a speculator.

Now here's another trader's adage, Mr. S. offers: a bushel of wheat must always sell for more than a bushel of corn. Right? Wrong! It wasn't so in 1969, 1970, and 1977. At these times the impossible happened, and wheat actually dipped below corn. At such a time, putting on a spread—long wheat, short corn—would have been quite lucrative. But one would still have to use some thought, since buying July 1969 wheat and selling July 1969 corn in June of 1969 wouldn't have given the spread time to work. In June of 1977, however, one could have bought September 1977 wheat and sold September 1977 corn at even money and then as the September contracts came due just have rolled over into future months.

And what would have been the compensation for these risks? Mr. E. is curious to know. Considerable, says Mr. S. Wheat, theoretically anyway, cannot stay below corn for long. Assuming a $500 margin requirement on the wheat-corn spread of 5,000 bushels each, one can see from the charts of that period that the spread went from zero to upward perhaps 70¢ or 80¢ in a year's time—depending on how one rolled over the spreads. That is, a bushel of wheat went for about 70¢ more than a bushel of corn. A 1¢ move on 5,000 bushels is $50, and that multiplied by 70¢ comes to $3,500 per spread (minus commissions)—on just $500, in a year!

But a trader must always be wary of counting his riches, Mr. S. goes on. There's the example of another spread situation that might not have worked out so nicely because the impossible happened again. Live hogs are slaughtered and then processed to wind up as, among other things, frozen pork bellies, from whence comes our bacon. Since hogs must be converted into pork bellies, the latter must always cost more per pound than the former. But wrong! exclaims Mr. S. When one checks the price charts, one sees that the July contracts closed about even in 1971. And in 1979 July pork bellies were actually some 6¢ to 7¢ under July hogs. So history was being made again, contradicting the soothsayers. And if a trader had done a long-pork-bellies–short-live-hogs spread for July, he might have been caught in hot oil. With a little knowledge and experience, however, a trader could have gone into a long-pork bellies–short-live hogs spread in the next "crop year" for hogs and then have done quite well, at least for a while.

A small speculator can search for signs for "once-in-a-lifetime" trading opportunities. But he would do well, Mr. S. cautions, to avoid any commodity *options* salesmen who try to convince him that here, right now, is his chance to make a small fortune and that never again will such an opportunity arrive. He gets the big rush, whether it's over gold or foreign currency or silver coins or whatever. Once he gets his money in, it'll be smooth sailing right into the port where the millionaires' yachts are anchored. But he may find that his cash was steamed away in a "boiler room."

Mr. E. asks to know about options. He knows they exist in stock but doesn't know how they would work with commodities. Well, says Mr. S., an option by itself is a perfectly legitimate concept under normal circumstances. For instance, if X owns an apartment building or a block of stock, he can sell an option to Y, giving him the right to purchase that property, within a time limit, for a set price. But in the case of commodity futures, it's a different story. Y can buy an option on a commodity contract from X, but X does not own anything. Now X can buy a futures contract, it's true, but remember that a futures contract is not real ownership but a promise to buy when the contract comes due.

And the question is, Why should Y buy an option from X when Y can buy the futures contract directly? says Mr. S. So X is a middleman with no real function. And he usually charges Y a much higher price than he should be paying or else—as has frequently been the case—X is a total crook, who would sell the options to the unwary and then if things went wrong simply run off with the funds.

Mr. S. would like to note, however, that in the past it was quite common to actually refer to a futures contract as an "option," as indeed it was, in a sense. But the term used that way has now become archaic. And there was an area of legitimacy with options, especially connected with "forward contracting." Recently, though, the term has been taken up and abused by fraudulent boiler-room, bucket-shop operators who used the high-pressure tactics of calling up potential customers and promising riches and continually pestering them in the hope of getting their money; meanwhile they did not cover themselves by actually buying the futures contracts for which they were offering options!

The CFTC and investigative reporters and federal agents have cracked down on these excesses and abuses practiced by options dealers, and some of the firms have been taken to court. Still more cases are under examination. Many of the options companies have solid-sounding names and use phrases like *deferred delivery* or *long-term forward contracts* to describe the dubious product they are selling. A number are legitimate and reputable enough, but it's hard for anyone—including the CFTC—to know which is which. Therefore it has been proposed that all options be traded on a recognized exchange in the United States under the CFTC's watchful eye. As it is right now, Mr. S. says, only foreign exchanges deal in options. The whole matter is being debated, with some people insisting that options should be outlawed altogether, since they are unsuitable for the public at large and inevitably offer money-bilking opportunities for the unscrupulous, who—alas—are ever with us.

Well, Mr. E. comments, there certainly have been a lot of new futures contracts developed in the last few years. Look at them all! The international currencies, T-bills, government bonds, and commercial paper. And he's been reading about the new Eurodollar, the European certificate of deposit that may be traded on the CBT. Surely most of the possibilities must be exhausted by now, Mr. E. asserts.

Ah, Mr. S. remarks, there are innumerable future futures constantly being proposed nowadays. That's why one should never underestimate the American economy—and American innovativeness! There's talk of adding the Italian lira to the IMM foreign currencies, and the Chicago Mercantile Exchange may take on fresh broiler chickens. The New York Mercantile Exchange may handle gasoline futures. Sunflower seeds contracts may be traded soon on the Minneapolis Grain Exchange and perhaps on the CBT, which may also have futures in southern plywood. The New Orleans Commodity Exchange could get very busy with rough rice, milled rice, cotton, and soybean contracts. And what with the increasing undependability in paper supply, there could be a futures contract in scrap paper. More of the exchanges are getting into the financial instruments, with the New York Futures Exchange specializing in them. Some exchanges are merging, and there's the probability that a few may open on the West Coast, thereby extending commodity trading for several more hours each day. Also, the Chicago Mercantile Exchange may start a branch in London, and the CBT will have one in New York.

Mr. E.'s head is whirling with this burst of news. How does a small speculator keep up with such changes and additions? he wonders. Just by keeping in touch with the market, Mr. S. answers. A good daily newspaper will have the latest commodity news among its business section's pages. And a speculator who's serious about what he's doing will also subscribe to several specialized financial or commodity journals or services. If he reads them faithfully, he'll have no trouble in knowing what's going on. The changes, Mr. S. admits, are coming thick and fast nowadays, and so no book can really hope to cover everything or have all the current lists and figures that a speculator needs. A general book's best service is to introduce a new speculator to the basic principles involved in speculating and to demonstrate a few conservative techniques to follow when trading. Exact trading specifics, especially in newly created situations, must be picked up elsewhere. There is plenty of literature around, available from brokerages and from the exchanges themselves, that gives the most up-to-date information and lists.

Now that the hedging mechanism is far better understood and appreciated, Mr. S. continues, more and more commercials are using it as insurance against adverse price changes. And there is also more pressure on the experts at the exchanges to devise new futures contracts to accommodate them. The tremendous success of the financial instruments in the seventies revolutionized monetary economists' thinking.

How so? wonders Mr. E. For one excellent example, Mr. S. replies, new portfolio futures are proposed. Portfolio? Isn't that a collection of securities, like stocks and bonds? Mr. E. asks. Exactly, Mr. S. responds. And the Chicago Board of Trade has developed a mechanism to speculate in the price changes of corporate stocks. Rather than have futures in individual stocks, though, the futures are for several major stocks placed in groups, called industry portfolios. There are ten of them: air transport, automotive, banking, chemical, drug, information processing, petroleum, photo-optic, retail, and telecommunications. Then there will be a futures contract in the entire collection—known as the composite portfolio. Also, Mr. S. goes on, the Kansas City Board of Trade is doing something similar with the Value Line Index, and the CME with the Dow Jones.

What a boon to stock market speculators! Mr. E. exclaims. This way, if they wish to speculate in price changes rather than just receive dividend income, they can do it directly in these futures, instead of having to bother with buying and selling the underlying stocks themselves. (And here Mr. E. realizes just how much he's learned about the difference between investing and speculating in the past few weeks.)

But basically one must always keep in mind the real value of the futures exchanges and contracts, Mr. S. interjects: they provide hedging opportunities for commercials. A typical group interested in hedging with these new stock futures would be a pension fund. The fund managers wish to make investments and realize a definite income; they certainly do not want to speculate on a change in price of the stocks they purchase.

So consider the problem they have right now, Mr. S. proposes. If the managers of a pension fund purchase $100 million in stocks, they may be satisfied with their interest income of $5 million or $10 million; but they are deathly afraid of a decrease in the value of their portfolio. That is why many pension funds are geared to earn only a very low percentage on their money; often less than half the current interest rate. It's a safety factor that takes into account any decrease in the value of their stock purchases.

Of course, Mr. S. continues, the value of the stocks can also go up. But a pension fund isn't in the speculating business; it just wants a nice, steady, and, above all, *reliable* income—with no loss in original capital. Now, Mr. S. reminds his listener, no insurance company in the world has the resources to insure a pension fund against stock prices' collapsing. As a matter of fact, the insurance companies themselves are in the same predicament. They too would like to place their reserves into stocks and bonds and have a guarantee of no price change. But prices *do* change.

Pension funds, then, Mr. S. concludes, can insure against a decrease in stock prices by selling futures on a commodity exchange. Then if stock prices go down, the fund will gain on the futures market what it lost in its cash holdings. And naturally a rise in prices will result in a loss in the futures but a gain in the cash. No longer having to worry much about price fluctuations, they can do what they're supposed to do: earn dividends on their investments.

There's a rather recent development that's favorable to speculators too, Mr. S. tells Mr. E. And that's the ease of buying such financial interest-earning investments as Treasury bills and commercial paper. Because of this, a brokerage firm can invest the unused portions of speculators' accounts in such funds, thereby earning some interest for them. Thus a speculator can open an account for commodity trading for $10,000, commit $2,000 to a particular trade, and earn interest on the remaining $8,000. Of course this unused portion will change day to day as the price of the commodity itself fluctuates, but many firms will handle the computations and paperwork for clients opening an account with a minimum amount.

The growth of futures trading, says Mr. S., has really been phenomenal in the past few years. The statistics show this dramatically. The number of contracts traded increased from 3.8 million in 1960 to 58 million in 1978! And the volume has been rising annually by 30%. The Chicago Board of Trade alone traded as many contracts in 1978 as were traded in *all* the exchanges in the United States in 1974. And the dollar volume in the commodity market—1 *trillion*—compares favorably indeed with that of the stock market, which is around 150 billion. The commodity market is obviously overtaking the stock market in activity. And yet, ironically, Mr. S. remarks, so many members of the general public hardly seem to know that it exists. Or if they do know, they wish it would go away!— because they simply haven't bothered to investigate and understand what it does for the American economy.

But now, Mr. S. says, glancing at his clock, it is time for his graduating apprentice to depart. He has guided him over the stepping-stones across the river. The uphill, winding road leading on to fortune he can walk upon only by himself. He now knows the way, the rules, and the routines. He has become acquainted with perils and pleasures ahead. Mr. S. bids him Godspeed on his journey, beginning soon!

The two men shake hands warmly as Mr. E. rises to go.

Oh, they are surely going to meet again. Next time, perhaps, at Mr. B.'s brokerage office.

CHAPTER SEVENTEEN

Mr. E. Goes Off
into the Sunset

A few months pass by, during which our Mr. E., the novice speculator, continues to study diligently the entire subject of commodity speculation. Extra interest is added by the enlivening paper trading he is doing on the side, by taking up would-be positions in the current trading on the various markets and building up his aptitude for both guesswork and maneuvering. When his mock account finally begins showing a robust profit, he decides he is ready for the real marketplace.

Easing up from his solitary pursuits, he attends his first Friday night poker game in . . . well, months. As he enters the home of the host, a neighbor, he is greeted with cheers and resounding back slaps. Where has he been all this time? he is asked. All his poker buddies had just about given up on ever seeing him again at a game.

Before they settle down to playing, Dr. M., the mathematician, goes over to shake Mr. E.'s hand and say hello. He has been much concerned that Mr. E. may have given up entirely on the hope of achieving financial betterment through money investment, he says. And does this include poker playing too? Heavens no! exclaims Mr. E. He has just been too busy to come over until now.

Busy? Dr. M. asks. With what? Is he going to night school and taking up a new profession? Oh no, says Mr. E. He has been studying, it's true. But he's not giving up his regular job. He's only adding another part-time profession. As—? Dr. M. inquires. Now, if anybody will be able to ap-

237

preciate what Mr. E. is going to do, this insurance actuary standing in front of him will.

As a commodity speculator, Mr. E. responds. Dr. M. looks startled. Astonished. Not entirely approving. But curious nonetheless. Well, that is a financial endeavor that he really knows next to nothing about, he says in a while. Is it really on the up-and-up?

Mr. E. laughs, naturally. Dr. M. did him a large favor some while ago, he says, when he introduced him to a number of matters having to do with money, gambling, probabilities, and insurance. It may interest him to know that their conversations really got him started in the direction he's going.

And actually, he adds, the two of them have something in common now: they are *both* in the insurance business!

Dr. M. is perplexed. Well, how can that be? Mr. E. can't even begin to tell him now, of course. But he'll be happy to drop by Dr. M.'s house maybe tomorrow to tell him about commodity speculation and its function in supplying price-change insurance to commercials who deal in the commodities.

And who knows? Dr. M. may even wish to consider becoming a trader himself.

Then on Monday morning, bright and early, before going off to work, Mr. E. comes by Mr. B.'s brokerage office. He fills out the necessary forms and hands Mr. B. a certified check for $10,000, with which he will open his commodity trading account.

And then he gives him his order, the first of many more to come. It says,

"_____"

Appendix

For Further Reading

Books

Angell, George. *Winning in the Commodities Market*. New York: Doubleday, 1979.

Angrist, Stanley. *Sensible Speculation in Commodities*. New York: Simon & Schuster, 1972.

Beard, R. E.; Pentikainen, T.; and Pesonen, E. *Risk Theory: The Stochastic Basis of Insurance*. New York: Wiley, 1977.

Belveal, L. Dee. *Charting Commodity Market Price Behavior*. Wilmette, IL: Belveal & Co., 1969.

Commodity Yearbook. New York: Commodity Research Bureau, Annual.

Epstein, Eugene. *Making Money in Commodities*. New York: Praeger, 1976.

Epstein, Richard. *The Theory of Gambling and Statistical Logic*. rev. ed. Chicago: Academy Press, 1977.

Hieronymus, Thomas A. *Economics of Futures Trading*. 2nd ed. New York: Commodity Research Bureau, 1972.

Krohl, Stanley. *The Professional Commodity Trader (Look Over My Shoulder)*. New York: Harper & Row, 1974.

Reinach, Arthur M. *The Fastest Game in Town: Trading Commodity Futures*. New York: Random House, 1973.

Shaw, John E. *A Professional Guide to Commodity Speculation*. Englewood Cliffs, NJ: Prentice-Hall, 1972.

Appendix

Springer, John L. *If They're So Smart, How Come You're Not Rich?* South Bend, IN: Regnery, 1971.

Teweles, Richard; Harlow, Charles; and Stone, Herbert. *The Commodity Futures Game: Who Wins? Who Loses? Why?* rev. ed. New York: McGraw-Hill, 1974.

von Neumann, John, and Morgenstern, Oskar. *The Theory of Games and Economic Behavior.* Princeton, NJ: Princeton University Press, 1953.

Articles

Billings, Robert. "Get Rich in Your Spare Time While Doing Absolutely Nothing (Almost)." *Playboy,* March 1978.

"How to Trade in Commodities." *Business Week,* 20 September 1976.

"How Futures Prices Can Be Used as a Predictive Device." *Newsweek,* 15 January 1979.

Periodicals

The following periodicals are free on request:

Monetary Trends and National Economic Trends. Federal Reserve Bank of Saint Louis, Box 442, Saint Louis, MO 63166

Monthly Economic Letter. Citibank Economics Department, 399 Park Ave., New York, NY 10022

U.S. Department of Agriculture Publications. (Economics, Statistics, and Cooperatives Service Bulletins, Crop Reports, Market News, Weekly Roundup of World Production and Trade, etc.) Washington, D.C. 20250

(subscriptions)

Commodities Magazine. 219 Parkade. Cedar Falls, IA 50613

Consensus. Box 19086. Kansas City, MO 64141

Journal of Commerce. 99 Wall St., New York, NY 10005

Wall Street Journal. Dow Jones & Co., 200 Burnett Road, Chicopee, MA 01021

To the Reader: Inclusion in any of the following lists of speculative-services firms does not constitute a recommendation.

About Brokerage Firms

There are basically three types of brokerage firms that handle commodity accounts:

1. *Total service.* These are the large commission houses that deal in stocks, bonds, and other areas of financial endeavors, as well as in commodities.
2. *Commodities only.* These firms limit themselves to commodity futures contracts. They buy and sell for their customers and also provide customers with information and advice. Their commission structure is similar to that of the total-brokerage type.
3. *Discount brokers.* For their customers, these firms will buy and sell con-

tracts—but only that. They will not offer advice. Their commissions may be up to 50% less than the other two types.

A comment here: at first one may think that the cheaper the commissions, the better. But commissions may be a relatively small part of the overall profits and losses in trading. The position trader, who trades perhaps infrequently, will not be as affected by commissions as the speculator who is in and out of commitments constantly.

Discount brokers don't provide advice. But speculators have to consider the value of any advice they are given. Bad advice, obviously, is worse than no advice at all. Futures commission merchants of all kinds do more than just execute orders. They hold your money, and a full-service firm may be able to place unused funds into interest-bearing securities. And they keep track of your contract positions, warning you when the delivery month is approaching. (The at-home speculator naturally wants to avoid taking delivery of a commodity. You would have to save a lot of commissions at a discount in order to pay for 22,500 dozen eggs!)

Here are some firms in each group. Some of the Type 1 and 2 firms named here have local offices that are listed in the yellow pages of phone books:

1. TOTAL SERVICE
   Bache Halsey Stuart Shields, Inc.
   Blyth Eastman Dillon & Co., Inc.
   E. F. Hutton & Company, Inc.
   Loeb, Rhoades, Hornblower & Co.
   Paine, Webber, Jackson & Curtis, Inc.
   Merrill Lynch, Pierce, Fenner & Smith, Inc.
   Shearson Inc.

2. COMMODITIES ONLY
   Ace American, Inc.
   Archers
   Clayton Brokerage Co. of Saint Louis
   ContiCommodity Services, Inc.
   Delphi Commodities, Inc.
   Delta Commodities Corp.
   First Commodity Corp. of Boston
   Maduff & Sons, Inc.
   PMA Commodities
   Siegel Trading Co., Inc.
   Weinberg Bros.

3. DISCOUNT BROKERS
   Chicago Discount Commodity Brokers (CDCB)
   175 W. Jackson Blvd.
   Chicago, IL 60604

Eastern Capital Corporation
One Washington Mall
Boston, MA 02108

Riverside Commodities
222 S. Riverside Plaza
Chicago, IL 60606

Murlas Bros. Commodities, Inc
5450 W. Fullerton Ave.
Chicago, IL 60639

Southern States Trading Co., Inc.
One World Trade Center
New York, NY 10048

Pacific Commodities
455 S. Broadway
Estacada, OR 97023

Commodity Pool Operators

These firms will pool an individual's funds into one account and manage that account:

Commodity Systems
150 E. Palmetto Park Rd.
Boca Raton, FL 33432

Pacific Commodities
455 S. Broadway
Estacada, OR 97023

ContiCommodity Services, Inc.
1800 Board of Trade Bldg.
Chicago, IL 60604

PMA Commodities
133 Federal St.
Boston, MA 02110

Dunn and Hargitt
22 N. 2nd St.
Lafayette, IN 47902

Yorkstone
41 State St.
Albany, NY 12207

New Orleans Advisors
Box 50371
New Orleans, LA 70150

Advisory Services

(On request, any of these firms will send information about their particular services and fees.)

Commodex
114 Liberty St.
New York, NY 10006

Commodity Sense
Box 625
Altamont, KS 67330

Commodity Research Bureau
One Liberty Plaza
New York, NY 10006

Contrary Opinion; Seasonal Patterns
Sibbet-Hadady Publications
380 E. Green St.
Pasadena, CA 91101

CSIC Group
Shearson Hayden Stone
9609 Wilshire Blvd.
Beverly Hills, CA 90212

Delta Financial Research
1724 Sherman Ave.
Evanston, IL 60201

First Commodity Corp. of Boston
11601 Biscayne Blvd.
North Miami, FL 33181

Bruce Gould
Box 16
Seattle, WN 98111

International Investors Services
200 E. 81st St.
New York, NY 10028

Jeremy Oates Ltd.
18–19 Fish Street Hill
London, EC 3R 6BY
ENGLAND

Keltner Statistical Service
1004 Baltimore Ave.
Kansas City, MO 64105

Lind-Waldock & Co.
15125 Ventura Blvd.
Sherman Oaks, CA 91403

MBH Advisors
Box 353
Winnetka, IL 60093

Parris and Company
649 West Oakland Park
Room 201-D
Fort Lauderdale, FL 33311

Tara (Texas Agricultural and
     Research Assn.)
3521 34th St.
Lubbock, TX 79410

Western Financial Management
3031 Tisch Way
Suite 803
San Jose, CA 95128

Wisconsin Research
Box 726
Janesville, WI 53545

Charting Services

These firms chart recent price action—they usually do not give advice:

Commodity Price Charts
219 Parkade
Cedar Falls, IA 50613

Commodity Research Bureau
One Liberty Plaza
New York, NY 10006

Comtrend
25 3rd St.
Stamford, CT 06905

Dunn and Hargitt
22 N. 2nd St.
Lafayette, IN 47902

IBEX Charts
Box 693
Seattle, WN 98121

Spread Scope
Box 41221
Los Angeles, CA 90041

Traders Press
Box 10344
Greenville, SC 29603

Appendix

Commodity Information Packages

The major commodity exchanges are usually quite generous to prospective small speculators. Write to their Public Relations Department (at the addresses given on the List of Commodity Exchanges in the U.S., p. 245 and request information about futures trading and the commodities on their exchange. The Chicago Mercantile Exchange has a booklet called "Commodity Scorecard" which would be highly useful in paper trading.

At your request, any of these firms will send you a package containing information about various commodity services and publications:

Commodity Action Cards
219 Parkade
Cedar Falls, IA 50613

Allan C. Davis
1617 Linner Rd.
Wayzata, MN 55391

Impact Postcards
Consensus Inc.
30 W. Pershing Rd.
Kansas City, MO 64108

Select Information Exchange
2095 Broadway
New York, NY 10023

Speer Books
20380 Town Center Lane
Suite 230
Cupertino, CA 95014

Traders Press, Inc.
Box 10344
Greenville, SC 29603

Wire Services

These firms provide Teletype and computer terminals linked directly to the latest market news and price action:

Ciscom
4232 Brandywine Dr.
Peoria, IL 61614

Comm Basic
7920 Chambersburg Rd.
Dayton, OH 45424

Commodity Communications Corp.
175 W. Jackson Blvd.
Chicago, IL 60604

Commodity News Service
2100 W. 89th St.
Leawood, KS 66206

Reuters
1700 Broadway
New York, NY 10019

Trans-Lux
110 Richards Ave.
Norwalk, CT 06854

VideCom of Comtrend
25 3rd St.
Stamford, CT 06905

The Commodity Futures Trading Commission

The Commodity Futures Trading Commission (CFTC) is the federal regulatory agency for futures trading. It was established in 1975 to supersede the Commodity Exchange Authority. The five commissioners are appointed by the president of the United States and are subject to Senate confirmation. The CFTC makes and enforces the rules under which the approximately one dozen commodity exchanges in the United States operate. It also oversees the operations of several thousand commodity exchange members, the nearly four hundred futures commission or brokerage houses, some sixteen hundred commodity trading advisors (CTAs) and commodity pool operators (CPOs), and about thirty-seven thousand registered futures commission merchants (FCMs).

The Commodity Futures Exchanges in the United States

ABBREVIATION(S)	NAME AND ADDRESS	MAIN COMMODITIES TRADED	VOLUME IN 1979
ACE	Amex Commodity Exchange 86 Trinity Pl. New York, NY 10006	GNMAs, T-bills	64,319
CBT	Chicago Board of Trade 141 W. Jackson Blvd. Chicago, IL 60605	Iced broilers, commercial paper, corn, GNMAs, gold, oats, plywood, silver, soybeans, soybean meal, soybean oil, T-bonds	33,870,680
CME (see also IMM)	Chicago Mercantile Exchange 444 W. Jackson Blvd. Chicago, IL 60606	Boneless beef, butter, feeder cattle, live cattle, shell eggs, skinned hams, live hogs, lumber, milo, pork bellies, russet and burbank potatoes, turkeys	19,930,798
CMX, COMEX	Commodity Exchange, Inc. Four World Trade Center New York, NY 10048	Copper, gold, silver, zinc	12,952,353
CTN, NYC, NYCE	New York Cotton Exchange Four World Trade Center New York, NY 10048	Cotton no. 2, crude oil, orange juice, propane	1,875,126
IMM (affiliated with CME)	International Monetary Mart 444 W. Jackson Blvd. Chicago, IL 60606	Copper, foreign currencies, gold, U.S. silver coins, T-bills (13 wks., 1 yr.)	

Appendix

ABBREVIATION(S)	NAME AND ADDRESS	MAIN COMMODITIES TRADED	VOLUME IN 1979
KCBT	Kansas City Board of Trade 4800 Main St. Kansas City, MO 64112	Milo, wheat (hard red winter)	1,037,018
MACE, MAX, MID	MidAmerica Commodity Exchange Chicago, IL 60604	Corn, gold, live hogs, oats, silver, cattle, soybeans, wheat	2,568,950
MGE	Minneapolis Grain Exchange 150 Grain Exchange Bldg. Minneapolis, MN 55415	Oats, durum wheat, spring wheat	328,799
NYCSC (new combine)	New York Coffee, Sugar & Cocoa Exchange Four World Trade Center New York, NY 10048	Cocoa, coffee "B" and "C", rubber, sugar nos. 11 and 12	2,510,179
NYFE	New York Futures Exchange 11 Wall St. New York, NY 10005	Financial Instruments	
NYM,	New York Mercantile Exchange Four World Trade Center New York, NY 10048	Swiss franc, gold, imp. boneless beef, heating oil, industrial fuel oil, palladium, platinum, Maine potatoes, U.S. silver coins	828,249
NOCE	New Orleans Commodity Exchange 308 Board of Trade Pl. New Orleans, LA 70130		
(Canada)	Winnepeg Commodity Exchange	Barley, flaxseed, gold, oats, rapeseed, rye, wheat	

TOTAL:	75,966,471
TOTAL 1978	58,462,172
INCREASE:	30%

The CFTC publishes research bulletins and a brief bibliography concerning futures trading. Also available are the following CFTC publications:

100—"Purpose of the CFTC"
101—"Reparations"
102—"Economic Purposes of Futures Trading"
103—"Farmers, Futures and Grain Prices"
104—"Reading Commodity Futures Price Tables"
105—"Glossary of Terms"

To obtain the materials, contact the CFTC's national office at the following address:

Commodity Futures Trading Commission
2033 K Street, NW
Washington, D.C. 20581
Telephone: (202) 254-5273

The CFTC also maintains the following regional offices:

Eastern Region
One World Trade Center, Suite 4747
New York, N.Y. 10048
Telephone: (212) 791-0790

Central Region
233 S. Wacker Dr., 46th Floor
Chicago, IL 60606
Telephone: (312) 353-5990

Suboffice
510 Grain Exchange Building
Minneapolis, MN 55415
Telephone: (612) 725-2025

Southwestern Region
4901 Main St., Room 208
Kansas City, MO 64112
Telephone: (816) 374-2994

Western Region
Two Embarcadero Center
Suite 1660
San Francisco, CA 94111
Telephone: (415) 556-7503

The CFTC also provides a consumer hot line—toll-free telephone service to answer questions concerning firms or persons dealing in commodity futures or options. Request CFTC reports or materials at the following hot-line numbers:

Continental United States:	800-424-9838
Alaska and Hawaii:	800-424-9707
Washington, D.C.:	202-254-7837

Index

Account executive, commodity. *See* Broker, commodity

Accounts, trading (at brokerage), 41, 211–13, 214, 236, 238

Actuals. *See* Cash commodities

"Actuarial" approach to futures trading, 105, 189, 207, 218. *See also* Money management

Actuaries, insurance: calculating risks and expectations, 17–18, 32, 192, 227

Agribusinesses as hedgers, 85–86

Arbitrage. *See* Spreads

"At the market" orders, 63, 72, 216

Banks: low interest paid by, 11, 21; requiring commercial borrowers to hedge, 174; using depositors' money, 10, 23

Bar charts, 105–6, 155–56, 157, 194

Barley, 29, 246

Bartering, 10, 127

Basis, 78, 153, 177–79, 180

Beans. *See* Soybeans

"Bear" or "bearish," 45, 46. *See also* "Short" position, as trader

Beef, boneless, 137

Beginner in commodity speculating. *See* Novice speculator

"Boiler rooms," 233. *See also* "Con games" in commodities

Bonds, government, 234. *See also* Treasury bills, etc.

Books about commodity speculation, xiii, xiv, 152, 187–90, 201, 214, 234, 239–40

Breakout (in price trends), 163

Broad tape (teletypewriter), 111–12

Broker, commodity: described in action, 64–66; functions of, 27, 64, 95–96; how to choose, 95–97, 240–41

Brokerages (commission houses), 22–25, 26–27, 53, 57–58, 62–66, 69–75, 81–92, 241. *See also* Accounts, trading; Commissions, brokers'; Orders, trading

"Bucket shops," 224–25, 233. *See also* "Con games" in commodities

"Bull" or "bullish," 45, 46. *See also* "Long" position, as trader

"Bulls" and "bears," origin of terms, 46

Buy-stop orders, 166

Buying futures contracts. *See* "Long" position

Index

"Buying hedge." *See* "Long" position, as hedger

Calculations, basic, in trading, 145, 154, 202, 208, 214, 218, 221, 222; how to calculate earning percentages, 211; equity in account, 211–12; inflation proportions, 205–6; margin deposits, 40, 142, 209, 218; margin maintenance, 74, 209–10; profitable price moves, 209–10; value of contract—*see* Contract value
Carrying-charge market, 177–78, 183, 184
Carryovers, 148
Cash commodities or markets, 59–60, 176, 178
Cash price (spot), 41, 42, 47, 59, 88, 95, 159, 177, 230
Cattle. *See* Feeder cattle; Live cattle
CBT. *See* Chicago Board of Trade
CEA (Commodity Exchange Authority), 94, 245
CFTC (Commodity Futures Trading Commission), 35, 94–95, 141, 225, 233, 245–47
Channel line (in price chart), 161
Charting approach. *See* Technical approach to trading
Charts, price. *See* Bar charts; Moving averages charts; Point-and-figure charts; Technical approach to trading
Chicago Board of Trade, xv, 38, 55–56, 57, 92, 117, 120, 134–39, 176, 184, 215, 224, 234, 235; clearinghouse of, 81–92; trading floor of, 53, 57–62, 68–81; trading volume of, 56, 236, 245
Chicago Mercantile Exchange (CME or "Merc"), 56, 62, 65, 116, 130, 135–37, 234, 235, 245
Chickens: fresh broiler, 234. *See also* Iced broilers; Poultry
"Churning," by brokers, 96
Clearinghouses or clearing corporations of exchanges, 41, 42, 62, 74, 81–92
Closing out contracts. *See* Contract canceling
CME. *See* Chicago Mercantile Exchange
Cocoa, 29, 74, 123, 133, 135, 143, 148
Coffee, 29, 133, 135, 143, 148, 150, 199–201
Comex. *See* Commodity Exchange, Inc. (New York)
Commercial paper, xiii, 131, 132, 139, 234, 236. *See also* Financial instruments

Commercials: defined, xii, 30; problems with price changes, 30–35, 42–43; taking positions early, 45, 90. *See also* Hedgers; Hedging; Price change insurance
Commissions, brokers': in commodity trading, 47, 182, 200, 211, 212, 232, 241; in real estate, 22; in stocks, 25, 47
Commitments of traders (chart), 153, 173–75
Commodities: basic groups of, 28–29, 115–32; contracts for—*see* Contracts, commodity futures; defined, 10–11, 27, 28, 115, 116–17; on the exchanges, 28, 30, 52, 115–32; letter symbols for, 71; new—*see* Future futures; popularity of particular, 170; substitutions in—*see* Substitutions in commodities
Commodity broker. *See* Broker, commodity
Commodity charts (specifications), 134–39, 245–46
Commodity commission houses. *See* Brokerages
Commodity contracts. *See* Contracts, commodity futures
Commodity Credit Corporation, 231
Commodity dollar, 128
Commodity Exchange Center (CEC), 56
Commodity Exchange, Inc. (New York) (Comex), 138, 245
Commodity exchanges: xi–xii, 34, 141, 215, 235; auction aspect of, 38, 61, 73; branches of American, 234; foreign, 133, 233; as nonprofit services, 54–55; origin of, 38, 55–56, 57, 224; public access to, 38–39; rules of, 52, 60; supervision of, 38–39, 52, 225; trading hours of, 53, 58, 83. *See also individual names of exchanges*
Commodity Futures Trading Commission. *See* CFTC
Commodity information sources, 194, 215, 234, 240–44
Commodity Research Bureau (CRB), 205, 206, 242–43
Commodity speculation (commodity market, futures market, futures trading, etc.) as a business, xi–xiv, 27, 55, 189, 201, 207, 229; compared with stock speculation, 36, 39–40, 47, 48, 236; from economic perspective, 37–39, 47–48, 226, 236; profits in—*see* Profit potential

in futures trading; public's lack of knowledge about, xii–xiii, 27, 39, 51, 103; as rational price determinant, 95, 116, 125. *See also* Commodity Speculators

Commodity speculators (or traders): blamed for higher consumer prices and inflation, 47, 51, 224; functions of—*see* Price change insurance, Liquidity; psychological facets of, xii, 26, 36, 45, 101, 211, 218, 225, 228; skills of—*see* Money management in trading; guesswork of—*see* Price predicting in futures; as insurance underwriters—*see* Price change insurance; tactics of, 203, 229—*see also* Game theory; using price and other technical charts, 152–54. *See also* Failed traders; Large traders; Novice speculators; Small speculators

Computers: in actuarial work, 18; doing trading calculations, 83, 89; limitations of, as price-change predictors, 107–8, 165–66, 192, 230; record keeping, 64–65, 66, 89, 165–66; for relaying information, 64, 65, 165

"Con games" in commodities, 187–90, 201

Congestion areas (P & F charts), 158

Consumer prices, effect of speculation on, 29, 30, 47, 51, 149–50

Consumption, 107–9. *See also* Demand; Production

Continuation charts, 159

Continuation patterns, 160

Contract buyer. *See* "Long" position

Contract canceling (closing out or liquidating), 40–42, 87–88, 89, 212, 213, 214

Contract months. *See* Delivery months

Contract seller. *See* "Short" position

Contract size, 73–74, 134–39, 141, 143–44, 215

Contract value, calculating, 40, 44, 141–42

Contracts, commodity futures: basic price units in, 73–74; defined, 34, 41; delivery months in, 34–35; evenly matched at exchanges, 41–42, 83, 84; history of, 37–38, legal obligations in, 84, 87–88; reality of, 51, 83, 85, 87–88, 90; specifications of, 34, 134–39, 140–44

Contrary-opinion traders, 175–76

Copper, 29, 125, 138, 144, 150, 230–31

Corn, 29, 77, 117, 119, 134, 141, 146, 231, 232. *See also* Grains

"Cornering the market," 52, 90–91, 94–95, 224. *See also* Price manipulation

Cotton, 29, 74, 124, 136, 234

Crop year, 178

Currencies, international (or foreign), xiii, 80, 130–31, 139, 196, 234, 226

Daily limit: 74, 90, 134–39, 141, 142–43, 196, 209; often removed close to delivery month, 230

Daily prices, 144

Day orders, 72, 216

Deliveries (in contracts): 34–35, 87–88; avoiding making or taking, 8, 87–88, 170, 208, 214, 230–31

Delivery months, 34–35, 40, 59, 69, 134–39, 141, 144, 160; letter symbols for, 71

Delivery registrations, 176–77

Demand: effect on price, 107; effect on supply, 108; elastic and inelastic, 109. *See also* Supply and demand

Department of Agriculture, U.S. (USDA), 45, 110, 240. *See also* Price supports and loans

"Discounted" future prices, 113, 147–48, 154

Dislocations or discrepancies in futures prices: traders looking for, 181, 186

Dollar, purchasing power of, 205–7

"Double reversal" price pattern, 66

Dow Jones Average Index, 23, 235

Eggs, shell, 56, 74, 121, 135, 141, 142, 149, 183, 231

Electronic price display boards. *See* Price display boards

"Enter open stop" (EOS) order, 217

Exchange memberships, 54–55

Exchanges, commodity. *See* Commodity exchanges

Expectation (mathematical concept), 16–18, 196

Experts, market: effect on trading action and prices, 229–30. *See also* Price predicting in futures

Failed traders, xii, 27, 35, 51, 80, 102–3, 146–47, 154, 189, 191, 195, 197, 201, 211, 223–24, 227–28, 233

Index

FCM (registered futures commission merchant). *See* Broker, commodity⁻

Feeder cattle, 29, 120, 137, 143, 183

Financial instruments, xiii, 52, 74, 79, 131–32, 234

Flaxseed, 117, 246

"Floating currencies." *See* Currencies, international

Floor traders and brokers, 53, 57, 69–70, 74–76

Food chain, 121–22, 150

Foreign currencies. *See* Currencies, international

Foreign trade, 32–33, 204

"Forward contracting," 233

Fractions in futures prices, 69, 144

Fundamental approach to trading, 105–14, 145, 146–47, 152, 192, 195, 230

Future futures (proposed or scheduled), 116, 233–36

Futures contracts. *See* Contracts, commodity futures

Futures market (or trading): 34, 37–38; compared with stock market, xii, 36, 39–40, 47, 48, 55, 236; as price discovery mechanism, 113. *See also* Commodity speculation

Futures prices, current, 203, 205, 207, 222. *See also listings under* Price

Gambling: attraction of, 11; differentiated from speculating, 11, 19, 26, 236; luck *vs.* skills in, 6; payoffs in, 12; probabilities in, 11–17

Game theory, applied to trading, 195–96, 213, 218, 220

Gasoline, as future futures, 234. *See also* Petroleum products

"Get-rich-quick" schemes and publications. *See* "Con games" in commodities; Money-making systems

"Ginnie Mae." *See* GNMA

GNMA (Government National Mortgage Association), xiii, 79–80, 131, 132, 139, 176

Gold, 29, 73, 120, 125–26, 138, 141, 144, 176, 208, 218–20, 232

"Good till canceled" (GTC) orders, 72, 96, 216

Government: encouragement of commodity speculation, 45, 132, 225; supervision of exchanges and trading—*see* CFTC

Grain elevators, 43, 60, 76, 169, 171. *See also* Storage

Grains: as commodity group, 28–29, 59, 73, 115, 117–20, 143; as good bet for spreads, 183; government price supports of, 118, 119, 204, 231–32; in history, 38, 56; orders quoted in 1,000-bushel units, 61, 66, 215–16; prices affecting livestock production and prices, 48; substitutions in, 33, 181. *See also listings under particular grains,* as Corn; Oats; Wheat

Hand signals of traders, 38, 61, 72–73, 74

Hedgers: defined, 35; needs at exchanges, 76, 171; not limited in contract holdings, 91; positions of, 35; as speculators, 42–43, 86, 121. *See also* Commercials; Hedging; Price change insurance

Hedging: described, 34–35, 42–43, 108; "selective," 169–70; speculators' role in, 44–45. *See also* Hedgers; Price change insurance

Hog-corn ratio, 153, 181, 185–86

"Hot lines": in brokerages, 63; at CFTC, 95, 247

Iced broilers (chickens), 29, 73, 120, 137, 176, 183, 196

IMM. *See* International Monetary Mart

Inflation: blamed on speculators, 226; causes of, 128–29; and futures trading, 55, 207–8; and proportion equation for current prices *vs.* past prices, 205–7

Insurance: basic concepts in, 16–18, 33, 173, 196; commodity speculation as a special form of underwriting—*see* Price-change insurance; risk transference in, 17–18, 189, 227

International Monetary Mart (IMM), 130, 138, 139, 141, 234, 245

Investing, differentiated from speculating, 25–26, 227–28. *See also* Real estate; Stock market

Kansas City Board of Trade, 117, 134, 184, 235, 245

Keynes, John Maynard, 201–2

"Killings," financial: examples of, 197–201. *See also* Profit potential in futures trading

Large traders (classification), 91, 141, 174–75, 228

Leverage: in commodity contracts, 40, 45, 191, 198; defined, 24; in real estate, 40; in stocks, 24–25, 39–40, 45; when working against speculators, 80, 191. *See also* Margin deposit; Margin maintenance

Limit days. *See* Daily limit

Limits, in orders, 72, 96, 216–17

Liquidation of futures contracts. *See* Contract canceling

Liquidity: aided by pit scalpers, 76; increased by commodity speculators, 29–30, 47, 90; in "thin" markets, 196

Live cattle, 29, 74, 116, 120–21, 137, 143, 183, 185

Live hogs, 29, 121, 137, 141, 143, 181, 183, 185, 232

Livestock feed, 33, 59, 112, 117, 121

Lloyd's of London, 31, 33–34

"Long" position: defined, 46; as hedger, 42, 44, 46–47, 73, 148; as trader, 46–47, 119, 166, 169–70, 197, 204, 210, 219–21, 231

Losses in trading: causes for large, 45, 223; minimizing, 45, 46, 196, 213; using stops in orders to limit, 216, 220, 221. *See also* Failed traders; Game theory in trading

Luck (or chance): in commodity speculating, xii, 191, 226; in gambling, 11. *See also* Price predicting in futures

Lumber, 29, 124, 125, 136, 185

Managed commodity accounts, 95

Margin call, 89

Margin deposit or requirement: in commodity contracts, 40, 142, 145, 209; increased by exchanges, 200; as performance bond, 38, 40; put up by hedgers too, 86; in stocks, 24, 39; using trading profits to pay for, in pyramiding, 198–200

Margin maintenance: to be considered when position taking, 210; in losing positions, 40, 46, 86, 146–47, 191

"Market, at the," "under," "over," etc., 63, 216

Market mechanisms in trading, necessity for understanding: *see* Novice Speculator; Failed traders

"Market" orders, 72

Market sentiment index, 153, 173, 175–76

"Marking to (the) market": defined, 47, 90, 230; as daily routine at brokerage, 41, 89–90, 212

Merchant-trader, as early commodity speculator, 11, 37–38, 56

Metals, 115, 125–26; precious, as basis for money systems, 126; as high-risk futures, 80. *See also* Copper; Gold; Palladium; Platinum; Silver

MidAmerica Commodity Exchange (Chicago), 62, 134, 137, 138, 141, 215, 246

Minimum price fluctuation, 61, 76, 134–39, 141

Minneapolis Grain Exchange, 117, 134, 184, 234, 246

Models, fundamental, 106, 152

Money: affected by inflation, 129; connection with production, 127–29; "counterfeited" by governments, 127–28; as medium of exchange, 10 - 11

Money-making "systems," xi, xiii, 7, 13, 188. *See also* "Con games" in commodities

Money management in trading, xi, 27, 36, 145, 189, 195, 201, 210, 219. *See also* Actuarial approach

Moving averages charts, 153, 163–64, 165

New Orleans Commodity Exchange, 234, 246

New York Coffee, Sugar and Cocoa Exchange, 122, 135, 246

New York Cotton Exchange, 135, 136, 245

New York Futures Exchange, 236, 246

New York Mercantile Exchange, 124, 135, 136, 138

New York Stock Exchange, 22, 23. *See also* Stock market

News, in causing price changes, 52, 109–13, 146, 148, 166, 202, 221

Novice speculator (beginner): best characteristics for success, xii, 102–4, 228; importance of preparatory period, xiv, 97, 102, 223, 237; long position probably safer for, 119, 207; need for wariness, 189, 196, 210–11; positions to consider, 119–20; psychological unsuitabilities in, 10, 26, 102–3, 225–26; reasons for high failure rate, xii, 27, 222–23, 228; situations to avoid, 46, 79, 80,

Index

Novice speculator (*cont.*)
131, 132–33, 201. *See also* Failed traders;
Paper trading

Oats, 29, 117, 119, 134, 141, 142, 196, 219–
21, 231
Oil, crude, heating, fuel. *See* Petroleum
products
Onions, 29
Open interest, 88–89, 144–45, 153, 169–70,
173
Open orders, 72
Opening price, 60
Opportunities, "once-in-a-lifetime," 231–
32
Options, commodity, 232–33
Orange juice (frozen concentrated), 123,
135, 142, 148, 196–97
Order transactions: how recorded at
exchange, 75
Order transmitting: 62–63, 64, 69–70
Orders, trading: built-in safeguards and
instructions in, 72, 96–97, 213; given to
broker, 65, 96–97; importance of
designing in advance, 215–17; letter
symbols and expressions in, 70–74;
notifying client of execution of, 62–63;
phrasing of, 63, 65, 69–70; problems in
filling, 63; relayed to exchange, 62–66;
special types, 215–18; time limit in, 216
Oscillators, 153, 164, 165
"Out-trades" in exchanges, 75, 83
"Overbought" contracts, 170, 175–76
Oversupply. *See* Surplus

Palladium, 29, 125, 126
Paper trading, xiv, 105, 208, 222–23, 237
Parlaying, in gambling, 13–15, 191, 224.
See also Pyramids
Partnerships, trading, 95, 226
"Perfect hedge," 44, 169
Petroleum products, 122, 124–25, 136. *See
also* Gasoline
Phoneclerks at phonedesks (in exchanges),
57–58, 63–64, 69–70
Pit brokers or traders, 70, 75, 202. *See also*
"Scalpers"
Pits, trading, 58–59
Plant breeding, 117
Plant diseases and pests, 32, 117–18, 203–4
Platform at trading pit, 60, 72, 73
Platinum, 29, 125, 126, 138, 144

Plywood, 29, 73, 124, 136, 176, 185, 234
Point-and-figure (P & F) charts, 105–6, 155,
156–59, 163
Points (in contracts), 76
"Pools," commodity, 95, 242
Pork bellies, 121, 137, 185, 232
Portfolio futures, industrial, 235–36
Position limit (reporting position), 141
Position traders, 46, 94, 202, 241
Positions, contract. *See* "Long" *and*
"Short" Positions
Potatoes (Idaho and Maine), 29, 74, 123–
24, 135, 143, 144, 159, 209, 215
Poultry, 29. *See also* Chickens; Eggs; Iced
broilers
"Premium," 72, 178, 217
Price: Spot, Cash, or Actuals. *See* Cash
price
Price behavior, 148, 152–67, 193–94. *See
also* Fundamental approach; News;
Supply and demand
Price-change insurance: 30–36, 55, 108,
113, 225, 229, 234–36
Price changes in commodities: caused by
news—*see* News; caused by traders,
207; effect on commercials, 30–36;
seasonal, 148; universality of, in
particular commodities, 31, 32–33, 148;
unpredictability of, 30, 31, 102, 165, 154.
See also Price predicting in futures
Price charts. *See* Charts, price
Price display boards (at exchanges), 39, 60,
69, 73
Price fluctuation, minimum, *See* Minimum
price fluctuation
Price manipulation, 38, 39, 52, 90–91, 94,
95. *See also* "Cornering the market"
Price move limits. *See* Daily limit
Price patterns, in charts, 158–167
Price per unit, 73–74, 134–39
Price predicting in futures: by market
experts, 111, 148, 154, 165, 229–30; by
speculators, 35–36, 41, 45, 46, 102, 113,
147. *See also* Small speculator
Price quotation tables, 142–44, 209
Price reversals, 120, 145, 156, 157, 160, 176
Price supports and loans, 118, 119, 204,
231–32
Price trends: detected through charting,
153; as production determinant, 47–48,
89. *See also* Trendlines, price; Price
patterns

Prices: on display boards, 73–74; in newspapers, 143–45; how to chart, 155–67

Probabilities: "biased," 191, 207, 226; in gambling (odds), 6, 11–15; in insurance, 16–18, 189; in speculating, 15–16, 46, 147, 191

Processors, commodity. *See* Commercials; Hedgers, "long"

Producers, commodity. *See* Commercials; Hedgers, "short"

Production: affected by prices, 47–48, 89, 125, 226; and consumption, 106–8, 127–29, 148

Production costs, 119, 149, 150

Profit potential in futures trading, xii, 35–36, 188, 197–201, 211, 223, 224. *See also* Commodity speculation, as a business

Propane, liquified, 124, 136

Purchasing power of dollar, 205–7

Pyramids in futures contracts, 45, 189–91, 196, 197–201

Quotations, price, how to read: on display boards, 39, 60; in newspapers, 40, 142–44

"Random walk," 193

Randomness in futures prices movements, 148, 165

Real estate, for speculating, 18, 19, 21–22, 39–40, 41

Record keeping by speculator, 214, 221

Resistance (in charting), 119, 121, 150, 158, 166

Retendering commodities, 231

"Reuters" (broad tape), 112, 244

Reversals. *See* Price reversals

Rice, 29, 234

Rings, trading. *See* Pits, trading

Risk capital, 208–9

Risk taking: in early commerce, 11; in everyday life, 15–18; in gambling and speculating, 6, 15; geared to profit percentages and payoffs, 11, 35–36; in insurance underwriting, 33–36

Risks, high, in futures trading. *See* Failed traders; Profit potential

"Rolling over," 79, 232

"Round turn," 47, 96, 182, 212

"Runners" (messengers) on trading floors, 57–58, 62, 69, 75

"Scalpers," 76, 171, 202

Scarcity (shortage, undersupply), 30, 32, 107, 119, 149, 207, 226

SEC (Securities and Exchange Commission), 24, 25

Sell-stop orders, 166–67

Selling futures contracts. *See* "Short" position

"Short" position: defined, 46; examples, as hedger—43–44, 46–47, 85, 169, 171; as trader—46–47, 119, 166, 197, 204, 210, 218–20, 231; risker for new traders, 119–20, 226

"Short squeeze," 230–31

Silver, 29, 109, 120, 125–26, 138, 141, 144, 176

Silver coins, U.S., 29, 74, 126, 141, 232

Small speculators, advantages and tactics of, 93–94, 102, 113, 147–48, 154, 174–75, 183, 186, 196, 202, 213

Society, benefit to, from commodity trading, 29, 30, 37–39, 47–48. *See also* Commodity Speculation as rational price determinant; Liquidity; Price change insurance

"Soft" commodities. *See* Currencies, international; Financial instruments

Soybean meal, 58, 73, 112, 134, 143, 176, 181, 185

Soybean oil, 58, 176, 185

Soybeans, 29, 58–59, 73, 111, 112, 117, 134, 141, 181, 185, 186, 231, 234

Speculating: defined, 15; differentiated from gambling, 11, 226; differentiated from investing, 26, 227–28, 235; institutionalized in insurance, 17–18

Split close, 144

Spot price. *See* Cash price

Spread Scope, 173, 179, 183

Spreads: advantages of, 78–79, 181, 185; defined, 77, 179; examples of, 78–79, 181–84, 232; types of, 79, 179–86

Stock market, 23–26, 36, 41, 46, 48, 55, 193, 235, 236

Stocks, corporate, 23–26, 39–40, 235–36

Stops, in orders, 72, 96–97, 216–17, 220, 221

Storage costs, 148, 177–78. *See also* Carrying-charge market

Straddles. *See* Spreads

Subscription services, 214, 240, 242–44

Substitution in commodities, 33, 184–86

Index

Sugar, 29, 74, 122–23, 133, 135, 143, 144, 146–47

Sunflowers, 117, 145–46, 234

Supply, factors that increase or reduce, 32–33

Supply and demand (economics), 28, 30–31, 41, 48, 93, 106–9, 116, 119, 149, 151–54, 192, 226. *See also* Demand; Scarcity; Surplus

Support (chart line), 119, 150, 158, 166

Surplus (oversupply, overproduction), 30–31, 32, 107–8. *See also* Supply and demand

Switchover day, 159

Syndicated insurance, 30–36. *See also* Price change insurance

T-bills, notes, bonds. *See* Treasury bills, etc.

Taxes in trading, 79, 214–215

Tea, 123

Technical approach to trading (chartist), 105–6, 145, 152–86, 192, 195

Technical rally, 166–67

Traders in exchanges: badges of, 56–57, 68, 75; behavior in pits, 51, 59, 60–61, 70, 72–73, 74–75; dress of, 56–58; filling orders, 63; hand signals, 38, 61, 72–73, 74; special language of, 61, 63, 65–66, 70; useful function of—*see* Floor traders and brokers; Scalpers; writing up customers' orders. *See also* Commodity speculators; Exchange memberships; Large traders

Trading floors (exchanges): CBT's, described, 57–62, 68–81; as public auction markets, 38–39, 61, 73; visitors to, 53–54, 68

Trading jargon, 63, 66, 72, 74, 215

Trading months. *See* Delivery months

Trading plan, benefit of designing and sticking to, xii, 102, 114, 120, 211, 213

Transactions, uncompleted, 212. *See also* Open interest

Treasury bills, notes, bonds, 131–39, 236. *See also* Financial instruments

Trendlines, price, 161, 194–95, 207

Troy ounces, explained, 126

Undersupply. *See* Scarcity

USDA. *See* Department of Agriculture

Value Line Index, 235

Value, contract, *See* Contract value

Variable limits, 74, 142–43

Volatility: in commodities, 170, 219, 220; in stocks, 25

Volume, in commodity trading, 153, 168–73; contrasted with stocks, 48, 236

Wall Street Journal, 144–45, 240

Warehouse receipts, 153, 176–77, 231. *See also* Delivery registrations

Wheat, 29, 32–33, 112–13, 117–18, 119, 134, 141, 150, 204, 215, 231, 232

"Whipsaws," 208

Winnipeg Commodity Exchange, 246

Women in commodity trading, xiv, 63–64, 66–67

Wool, 29, 124

World Trade Center (New York), 56

Yen, Japanese, 130, 139

"Zero-sum game," 16–17, 47, 228–29